T0070280

ELT Methods and Approaches: Experiments and Observations

TAJ MOHAMMAD
AND
SOADA IDRIS

ELT METHODS AND APPROACHES: EXPERIMENTS AND OBSERVATIONS

Copyright © 2022 Taj Mohammad and Soada Idris.

All rights reserved. No part of this book may be used or reproduced by any means, graphic, electronic, or mechanical, including photocopying, recording, taping or by any information storage retrieval system without the written permission of the author except in the case of brief quotations embodied in critical articles and reviews.

iUniverse books may be ordered through booksellers or by contacting:

iUniverse
1663 Liberty Drive
Bloomington, IN 47403
www.iuniverse.com
844-349-9409

Because of the dynamic nature of the Internet, any web addresses or links contained in this book may have changed since publication and may no longer be valid. The views expressed in this work are solely those of the author and do not necessarily reflect the views of the publisher, and the publisher hereby disclaims any responsibility for them.

Any people depicted in stock imagery provided by Getty Images are models, and such images are being used for illustrative purposes only.
Certain stock imagery © Getty Images.

ISBN: 978-1-6632-3799-6 (sc)
ISBN: 978-1-6632-3800-9 (e)

Print information available on the last page.

iUniverse rev. date: 04/21/2022

In the Loving Memory of

Prof. John Charles Miller

Contents

Foreword

ELT METHODS AND APPROACHES: EXPERIMENTS AND OBSERVATIONS narrates the experiments and observations of different methodological approaches in English Language Teaching. At the beginning of each chapter, the authors provide a conceptual framework of each method and approach supported by well-known critics and scholars in the field. Such a theoretical background to most of the methods and approaches in English Language Teaching may attract students, research scholars and classroom teachers.

The authors have used their own personal experiences in writing this book, an amalgam of theory and practice in English Language Teaching. They emphasize the application of those methods and approaches in a particular EFL/ESL situation. That is what seemed to motivate the author to write this book, a different source in that it not only provides the conceptual framework of different methods, approaches and techniques but also executes and experiments with them in EFL/ESL situations. The work is unique as it not only experiments with different methods and approaches but also observes what practical challenges learners and teachers face during their implementation as well as how these difficulties can be addressed and overcome.

This text has provided adequate scope for learners, the target group to integrate them into the research. They have actively participated in the creation and formation of this book. The authors have included learners' feedback on the execution, approach and technique. Their feedback is important in assessing whether a method or approach is successful in a specific EFL/ESL environment. Learners' feedback has assisted the authors as they present, discuss and assess the advantages and disadvantages of each method. The authors have shared their personal experiences with different EFL/ESL learners in three countries, the United States of America, Saudi Arabia and India.

John C. Miller, D.M.L.
Professor Emeritus Languages and Cultures Department
University of Colorado, Colorado Springs (USA)

Preface

There have been various books on methods and approaches in English Language Teaching. However, there are very few books, which deal with the experiments and observations of different methods and approaches in the classroom in a particular situation. This book addresses the principles of different methods, approaches in details, and presents feedback from students on every method and approach. The book includes experiences of teacher in different countries like Kingdom of Saudi Arabia, United States of America and India. The book presents the theoretical details about methods and approaches followed by their experiments and observations in an EFL/ESL situation. The book responds not only to teachers' opinions about the success rate of a particular method or approach but also simultaneously analyses students' opinions about the particular method and approach. Students are given a questionnaire based on a Likert scale to put forward their opinion against every statement based on the principles of each method and approach. Most of the statements in the questionnaire comprise of the contents taught in the classroom. The analysis of students' questionnaire is depicted in form of graphs to clearly display the success rate of each method and approach.

The book has presented and analyzed a single EFL/ESL situation based on every method and approach. However, the analysis, experiences and observations demonstrate that these situations cover a wide range of issues of EFL/ESL learners/teachers worldwide. The book can be a resource for the EFL/ESL teachers as well as learners in different parts of world. It illustrates that methods are not obsolete and probably can never be. Each method has some advantages and disadvantages based on the situation in which it is used. Teachers must be oriented to different methods and approaches as it helps them to understand their classroom situations in a better way. Some methods prove to have a higher rate of success while others have a lower rate. The success of each method and approach also depends upon how a teacher utilizes them in a particular situation. The book provides learners an opportunity to raise their voice and be a part of not only teaching/learning process but also of research. The book has metaphorically stressed the fact that methods are not dead, but are reborn from time to time though residing in new bodies. Methods have characteristics common to each other. For example, the post-method era includes various characteristics which are part of other methods like 'autonomous learners' already proposed by the silent way. Different methods are used throughout the world in a variety of teaching/learning situations. They all provide learning instructions with the same desired output to an extent. This book has provided a different perspective to look at methods, approaches and techniques. It supplements methods and approaches with student surveys in a particular ESL/EFL setting highlighting the advantages and disadvantages of the use of those methodologies and techniques in a specific situation in the classroom.

Acknowledgments

The book *ELT Methods and Approaches: Experiments and Observations* is written with an intention to express thanks to the late Prof. J.C. Miller who guided me through the path of my academic journey. I am equally thankful to Mr. Robert Bixler who has always been a source of inspiration to me. My heart is full of appreciation for Late Mr. Rais Uddin Siddiqui, Late Mr. Mahfooz Khan, my father, Late Mrs. Shahin Akhtar, my mother, Mr. Intisar Husain, Mr. Irfan Khan, Mr. Naseer Ahmed, Mr. Qadeer Ahmed, Mr. Majid Hussain, Dr. S.U. Chishti, Late Dr. Ejaz Hasan Khan, Dr Mohammad Askandar Iqbal and Mr. Ghayas Ahmed Khan who motivated me to join the AMU, and guided me through my journey. I am also highly thankful to my esteemed teachers, Prof. A.R. Kidwai, Prof. Mohammad Asim Siddiqui, Prof. Sami Rafiq, Prof. M.M. Adnan Raza who have always been a source of inspiration and guidance to me. I owe a lot to my friends Dr. Jalal Ahmed, Dr. Aadel Yousuf Khanday, Mr. Bilal Ahmed Itoo, Dr. Mohamamd Faiz, Mr. Mohammad Younus, Mr. Zeeshan, Late Sarfaraz Khan, Mr. Jameel, Dr. Momtazul Islam, Dr. Rehan Khan, Mr. Shehzad Ahmed, Dr. Haris Qadeer and my well-wisher Prof. S.M. Hashim and Prof. Syed Mohammad Amin, Dept. of Urdu, AMU, Aligarh. I am also highly obliged to my colleagues Dr. Abdul Aziz Aboud Asiri, dean PY, Dr. Sami Alqouzi, dean, College of Languages, Dr. Faisal Al Najmi, vice dean of academic affairs, and all other colleagues whose names could not be mentioned but whose support and contribution are always appreciated. Finally, I express my heartfelt gratitude to the anonymous reviewers of this book whose guidance and comments were highly significant.

CHAPTER 1

Introduction

Approach, Method and Technique are interrelated to each other and are very common terms in English Language Teaching. Approach is an abstract concept while method is a concrete one. Approach is a set of beliefs while method is instrumental in implementing the particular beliefs related to an approach. Techniques refer to classroom activities and procedures usually pertaining to a method and approach. For Richards and Rodgers (1986), method is used as an umbrella term comprising approach, design and procedure. Similarly, Prabhu (1990) considers method as classroom activities and their underlying theories.

Defining the concept of method, Bell (2003) makes a distinction between method (with a lowercase m) and Method (with an uppercase M). The former refers to classroom practices, while the latter means, "a fixed set of classroom practices that serve as a prescription and therefore do not allow variation" (p. 326). However, it is a real challenge between what theories propose and how teachers implement them in the classroom. According to Kumaravadivelu (2006), "The term *method* is used indiscriminately to refer to what theorists propose and to what teachers practice" (p. 60).

There are several methods and approaches used for teaching English. There is no best method as all language teaching methods differ from learner to learner and situation to situation. Within the teaching method framework, the approach is constituted by those theoretical principles on which the curricular design is based (Richards & Rodgers, 1986). Thus, an approach is usually understood as the body of linguistic, psychological and pedagogical theories, which inspire the teaching practice. Stern (1983) refers to "foundations/theoretical assumptions and to a level-inter level- between theory and practice where the educational linguistics theory and research take place" (p. 43-50).

As discussed above, approach usually includes a set of beliefs in form of theory. It refers to at least three various theoretical views of language: the structural, the functional and the interactional. The structural view defines language as a system of structurally related items. It views language as a product of different units like phonological (phonemes), grammatical (clauses, phrases, sentences, etc.) and lexical (function word and structure word). These views of language are usually embraced by the Audiolingual Method, the Total Physical Response and the Silent Way.

The second view of language is a functional view, which considers language as a vehicle of expression of functional meaning. The Communicative Language Teaching conforms to the same belief of language. This theory emphasizes semantic and communicative aspects rather than grammatical characteristics of language. Wilkins's Notional Syllabuses (1976) as stated by Richards and Rodgers (2001), "includes not only elements of grammar and lexis but also specifies the topics, notions and concepts to communicate about" (p. 21). The third view of language, interactional view, perceives language as a vehicle for interpersonal relations and social interactions between individuals. Here language is the product of society and society cannot exist without language. Therefore, the language is used to maintain social relations and it is the lingua franca of a society.

These different views of approach provide a theoretical framework to Second Language Teaching (SLT). Method is a specific set of rules, which are used to teach the second language in the classroom. In order to learn and teach a second language, the curriculum has a variety of components, which are characterized under methodology. As far as methodology is concerned, it consists of many components as Stern's (1983) concept of *methodology* can be identified with *design*. It involves *content, objectives, materials, procedures* and *assessment* – under the acronym of C.O.M.P.A. Together with *organization*, it constitutes the *practical level* of *the general model for second language teaching* (p. 44).

A cursory glance over the history of methods and approaches will affirm that methods and approaches to language teaching have been a continuous process until 2000s, the year, which announced post-method era in language teaching.

Language teachers are aware that there have been various methods of teaching English language evolving from time to time pertaining to the aim of making learning easier for students. At the core of developing methods and approaches, there had been a sincere effort to make the learning of second language more enjoyable and fruitful. As there is long history of the development of methods, and approaches, they went through the touchstone of the popular practices of language teaching of their time to ensure their efficiency in language proficiency. Contrary to the common expectations, not all methods were the product of academic setting in a formal situation. Some of them were originally the product of the non-academic requirements of a historical period and were developed accordingly. It further confirms our belief that necessity is the mother of invention as various methods came into existence as per the necessities of a particular period. Interestingly, methods were not used only to teach students in the classroom as language learners might pertain to believe.

Teaching methods cannot be confined only to classroom in a traditional setting facilitating the mode of interaction, communication and teaching learning between teacher and student. For example, Grammar-Translation Method (see chapter 2) had a very non-academic origin. It had nothing to do with the classroom teaching (in the beginning) as it is used now in several language schools and institutions. It was purely the product of wartime. It had no roots in an academic environment. It was never intended to discover this method to address the language issues of the students in a classroom especially of second language learners. The leading exponents (Johann, Seidenstucker, Karl Plotz, H.S. Ollendorf, and Johann Meidinger) of this method propound that Grammar Translation Method was the offspring of German scholarship. The main objective of this method, as W. H. D. Rouse opines, was "to know everything about something rather than the thing itself" (qtd. in Richards and Rodgers 2001, p. 5). It was first known in the United States as the Prussian Method. It was primarily the product of the 19th century and was widely used in the First World War to learn the second language. It was particularly used to teach the army men so that they could understand the language of the country they are fighting against or for. The main goal of this method was to learn through the literary text of a foreign language in order to be familiar with the syntactical properties as well cultural hegemony of a language and nation. The method precisely focuses on the detailed analysis of the grammar rules of a language followed by memorization and rigorous practices through drilling in order to manipulate the morphology and syntax of the foreign language. Stern (1983) has rightly opined, "The first language is maintained as the reference system in the acquisition of second language" (p. 455). In this method, the teacher provided a direct translation of particular words in mother tongue. They also motivated learners or army men to translate the language of everyday usage so that they could communicate with the locals. They also learnt specific vocabulary in the target language, which they could use to code and decode the messages in the target language. There was a lot of use of bilingual dictionary in order to translate vocabulary from first language to second language. As the sentence is the basic unit of teaching and language practice, much of the focus lies in translating sentences from first language to second language (Howatt 1984, p. 132). Different components of sentences like subject, verb, object, parts of speech and morphology are taken into consideration and are part of teaching application. Accuracy is given primary importance. There is no room for mistakes. Howatt (1984) rightly states, "Students are expected to attain high standards of translation because of the high priority attached to meticulous standards of accuracy which, as well as having intrinsic moral value, was a prerequisite for passing the increasing number of formal written examinations that grew up during the century" (p.132). Grammar is taught deductively. The rules of grammar are explained and analyzed in details followed by rigorous practice of the same in form of sentences. Interestingly, this method, which was invented to teach the army men, was later on adopted by the academicians to teach English language in the classroom. When it became the part of the classroom teaching, it followed the same approach of grammar and translation. There was a lot of emphasis on reading and writing and there was almost no focus on developing listening and speaking skills of the target language. Resultantly, students were very good in reading and writing but very poor in listening and speaking. Unfortunately, this method was not much successful because it almost skipped the listening and speaking skills. As it did not follow the natural approach of language learning, this method could not achieve popularity in academic circles. This method dominated European and Foreign Language Teaching from the 1840s to the 1940s and still continues to be used in some parts of the world with and without a few modifications. Toward the mid-19th century, there were several factors, which backed the rejection of the Grammar- Translation Method. The main cause of rejection of this method was less focus on communication. Thus, the increased demand of communication among Europeans made them indifferent to the use of Grammar-Translation Method. At the same time, many conversation books and phrase books began to circulate in the market for private studies. Then, there was time to change this traditional method, which probably seemed to be obsolete in academic settings.

The Frenchman C. Marcel (1793-1896)'s idea that child learning can be followed as a model for language teaching was a turning point and cause of the major shift from Grammar Translation Method to Natural Method of language acquisition. The second language can be acquired the same way as a child acquires his/her first language (as qtd. in Richards and Rodgers 2001, p.7). Well, it seems to make sense. The Englishman T. Prendergast was one of the firsts to advocate the view of natural learning as a child does and proposes the first "structural syllabus". He advocated that language is a tool to be used in different situations, as basic structures are recurrent in many day-to-day life situations. The Frenchman F. Gouin (1831-1896) is perhaps the best known of these mid-nineteen century reformers in foreign language teaching. He developed an approach to foreign language teaching based on his observations of children's use of language. He believes in presenting language rules in a context, as language cannot be decontextualized. Language can be learnt in a proper context in which it is used. These were some of the observations and ideas, which stressed the need to improve the language teaching practices and finally led to the birth of reform movement in language teaching. (as qtd. in Richards and Rodgers 2001, p.8).

From the 1880s, linguists such as Henry Sweet (an English philologist, phonetician and grammarian), Wilhelm Vietor (a German phonetician and language educator, a central figure in the Reform Movement in language education of the late 19th century), and Paul Passy (a French linguist, founder of the International Phonetic Association in 1886) in France became instrumental in providing the intellectual leadership to give reformist's ideas a wide range of acceptance among the academicians. There was a complete revolution in the discipline of language. Phonetics- the scientific analysis and description of the sound systems of language was established which gave a new dimension to the speech process ultimately emphasizing the communicative needs of a language. The International Phonetic Association was founded in 1886, and its International Phonetic Alphabet aimed to enable the sound of any language to be accurately transcribed. All these developments led to natural methods of teaching ultimately known as the Direct Method. (Richards and Rodgers 2001, p.10-11).

The fervent supporters of the Direct Method (see chapter 3) introduced it in France and Germany, which was officially approved in both the countries. L. Sauveur (1826-1907) used concentrated oral interaction in the target language to learn the language in context. Sauveur and other supporters of this method advocated that language could be taught without translation or without taking the help of mother tongue of the learners, which was of course, a rejection of the Grammar Translation Method.

Direct Method completely discarded the use of mother tongue in the classroom. Resultantly, there was a shift from the traditional way to modern ways of teaching. This method stressed the use of only the target language in the classroom. There was more emphasis on speech and less emphasis on accuracy theorizing that the basic function of a language is speech. The language teaching was patterned on the natural way of learning a language as a child is naturally programmed to develop the linguistic capabilities. The method was based on behavioral learning, as there was repetition of structures in the target language. Students learnt language through repetition and its use in a proper context. The proponents of this method rejected the Grammar Translation Method completely and labeled it as unnatural way of learning a language. They argued that language can be learnt in a natural way and not through unnatural ways or means as a traditional method is supposed to do. A child can learn the second language the way he learns first language. As there is no structured teaching of the native language, the same strategy should be adopted while learning and teaching the second language. In an academic setting, e.g. a classroom, they permitted only the use of target language, which yielded the desired results to some extent. However, many slow learners were still confused and could not pace with the classroom. The direct method too had its shortcomings and was not perfect for all teaching-learning situations.

By the 1920s, the use of the Direct Method in noncommercial schools in Europe had consequently declined. Although this method enjoyed popularity in Europe, it was not embraced universally. The British applied linguist Henry Sweet found this method lacking in methodological basis though it provided innovation at the level of teaching procedures. He supported a more principled approach to language teaching that could serve as the basis for teaching techniques. In the 1920s and 1930s, they schematized the language-teaching principles proposed earlier by the Reform Movement, which subsequently led to the birth of Audiolingual Method (see chapter 4) in the United States and the Oral or Situational Language Teaching in Britain. The most active period in the history of approaches and methods was from the 1950s to the 1980s. The 1950s and 1960s gave birth to the Audiolingual Method and Situational Method, which were both superseded by the Communicative Language Teaching (see chapter 9).

As the Audiolingual method stressed how audio-visual aids can be applied to learning a language. Language learning is facilitated by the recorded audios where audio tape recorders are used in order to teach a language. Here teacher plays the role of a music orchestra director. The main emphasis is on oral use of language rather than the written use of language.

Carroll (1963) states that the audiolingualism was developed from the principle that "a language is first of all a system of sounds for social communication; writing is secondary derivative system for the recording of spoken language" (p.1963). As the primary function of language is communication, this method encourages communication through oral drills, which require repetition and habit formation in order to learn a language.

The Audio-Lingual method teaches language through dialogues that focus on habit formation of students. To achieve communicative competence in target language students are required to form new habits in target language and overcome old habits of native language (Freeman, 2000). Thornbury (2000) expressed similar opinion about audio-lingual method and mentioned, 'language simply as form of behavior to be learned through the formation of correct speech habits' (p. 21).

It aims to improve students' speaking skills. Language items are presented to students in spoken form without any orientation to the mother tongue so that they can learn language skills successfully without interference of the mother tongue. The goal of the Audio-Lingual Method is teaching vocabulary and grammatical patterns through dialogues, to enable students to respond quickly and accurately in spoken language. There is no rigorous practice of attempting grammatical exercises. Grammar is acquired in a natural way. The dialogues are learnt through repetition and such drills as backward build-up, chain, substitution, transformation, and question-and-answer are conducted based upon the patterns in the dialogue (Freeman, 2000).

Next in queue, the Silent Way Method of teaching (see chapter 5) completely discouraged the teacher's talk time in the classroom. This method replaced teacher's talk time (TTT) with students' talk time (STT). Teacher's talk time was almost zero in the classroom, as he did not speak at all.

The teaching in the classroom was facilitated through charts, wallpapers, Fidel charts, etc. Teacher uses realia to convey the message in language teaching. He or she also provided a classroom with a wide range of learning materials that ensured students' exposure to the target language. There was more encouragement for learners' involvement in the classroom. The purpose of the Silent Way is to let everyone have the opportunity to experience themselves as independent, responsible, and autonomous learners (Stevick, 1996). Realia (objects and material from everyday life used as teaching aids) was the main tool in the classroom to use to facilitate language learning. The teacher conveys his message through charts. He points towards a particular chart or wallpapers etc. to direct learners in the classroom. This method also did not yield the desired results, as it did not prove to be an effective way of teaching. Students need the teacher for their various problems, to ask question, or have discussion with them. Cael (2010) states:

> The Silent Way Approach asks that teachers help students become aware how native speakers use the language, establishing that the goal is to come closer to the native speaker's usage of the language rather than adapting or inventing a personal and individual way of using a language. From the initial stage of instruction, the Silent Way focuses the learner's attention on accurately producing individual sounds, stress patterns, intonation, and aspects of connected speech (linking and pausing) in a way that approximates how English is actually spoken. (p. 12-13)

After this method, another method of teaching, Desuggestopedia, (see chapter 6) came into existence, focusing on the psychological aspects of language learning. The method postulates that learners are not able to focus because they have some psychological fears regarding learning a language. These fears can be attributed to the fear of a new language or adjusting themselves in a new situation or feeling reticent to ask questions to teachers and clear their doubts. Students feel hesitant to ask questions, as they feel afraid in the class. Suggestopedia is a method of teaching which focuses on desuggesting fears of students. It creates a psychological environment for students that help them remove imaginary fears regarding learning in the classroom. Students feel motivated to ask questions and do not feel anxious with the presence of teacher in the classroom. It was more of a psychological method than an educational or academic one. It desuggests negative emotions of students and creates a positive attitude. In order to carry out this method, teachers use different relaxation techniques to make students feel relaxed. Students learn better, when they feel relaxed and have no negative emotions or fears. This method also helps increase psychomotor and cognitive abilities of emotionally disturbed and learning disabled children. Language is acquired through problem solving skills. This method develops the communicative competence of students by increasing their confidence. As the method aims to remove imaginative fears of students, it uses easy and natural learning activities. Using this method in foreign or second language teaching, as it was mainly applied, can accelerate language learning three to five times faster than conventional methods (Lozanov, 2009).

The Community Language Learning Method (see chapter 7) succeeded this method. Charles Curran, a Jesuit priest with background in Clinical Psychology and Counseling, developed this method. The method has its roots in counseling learning between priest and clients, language learners. The same method has been adopted in Community Language Learning to teach foreign languages. Students are treated as clients, and teachers are considered counselors. The method is based on human relationship. There is no particular syllabus used in the classroom. Teachers rely heavily on mother tongue as a medium to teach target language through grammar and translation. As the method borrows more from the Grammar-Translation Method and does not seem to be quite interesting or motivating, teachers sometime use tape recorder in order to record the message of the clients or students and then play it, which makes the classroom more lively and interactive. This method makes students feel more relaxed and motivated, as they are not afraid to ask any question to their teachers. Teachers are usually well versed in the mother tongue of students and use it to teach in the classroom. Learners do not feel any anxiety or hesitation as teacher is well familiar with their mother tongue and accordingly could differentiate the language intricacies. It is a method exclusively based on English for communication and is enormously learner-focused. Although each course is unique and student-dictated, there are certain criteria that should be applied to all CLL classrooms like those that students must be motivated to practice the accurate pronunciation. Teacher also speaks when necessary to correct learners in a very polite way. Marion E. Bunch (1977) states:

> Learning is a basic and central component of the distinctive activities that constitute the subject matter of psychology. Learning including retention, on which it depends, is at the heart of perception, thinking, imagination, reasoning, judgment, attitudes, personality traits, systems of values, and the development and organization of the activities that constitute the personality of the individual (qtd. in Nurhasanah, 2015, p.84).

Community Language Learning was succeeded by Total Physical Response Method (see chapter 8) developed by James Asher. It incorporates the principles of the Comprehension Approach, which stresses the fact that language learning should start first with understanding and then producing. It incorporates the concept that the child first listens to the language around him as part of receptive skill. Then the child starts speaking their mother tongue as part of productive skill. Asher had the same notion when he reasoned that the quickest and less stressful way to learn the target language is to follow the commands of teachers with zero use of mother tongue. As the primary function of language is to follow commands, Total Physical Response emphasizes the physical activities of students. Zhang Qiu (2006) states, "Children like playing games. In TPR lessons, teachers design distinct games which can stimulate students' interest and motivate them to learn effectively" (as qtd. in Qiu 2016, p. 20). This method is extremely useful for unmotivated students who are the passive learners. It is a method based on the coordination of speech and action. It provides space to passive learners to be physically active in the classroom. The learners follow the commands of teachers, which motivate them to act physically in the classroom. Thus, meaning is conveyed through actions. Target language is supplied in chunks to students. Students can learn sentences in target language by rapidly moving their bodies. Students observe action of teachers and imitate them. Spoken language is emphasized over written language. Asher (1969) attempted "to find out the reasons why TPR could promote high-speed understanding and improve a good memory. He excluded some factors, which might affect the effectiveness of TPR. These factors include location, which means the location of the teaching instruments in the room during exercise; interflow, which means the learner gets into action before he has finished listening to instructions; sequence, which means that the instruction may indicate what the latter one is" (p.3).

Communicative Language Teaching (see chapter 9) succeeded this method. It is a reaction to traditional approaches of teaching like the structural approach where 'form' matters more than 'function'. This approach puts more focus on communicative aspects of language teaching. It makes the language live and practical. This method stresses on the fact that language cannot be learnt in isolation. Language needs a context in which it is used. Communicative Language Teaching (CLT) emphasizes contextual use of language. Language cannot be practiced in isolation. That is why Communicative Language Teaching focuses more on communicative aspects rather than the structural aspects of language. As the primary function of a language is communication, Communicative Language Teaching focuses on communication in real life situations. This approach has bridged the gap between a teacher and student. It encourages more informal interaction between students and teachers. Moreover, Communicative Language Teaching follows a learner-centered approach where learners take the charge of their own learning and the teacher is just a facilitator. Motivation plays a significant role in communicative language teaching. Brown (2002) stated that motivation is the most important factor to learn English. It provides a real purpose in learning English and a reason to continue learning. Teachers can measure students' motivation and transform them from unmotivated to motivated students. In order to contextualize the language in a CLT classroom, the teacher may use different approaches such as content-based, task-based and participatory strategies, which are nonetheless an extension of the CLT itself.

The difference between Communicative Language Teaching and Content-based, Task-based and Participatory Approaches is a matter of focus. It may be considered as different dimensions of Communicative Language Teaching. It integrates the learning of language with the learning of some other content, often academic in subject matter. The subject matter content is used for language teaching purposes. Student's previous knowledge is taken into consideration while teaching in the class. It bridges the gap between the previous knowledge and current knowledge on the topic. Learners feel motivated when they perceive the relevance of their language use. In this approach, as Communicative Language Teaching aims, vocabulary is learnt through contextual clues. Content-Based Language Teaching (see chapter 10) encourages students to take charge of their own learning. Teacher may take subject matter from any subject but that must be in English, the target language. Then the teacher may help students by describing some of the key terms associated with the subject matter, which might be unseen for students. It triggers the background knowledge of the students on the given topic. There is no predetermined linguistic content. The focus is more on procedure rather than the product.

Task-Based Language Teaching (see chapter 11) also known as Task-Based Instruction proposed by Prabhu (1987) advocates real life situations for language learning. In a Task-Based Language Teaching (TBLT) class, learners are given real life situation task like visiting a doctor, bank, railway, etc. TBLT encourages group and pair learning. Teacher gives a specific task to students to complete. The focus is more on completion of tasks and less on grammatical structures and accuracy. As the preoccupation with accuracy leads learners to focus more on form rather than function, TBLT focuses more on function rather than form. It aims to provide learners with a natural context for language learning. Teacher goes through a pre-task with students before they work individually. Students complete a task and engage in authentic speaking and listening, which enable them to develop their comprehension and speaking skills. Students have input into the design and the way of completing the task. This gives them more opportunity for authentic and meaningful interaction.

Participatory Approach (see chapter 12) was originated in the early '60s with the work of Paulo Freire (a Brazilian educator and philosopher). The goal of this approach is to help students understand the social, historical or cultural forces, which affect their lives. It helps students to take an action and make decisions in order to gain control over their lives. This approach tries to establish a connection between the academic life and real life, the classroom and the world outside. Learning is connected; it does not disassociate itself from authentic use of language. It provides a real context to students in which language must be used. The curriculum in this approach is the result of an ongoing context-specific problem-posing process. Education is most effective when it is experience-centered. Participatory approach ensures that students must experience what they learn.

It is more like content-based approach in the sense that contents are again focused in this approach and play an important part in language learning. However, it is slightly different from Content-Based Approach as it primarily focuses on real life experiences, personal experiences and situations one might face in everyday life. It assures that all the participants are actively taking part in the learning. The participants get more excited to participate in the class because it assesses different experiences of the learners and how they respond in that particular situation. Language is learnt more naturally when the focus is on its usage in daily life. This approach engages learners' minds while the teacher addresses their linguistic challenges.

Like other participatory approaches, Cooperative Language Learning (see chapter 13) also motivates learners for cooperation and involves their concerned teachers to learn a language. However, cooperative language learning (CLL) is different from participatory approaches as it strictly follows some principles. For example, it stresses the group formation of students but the groups must be heterogeneous. Students should belong not only to different academic level but also to different socio-cultural, political and ethnic backgrounds. Teachers should organize the three-, four-, or five-member groups so that students are mixed as heterogeneously as possible, first according to academic abilities, and then on the basis of ethnic backgrounds, race, and gender. Students should not be allowed to form their groups based on friendship and personal liking. When groups are maximally heterogeneous, students tend to interact and achieve in ways and at levels that are rarely found in other instructional strategies.

They also tend to become tolerant of diverse viewpoints, to consider others' thoughts and feelings in-depth, and seek more support and clarification of others' positions (Robert, n. d.). CLL emphasizes more cooperation with each other to gain knowledge and learning. Cooperative learning is the structured, systematic instructional technique in which small groups work together to achieve a common goal (Slavin, 1991). Cooperative language learning encourages mutual learning by motivating learners to have face to face interaction with each other. Learning together is a cooperative learning strategy created by Morton Deutsch, one of Lewin's graduate students, in the late 1940s. Learning together was originally designed to help train teachers on how to use cooperative learning groups in the classroom at the University of Minnesota in 1966. In the learning together strategy, cooperative effort includes five basic elements: face-to-face interaction, social skills, group processing, positive interdependence, and individual accountability (Johnson and Johnson, 1989).

As discussed above, various methods and approaches have evolved over time. All these methods and approaches dominated the stage of language teaching for a particular period and then other successive methods and approaches had replaced them. Opting for a particular method continued until when Kumaravadivelu (Professor Emeritus at San José State University, California) introduced the Post-Method era (see chapter 14). Kumaravadivelu (2003, 2001, 1994) states that the post-method pedagogy helps us to move beyond methods. The post-method (see chapter 14) condition suggests us to restructure our view of language teaching and teacher education. It invites our attention to review the character and content of classroom teaching in all its pedagogical and ideological perspectives. It drives us to reconceive our teacher education by refiguring the reified relationship between theory and practice (Kumaravadivelu, 2006). To implement it, three parameters are indispensable: particularity, practicality and possibility. Considering the particularity dimension, it is meant to respond to situational learning (Elliott, 1993). It motivates teacher to consider various aspects like specific situation, learning styles, and special learning context, etc. Teacher needs to analyze and reanalyze everything to come to a method, something that works for the group of learners in the institutional setting.

Regarding practicality, it encourages and enables teachers themselves to theorize from their practice and practice what they theorize (Kumaravadivelu, 1999). It provides teachers with enough liberty to implement their own experiences, which they might think, would inevitably benefit learners. Interestingly, teachers do not learn this from books rather it is the product of their own personal practices and experiences in the classroom. Becker (1986) states that particularity is something to be achieved. It means that we test and retest various techniques to assess what works and what does not. Prabhu (1990) states that there should be a relationship between the teaching context and the applied methodology.

The parameter of practicality motivates teachers to practice their own set of beliefs, which they get out of their experiences with language teaching in the classroom. Theory and practice continually and mutually inform and re-inform each other. It also calls for reflective teaching and action research i.e. trying to improve practice rather than producing knowledge. Pedagogical thoughtfulness is another term, which is related to the practicality parameter (Manen, 1991). So, it is a reflection of teacher on his own experiences in the classroom inspired by his personal beliefs and set of theories. Kumaravadivelu states (2006):

> The parameter of practicality, then, focuses on teachers' reflection and action, which are also based on their insights and intuition. Through prior and ongoing experience with learning and teaching, teachers gather an unexplained and sometimes explainable awareness of what constitutes good teaching (p.173).

The last parameter is possibility, which means that the method should be appropriate socially, culturally, and politically. It is related to identity formation and social transformation (Kumaravadivelu 2001, 2003). As learners have different identities, the teacher must respect variety in their identity. No learner should feel offended in the classroom.

The 2000s introduced the post-method era: a shift from using methods in the purist sense to recognizing that the nature of language learning is complex and non-linear. One particular method cannot be successful for all learners. Thus, the idea of implementing a particular method on learners lost its importance. The Post-method era did not search for an alternative method rather an alternate to method. Resultantly, the post-method era introduced many concepts, which were not practical though part of theory of various methods and approaches developed previously. The Post-method era provided the concepts of autonomous learner and autonomous teacher. It provided more freedom to teacher as well as learner. Teachers were free to follow any strategy or technique of teaching and learning suitable for the learners and they could switch from one technique to another. Teachers were also not bound to follow a particular method of teaching. They were free to adopt any technique or approach which could benefit learners at large. The Post-method era emphasized the context and identity. The context of language learning, including the use of pragmatics, cultural and social awareness, is an important aspect to be considered. Teachers must also take into consideration the identity of students, which plays an important role in a language classroom. As discussed above, students come with different socio-cultural, political and ethnic backgrounds, which create variety in their identity. Post-method era stresses that in a globalized world, the distance between the countries has been bridged. A language classroom may host global learners with multiple cultural, national, political, ethnic identities. The post-method era teacher takes into consideration these different identities of learners to effectively carry out teaching and learning in the classroom. Though post-method era does not necessitate following and implementing a single method, it has presented multiple other concepts and notions that teacher has to take into account while teaching in a language classroom. In a way, post-method era teacher is free to create his own experiences in the classroom. However, he must be certain that no strategy or technique counters the interests (social, political, racial, religious, personal etc.) of learners.

As discussed above, it is observed that most of the theorists have presented different theories about methods and approaches. All of them have certain principles and rules, which teachers are supposed to follow to successfully implement a particular method in the classroom. There have been various books on methods and approaches in English Language Teaching. However, there are very few books, which deal with the experiments and observations of different methods and approaches in the classroom in a particular situation. This book addresses the principles of different methods, approaches in detail, and presents feedback from students on every method and approach. The book includes experiences of teachers from different countries like Kingdom of Saudi Arabia, United States of America and India. The book presents the theoretical details about methods and approaches followed by their experiments and observations in an EFL and ESL situation. The book responds to not only teachers' opinions about the success rate of a particular method or approach but also simultaneously analyses students' opinions about the particular method and approach. Students are given a questionnaire based on a Likert scale to put forward their opinion against every statement based on the principles of each method and approach. Most of the statements in the questionnaire comprise of the contents taught in the classroom. The analysis of students' questionnaire is presented in form of graphs to clearly display the success rate of each method and approach. For the ease of analysis and discussion, 'agree' and 'strongly agree', scales are merged in the analysis and discussion sections. As the teacher primarily designs the questionnaire, it is not possible to include students' overall point of view about the teaching of each method or approach. That is why the teacher has also provided a set of open-ended question to students so that they can express their opinion about each method in detail. During the open-ended session, teachers also interviewed students and discussed with them difficulties, doubts or queries they had during the classroom teaching. Students also explain the reasons why they liked a particular method or approach implemented in the classroom.

The book has presented and analyzed a single EFL and ESL situation based on every method and approach. However, the analysis, experiences and observations demonstrate that these situations cover a wide range of issues of EFL and ESL learners worldwide. The book can be a resource for teachers as well as learners in different parts of world. It illustrates that methods are not obsolete and probably can never be. Each method has some advantages and disadvantages based on the situation in which it is used. Teachers must be oriented to different methods and approaches as it helps them to understand their classroom situations in a better way. Some methods prove to have a higher rate of success while others have a lower rate. The success of each method and approach also depends upon how a teacher utilizes them in a particular situation. This book provides learners an opportunity to raise their voice and be a part of not only teaching and learning process but also of research. The book has stressed the fact that methods are not dead, but are reborn from time to time residing in new bodies. Methods have characteristics common to each other. For example, the post-method era includes various characteristics which are part of other methods like 'autonomous learners' already proposed by the silent way. Different methods are used throughout the world in a variety of teaching and learning situations. They all provide learning instruction with the same desired output to an extent. This book has presented the methods and approaches in a new way. It supplements methods and approaches with student surveys in a particular ESL and EFL setting highlighting the advantages and disadvantages of the use of those methodologies in the specific classroom.

CHAPTER 2

The Grammar-Translation Method

In the nineteenth century, the Classical Method came to be known as the Grammar Translation Method. This Method began in Germany, or more precisely, Prussia, at the end of the eighteenth century. It became a very popular and favored methodology of the Prussia Gymnasien after their expansion in the early years of the nineteenth century. Richards and Rodgers (2001) rightly state, "Grammar Translation Method dominated European and foreign language teaching from the 1840s to the 1940s, and in modified form it continues to be widely used in some parts of the world today" (p6).

The method primarily focused to teach languages by grammar and translation. Grammar was the key concept in learning a new language. No second language was presumed to be learnt without sound knowledge of the target language. In the 18th century, the highly educated class acquired reading knowledge of a foreign language by studying grammar and applying this knowledge to the interpretation of texts with the use of a dictionary. Most of them were very well read people and had a good command over classical grammar. They were very well trained on how to use the familiar aspects of first language on the second language. Richard has rightly said about this aspect of grammar, "it was assumed that language learning meant building up a large repertoire of sentences and grammatical patterns and learning to produce these accurately and quickly in the appropriate situation" (as qtd. in Boumova, 2008, p. 12).

However, scholastic methods of this kind were not well suited to the competencies of younger school pupils and they were self-study methods, which were unsuitable for group teaching in the classroom (Chang, 2011)

This might be one of the sharpest criticisms of this method but it was a very popular method of its time. The Grammar-Translation Method also known as the classical method is one of the eldest methods of language teaching. It was the first ever method used to teach a foreign language. The Grammar-Translation Method, as the name suggests, is based on grammar and translation from native language to target language and vice versa as Richards and Rodgers (2001) opine, "Much of the lesson is devoted to translating sentences into and out of the target language, and it is this focus on the sentence that is a distinctive feature of the method" (p.6). The focus is on the translation that inculcates in itself the grammar of target language. This is twofold method. It develops two languages simultaneously, the native language and the target language. Learners learn not only the use of target language but also of their own native language. The method provides learners with an opportunity to learn their own mother tongue in a much better way which otherwise would not have been possible for them. Mother tongue was just like a reference for everything they did. Stern (1983) has rightly stated, "The first language is maintained as the reference system in the acquisition of the second language" (as qtd. in Richards and Rodgers, 2001, p.5). It is purely a grammar-based method where grammar is used as a medium to learn the target language. This method encourages rigorous practice through grammar exercises, mostly in isolation, to practice each item of grammar separately like, tenses, articles, preposition, article etc. so that students can form grammatically correct sentences. Thus, this method is a good one to develop grammatical competence among learners. Richard states:

> Grammatical competence refers to the knowledge we have of a language that accounts for our ability to produce sentences in a language. It refers to knowledge of building blocks of sentences (e.g. parts of speech, tenses, phrases, clauses, and sentence patterns) and how sentences are formed (as qtd. in Boumova, 2008, p. 1).

It is a teacher-centered method and teacher takes the charge of learning in the classroom. There is a lot of use of mother tongue in the classroom. All the rules of target language are explained in mother tongue. Teacher tries to provide all the grammatical equivalences of target language in to native language. Teacher presents the best contrastive analysis of both the languages in the classroom. There is hardly any focus on listening and speaking as language is hardly spoken or listened to in the classroom. In a way, it can be said that there is no communication in target language in the classroom and teachers usually focus only on literary passages and texts as Nagaraj (1996) states, "The learner is therefore exposed only to literary language. Communications skills are neglected with little attention to correct pronunciation" (p.4). Chang (2011) has rightly remarked about this method:

> The traditional grammar teaching method has its disadvantages, which prevent the students from developing their communicative competence. Firstly, the traditional grammar teaching method is teacher-centered. As a result, the majority of the classroom time is spent on the teachers' elaborate explanation of English grammar rules, while all the students are either listening or taking notes. Thus, little attention is paid to the development of English communicative competence (p. 13).

However, this method got so much popularity in 18th century because it hardly leaves any room of confusion for the learners as all the rules are explained in the target language. In order to understand how this method is implemented in the classrooms even today, let us step into a classroom in India where teacher is using Grammar-Translation Method to teach a class of intermediate level.

Experience

It is an intermediate class in a senior secondary school in UP, India. Teacher is teaching Present Indefinite Tense in the classroom. He describes students how to identify present indefinite tense. This identification is provided in Hindi language. Teacher explains present indefinite tense that usually ends in *'ta hai'*, *'ti hai'*, *'te hain'*. *'Ta hai'* stands for masculine gender and singular noun or pronoun. *'Ti hai'* stands for feminine gender and singular noun or pronoun. *'Te hain'* stands for masculine gender and plural noun or pronoun. *'Ti hain'* stands for feminine gender and plural noun or pronoun. The second rule teacher asks student to write about the use of verb 1st and verb 1st with 's' or 'es'. Teacher explains with he, she, it and singular 's' or 'es' is added into the first form of the verb while with I, we, you, they and plural 's' or 'es' are not added into it. For example, he says in Hindi *woh ghar jata hai*. He translates it as 'He goes to school'. He provides them with around eight sentences to practice on the same pattern. Then he switches to plural subject and singular verb structure. He explains to students that subjects like I, we, you, they and plurals do not take 's' or 'es' at the end of the first form of the verb. He asks students to write a sentence into Hindi like *hum kitab padte hain*. Then he asks students to translate it. They translate it as 'We read a book'. Teacher gives around ten sentences in Hindi and asks the students to translate them into English. Teacher names them as affirmative sentences and provides a structure like,

SUBJECT   +   VERB 1ST   (S OR ES)   +   OBJECT
↓   ↓
(with I, we, you, they and plural subject) (with he, she it and singular subject)

He asks the students to memorize the rules and verb forms with 's' or 'es'. Then switches the class to teach the negative sentences based on the present indefinite tense. Following the same steps, he explains students the identification of the tense like it ends with *ta hai, ti hai, te hain*. The only difference is that it uses the negative word *'nhi'* in Hindi that makes it negative statement. Teacher explains 'does not' is used with he, she, it, singular while 'do not' is used with I, we, you, they and plural in the sentences as an equivalent to *'nhi'* in Hindi. He provides students with a structural pattern of negative sentences like this,

SUBJECT   +   do not / does not   +   VERB 1ST   +   OBJECT
↓   ↓
(with I, we, you, they and plural subject)   (with he, she, it and singular subject)

Teacher explains students that there is no addition of 's' or 'es' in the first form of the verb in negative sentences. Teacher provides students with around ten examples that they translate into English. With a few confusions of singular and plural, students were able to translate all the sentences. Teacher supplied students immediately with correct translation wherever he found errors.

Then teacher explains how interrogative sentences are formed in Present Indefinite tense. The same way, he first provides with the identification of the tense like it starts with '*kia*' in Hindi. Unfortunately, there is no equivalent of Hindi word '*kia*' (Yes, No question) in English when it comes in the beginning. Teacher just explains when there is '*kia*' in Hindi sentence; we do not need to translate it. Teacher explains here Yes, No questions in English.

For example:

KIA WHO GHAR JATA HAI?
Is translated as
Does he go to home?

However, teacher explains students if '*kia*'(what) word is in the mid of a sentence like *who kia likhta hai*, its English is used in sentence and is put in the beginning of a sentence like,

WOH KIA LIKHTA HAI?
Is translated as
What does he write?

Therefore, he provides students with two structures: one with YES, NO question and another with WH (information question). Here too, he explains students that 'does' is used with 'he', 'she', 'it' and singular while 'do' is used with I, we you, they and plural subjects. He provides students with two structures like:

Does / do + Subject+ verb 1st + Object+? (YES/ NO question structure)
What, where, when, how, which, whose, how + does / do + Subject+ verb 1st + Object+?
(Information question structure)

Then teacher explains interrogative+ negative sentences with a minor addition of 'not' in the previously provided structure like

Does / Do + Subject+ not+ verb 1st + Object? (YES/ NO question structure)
What, where, when, how, which, whose, how + does / do + Subject+
not+ verb 1st + Object? (Information question structure)

Teacher provides students eight sentences to practice in the class while he gives 20 sentences along with ten forms of verb to practice at home as a homework. The class ends here.

Observation

Teacher observed that students took interest in translation from native to target language. They understood each and everything about the present indefinite tense, its identification, usage, rules etc. There was no room left for confusion and students understood rules as they were explained in their native language. Students memorized the identification of tense, its rules and forms of verbs with 's' or 'es'. Teacher emphasized on accuracy and students made least mistakes while translating from native to target language. As far as the summative assessment is concerned, students were assessed on accuracy in their formal examination. The examination pattern required in-depth knowledge of subtle grammar rules and their application in the form of sentence and paragraph translation, as Howatt (1984) rightly says about the accuracy in this method, "the high priority attached to meticulous standards of accuracy which, as well as having an intrinsic moral value, was a prerequisite for passing the increasing number of formal written examinations that grew up during the century" (p. 132). The classroom covered two skills: reading and writing. Richards and Rodgers (2001) rightly state, "Reading and writing are the major focus; little or no systematic attention is paid to speaking and listening" (p.6). It is true that there was no scope to practice other two skills like listening and speaking so that they can improve their communicative competence. Memorization of rules makes them feel indifferent to communicative use of language as Chang (2011) states, "Memorization and rote learning are the basic learning techniques, which cannot help to arouse students' interest, build their self-confidence or improve their communicative strategies in English learning and even makes them fear English grammar learning" (p. 13-14)

Teachers primarily use deductive method in order to teach through Grammar-Translation Method. Teachers explain and analyze the rules followed by rigorous practice. Rao and Ediger (2014) rightly state, "The rules and principles of Grammar are thrust upon the children and this grammar is taught through deductive method which is rule conscious. So, memorization of grammatical rules, paradigms, bilingual word lists and application of these in translation constitute the essence of this method" (p.94). Students were given homework, which they were supposed to complete the next day. Teacher observed that it was easier to explain the rules in mother tongue rather than the target language, as they could not understand the target language at all. Explaining the rules in target language led some of the learners to confusions. Students asked why we do not use English of 'kia' word in Hindi if it comes in the beginning. Teacher seemed to have no answer for this question, as there cannot be complete replacement of one language with another one. It seems as two languages were taught at the same time in the classroom. English was taught through Hindi. The classroom lacked activities and exercises only in listening and speaking skills; otherwise, it was a good class. The classroom did not follow the natural hierarchy of language learning like listening, speaking, reading and writing.

However, it was teachers' perspective regarding the application of Grammar Translation Method. Everything was narrated through the experience of the teachers. No voice of students is heard during the implementation of the method. Teacher narrated the experiences of the students as he felt them to be. Nevertheless, students were not given any chance to raise their voice. Success of this method cannot be truly measured until students, the target group, are given an opportunity to express their opinion and share their experiences. In order to record students' observation and experiences, a questionnaire set was given to them focusing on the key elements of Grammar Translation Method especially on the contents, which were taught in the classroom. In addition to the questionnaire, students were also interviewed with a set of open-ended questions to assess whether students had any query, doubt or confusion, which were not the part of the questionnaire. The open-ended questions provided enough space to students to put forward their opinion frankly.

Analysis of Students' Feedback

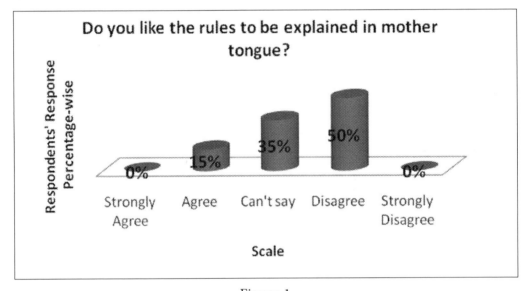

Figure 1

It was the first question (fig.1) directly put forward to the students. They were asked in the questionnaire if they liked the rules to be explained in their mother tongue. Their responses reveal that there is none who strongly agreed to the statement. Only 15% participants (a minority) felt that they liked the rules to be explained in mother tongue. 35% of the participants had no idea. 50% (a majority) of the participants disagreed.

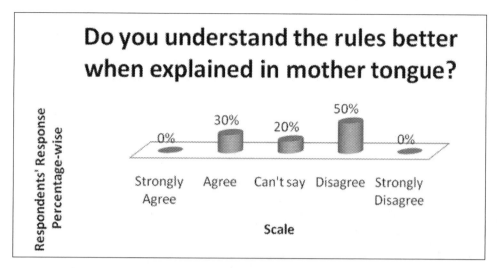

Figure 2

The second statement (fig.2) in the questionnaire was intended to rate whether students understand the rules better when explained in mother tongue. The result displays that there is nobody who strongly agreed to the statement. However, 30% of the participants opined that they understood the rules better when explained in mother tongue. 50% of the participants disagreed though 20% of the participants had no idea.

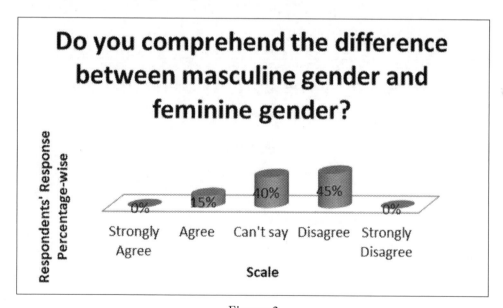

Figure 3

The third question (fig.3) aimed to know whether students comprehended the difference between masculine and feminine gender. The data shows that there is none who strongly agreed to the statement. 15% of the participants are of the opinion that they comprehend the difference between masculine and feminine gender. 45% of the participants disagreed to the statement though 40% of the participants had no opinion.

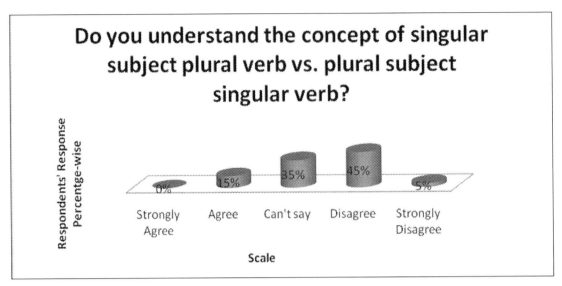

Figure 4

The fourth statement in the questionnaire (fig.4) if they understand the concept of singular subject plural verb versus plural subject singular verb exhibits that 'strongly agreed' is not assigned any value. There are 15% of the participants who agreed they understood the concept of singular subject plural verb versus plural subject singular verb.45% of the participants disagreed to it though 35% of the participants had no opinion. 5% of the participants strongly disagreed to the statement.

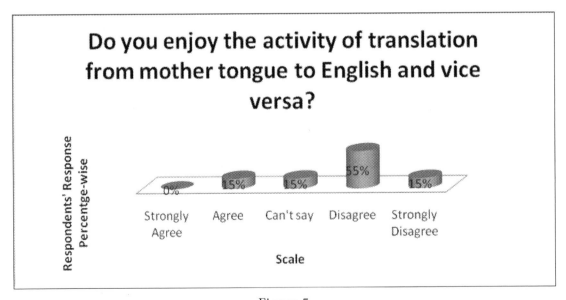

Figure 5

The fifth statement in the questionnaire (fig.5) if they enjoy the activity of translation from mother tongue to English and vice versa divulges that there is none who strongly agreed to the statement that they enjoyed the activity of translation from mother tongue to English and vice versa. 15% of the participants agreed with the statement though the same number (15%)

of the participants did not express their opinion. 55% of the participants disapproved and 15% of the participants strongly disagreed with the statement.

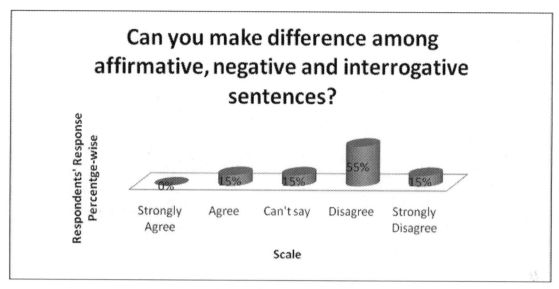

Figure 6

The sixth statement in the questionnaire (fig.6) if students can make difference among affirmative, negative and interrogative sentences discloses that there is none who strongly agreed to the statement. 15% of the participants concurred that they could differentiate among affirmative, negative and interrogative sentences. 15% of the participants were not sure about it. 55% of the participants disagreed. 15% of the participants strongly disagreed.

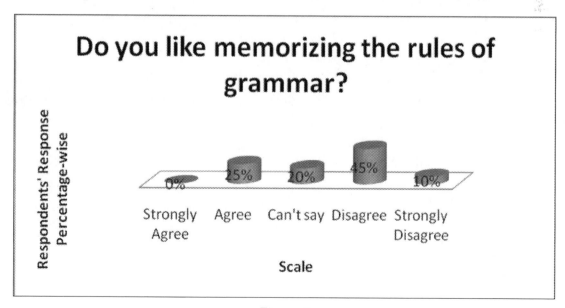

Figure 7

The seventh statement in the questionnaire (fig.7) if students like memorizing rules of grammar show that there is none who strongly agreed to the statement. 25% of the participants concurred that they liked memorizing rules of grammar. 20% of the participants were not sure about it. 45% of the participant disagreed. 10% of the participants strongly disagreed.

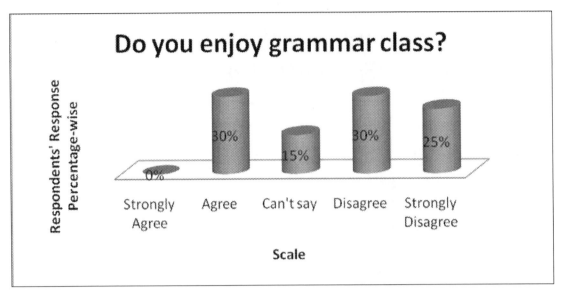

Figure 8

The eighth statement in the questionnaire (fig.8) if they enjoy grammar class unveils that there is none in absolute agreement to the statement that they enjoy grammar class. 30% of the participants agreed while there are 15% of the participants who did not state an opinion. 30% of the participants did not agree with the statement and 25% of the participants had absolute disagreement.

Interview Questions

Twenty samples were selected out of 30. The participants responded to the following questions in the interview:

1. Mention some difficulties faced in a grammar class:

2. Mention some confusions, doubts or queries you had

Table-1: Results of Interview Question no.1

Q.1.	Number of participants	some difficulties faced in a grammar class
	5	No session for students to know their problems
	6	Students were not given chance to state the extent they liked the class

| | 5 | Teacher did not engage the learners in teaching process
It was a totally teacher-centered class |
| | 4 | Teacher practiced certain sentences like *woh ghar jata hai, sita gana gati hai*
Teacher did not provide variety of sentences |

Table-2: Results of Interview Question no.2

Q.2.	Number of participants	some confusions, doubts or queries
	5	How can *I* be a plural. It is singular *You* can be both a singular and a plural Why *you* is always treated as plural
	6	Why do we not use English of the word *kia?* *Does not* is used with singular while *I* and *You* both can be singular
	5	How can we use *do* or *does* in the beginning of a sentence to denote English of Hindi word *kia* while in Hindi its meaning is *what* that is totally different
	4	When *kia* comes in the mid of a sentence in WH questions, its English *what* is used in the beginning of a sentence. Why do not we use its English in YES, NO questions

Discussion and Conclusion

The analysis of students' responses through questionnaire displays the difference between claimed control and actual performance. During the implementation of the method, teacher claimed this method to be a big success while the analysis of the data exhibits opposite results. There is a remarkable difference between what teachers claimed about the success of this method and what it actually turned out to be.

There is a major gap between what teacher observed and what students expressed. If we scan teachers' observation regarding the success of this method, it turned out to be a great success. However, one needs to go into details what aspects teacher took into consideration while he or she assumed the method to be a big success. Teachers provided students with some identification of the tenses in their mother tongue, which they correlated to the target language. They might have memorized certain rules of singular subject plural verb vs. plural subject singular verb. On this basis, they might have translated a few sentences, which cannot guarantee that students learnt the use of tense that might help them learn the target language. Students might have bred so many confusions, which they did not dare to ask their teacher, but they expressed them in interview sessions. For example, teacher states: singular subject takes plural verb and plural subject has singular verb. Teacher' explanation of masculine and feminine gender also owes a lot to its correlation with mother tongue. Students were confused as they expressed in interview in response to question 2. They were unable to comprehend how *I* can be treated as a plural though it is singular. The same is the case with the pronoun *you* which could be both singular and plural. Why is it always treated as plural? The same denotes to negative and interrogative sentences. Students were confused why ***does not*** is used with both singular and plural pronouns i.e. *I* and *you*. Here they probably consider *I* and *you* as singular. Another important query students had was: why English of the Hindi word ***kia*** is not used while coming in the beginning of a sentence though its English is used when it comes in the mid of a sentence. These were some of the difficulties students had regarding the understanding of the tense. These doubts of students were not cleared by the teachers as there was no satisfactory answer to these questions. One of the most considerable facts with Grammar-Translation Method is that it hardly has any scope for innovation and experiment with new techniques. Teachers blindly follow the textbook as if it is the Bible for the learners. They hardly use their mind to make some innovations in teaching. Nagaraj (1996) rightly opines about this method, "In this method, the teacher is totally dependent on the text as s/he follows the given lessons and exercises in it rigidly. S/he has little scope for innovative planning to incorporate the actual needs of the learners in the classroom" (p.4). There is no scope to take into account learners' needs or address the issues they have. Translation produces many doubts in learners, which are not regarding English language as the interview with students suggests, rather these doubts were the product of the translation of one language to another. Students had these issues because they were not only learning one language rather two languages at a time. They focused more on comparing and contrasting two languages rather than learning about target language. Teachers' conscious focus was not only to teach them one language, target language, rather to teach them two languages: target language consciously and their mother tongue unconsciously which they never got a chance to study since their birth. Freeman (2000) rightly asserts about this method that, "through the study of the grammar of the target language, students would become more familiar with the grammar of their native language and that this familiarity would help them speak and write their native language better" (p.11). However, this familiarity leads to much confusion when there were so many grammatical items of which no comparison was there in the target language. There is no complete structural replacement of one language with another one. Students concentrated more on finding out the equivalence of one language with the other one rather than learning the second language. These doubts were the result of teaching two languages at the same time.

As far as teacher's approach and technique are concerned, students were not very much satisfied with them. It is quite interesting to see that the self-proclaimed teacher predicted that students liked his way of teaching while the data collected through the questionnaire and interview state the facts otherwise. Many of the students stated in the questionnaire that they did not like grammar class. Some of the students had not decided about whether they liked this class or not. Many of the students straightforwardly admitted that they did not like the grammar class. The same is also stated in the interview set of questions as stated in response to question one. Students stated that they were not given a chance to participate in the classroom. It shows that teacher followed teacher-centered approach where teacher was all in all in the classroom. He was the in-charge and not the facilitator of language learning process. Freeman (2000) rightly states about the approach of this method, "The teacher is the authority in the classroom. The students do as she says so they can learn what she knows" (p.17). Teacher was like a priest giving a sermon and students were like the pupils of a saint who only had to listen to silently to what a priest says and had no power and right to question them. Students were not given a chance to put forward their problems. Another issue that students raised regarding the practice of the same sentences denotes to lack of innovative techniques on part of the teacher. Teacher provided only one type of practice to students. There was a lot of repetition and no variety of sentences was provided to students. It minimized and limited their exposure to second language learning acquisition.

CHAPTER 3

The Direct Method

The Direct Method of teaching came as a reaction to the Grammar-Translation method in the 19th century. Grammar-Translation method taught language through grammar rules, syntactic structures, excessive use of mother tongue, and translation from first language to the second language. This method requires rigorous practice in target language through translation of individual sentences, literary passages, and short paragraphs without providing a context. All these exercises to learn a language are termed as 'unnatural way' of learning a language. The argument behind this theory is supported by the fact that a child learns his or her first language in a natural environment and in a natural way without any formal training. They do not go to any school to learn a language. They do not use any book whether of grammar, stories, or literature in order to learn the first language. A child through his environment usually acquires first language. Whatever he listens to in his environment, he speaks the same language. For example, a child born in an English speaking country naturally speaks English language. He does not memorize grammar rules, verb forms, syntactical structures, morphological and phonological aspects of a language etc. A native speaker of a language is well versed in all the grammatical components of language without being consciously taught and without being consciously aware of his knowledge in the native language. They are unaware of these mental operations, which take place in their mind unconsciously. Satya (2008) writes about these mental operations, "Such mental operations are part of their grammatical sub-consciousness and may be called psycho-grammatical in so far as they imply workings of the mind (psych) aimed at generating linguistic (grammatical) structures" (p.45-46). A native speaker never gets any training in order to train his or her mind to produce the second language nor does he attend a lesson in his or her language. Nevertheless, he has a good command over the language as a speaker and listener of the language without joining a formal teaching program. He can easily comprehend his native language. He can decode the message in his native language without being trained in the art of translation. As far as reading and writing skills are concerned, a native speaker needs classes for them but there are no classes to develop listening and speaking skills.

Francois Gouin (a French linguist and a pioneer of language acquisition studies) who tried to build a methodology on this concept of child learning presents the same model of language learning. In 1880, he wrote a book called the *Art of Teaching and Learning of Languages*. According to this book as Nagaraj (1996) states, "a foreign language could be taught using a series of simple events. The teacher described each event in the foreign language and set reading and writing tasks on these lessons. The teacher used *full sentences* in the foreign language as input rather than words and phrases; no translation was used" (p.71). Other reformers like

Sauveur also turned their attention to naturalistic principles of language learning laying the foundation for natural method of language learning. He opined that foreign language, as we discussed above, can be taught without the help of the native language of learners. In order to learn the second language without the help of the mother tongue, one needs to communicate the message through demonstration and action as a child does when he or she learns first language. Mart (2013) asserts, "The Direct Method will enable students to understand the language which will help them to use the language with ease; moreover, as L1 is not allowed students learn the language through demonstration and conversation which will lead them to acquire fluency" (p. 183). There is a lot of use of visual teaching materials in Direct Method as it motivates learners to speak the language. Kruidenier J, (2002, as qtd. in Chen 2011, p. 72) states that with no recourse to the students' native language, the meaning of target language will be conveyed directly by demonstration and the implementation of visual teaching materials. Students, therefore, can overcome the habits of their native language and mentally form the new habits of English. The German scholar F. Franke (1884 as quoted in Richards and Rodgers, 2001, p. 11) wrote on the principles of direct association between forms and meaning in the target language. He believes that language can be taught by using it actively in the classroom. There is no use of rigorous practice of memorizing the rules of target language and then implementing them in the classroom to learn the target language. Learners would themselves induce the grammar rules from the structure they use to communicate their message.

These natural language learning principles prepared the foundation for the formulation of the Direct Method and can be synonyms with Natural Method. As its approach was to naturally learn a language, it got wide publicity and popularity in France, Germany, US and other parts of the world. Grammar-Translation Method lost its popularity because it lacked the basic function of a language that is communication. If any teaching method lacks in training the students to train in communication, it cannot survive longer. It was proved when the Direct Method replaced this method because the very essence of the Direct Method was communication. It emphasized more on communication rather than any other aspect of language. This Method follows the natural hierarchy of language learning; listening, speaking, reading and writing. Listening plays a vital role in the language acquisition, as it is the first step in learning a language followed by other skills. Therefore, there is a lot of listening in the environment a child lives and finally he speaks the language that he listens to in his environment. E. G. Kitson rightly states, "Learning to speak a language is, by far, the shortest road to learning to read and write" (as qtd. in Rao and Ediger, 2014, p. 100). Rivers summarizes the characteristics of the Direct Method as "students learn to understand a language by listening to a great deal of it and that they learn to speak it by speaking it- associating speech with appropriate action" (Rivers, 1968, p.18).

The problem with the Grammar-Translation Method is that it has no scope to develop communication among students. Freeman (2000) rightly asserts, "Since the Grammar-Translation Method was not very effective in preparing students to use the target language communicatively, the Direct Method became popular" (p. 23). Unlike Grammar- Translation method, Direct Method stresses on using the language directly without providing any translation in target language. So, a lot of time and energy were saved on memorization and drilling which is a very unnatural way of learning a language. Language cannot be treated like History. In History, one memorizes the facts to pass the examination and score better grades. This method cannot be applied on language learning and teaching as language is completely different form History or other disciplines, which focus on memorization. Direct Method got extreme popularity because it proposes that language must be learnt in a natural way as one learns one's mother tongue without memorization of grammar rules and translation from mother tongue to the target language as Stern believes that Direct Method is characterized by the use of the target language as a means of instruction and communication in the language classroom, and by the avoidance of the use of the first language and of translation as a technique (Stern, 1983). One does not learn grammar rules to learn the mother tongue as it is acquired naturally. A child learns his mother tongue unconsciously. He doesn't make any conscious effort to learn the mother tongue. In fact, it will be more difficult for him to acquire the language if it comes through memorization and drilling. It will create more impediments in language learning. Rao and Ediger (2014) have rightly stated, "It is clear that we learn our mother tongue more naturally and unconsciously. When we try to teach by rules, the rule consciousness will make the learner halt and falter at every step and come in way of his progress rather than help him to pick the language" (p.72) Concisely, it can be said that direct method believes in language acquisition rather than language learning. In this method, students are given maximum exposure to the target language so that they can acquire the language in their environment. Direct method completely discards the use of mother tongue in the classroom in order to learn the target language as Rao and Ediger (2014) state, "Mother tongue is not allowed in the classroom. So, Direct Method discourages the intervention of mother tongue since the aim is to enable the child to understand directly what is spoken, read and expressed directly"(100-101).

By the 1920s, use of the Direct Method began to lose its grounds in noncommercial schools in Europe. In France and Germany, it was mixed with some grammar controlled activities. It means it borrowed some of the practices of the Grammar-Translation Method to which its advocates had harshly criticized in the advent of Direct Method. Here we agree to Rao and Ediger (2014), "The rules of grammar should not be taught separately, but they also should not be totally ignored. In fact, teaching of grammar is necessary and sometimes essential; the only difference is the way of teaching" (p.72). Here, they stress on the way of teaching. The stress is on the importance of teaching grammar inductively. Learners must be given some examples of sentences without analyzing the rules as we do in deductive method. Students themselves will form the rules out of the sentences and its effect will be more lasting.

In order to assess the practical application and outputs of this method, one study is shared here which was conducted at an intermediate level class in the PY section of Najran University, KSA. In this class, contrary to the usual practices, teacher is using Direct Method in the classroom.

Experience

The topic of the lecture is Present continuous / progressive tense. Teacher has to make students understand what present continuous tense is and how it is used in a particular situation to communicate their ideas. There are twenty students in the classroom. Teacher distributes a bottle of water and a piece of cake to every student. It was a quite an unusual practice as it never happens in the classroom, as students reported. Teacher uses these audible items as realia (objects and material from everyday life used as teaching aids) in the classroom. Students open the packet of cake. Teacher asks them: what are you doing? They say cake open. Teacher encourages them to use a complete sentence like "I am opening the packet of cake." Then teacher says I am taking the cake out. Students repeat the same with the teachers. Teacher writes some words (verb, objects, subject) on the white board with different color pens like drink water, eat cake, share with others, close bottle, clean mouth, I feel etc. Teacher asks them to form sentences with these words and he lets students feel free without realizing them that teacher is in the class. He encourages students to help each other and strictly prohibits use of mother tongue in the classroom. He takes round in the classroom and ascertains that students are using target language in the classroom. Students make sentences like *I am drinking water, I am eating cake, I am sharing it with others, I am closing bottles, I am cleaning my mouth, I am feeling good.* They do the same action simultaneously as they speak the sentences. Students learn the use of these sentences in the classroom.

Then teacher shares a picture with students to further practice present continuous tense and asks them to describe it in English, the target language.

Students feel enthusiastic to see the picture and describe the pictures with some incorrect formation of sentences. Teacher does not interrupt students for accuracy and encourages them to come up with different description of the picture. Some of the sentences students spoke (based on the picture) are as follows: Friends *are sitting with each other. Some people eating snacks. They are enjoying at coffee shop. They are laughing. They are talking to each other. They are drinking together. They are eating food.*

Observations

Teacher observed that students were enjoying the teaching in the class. They were using the language for the real communication. Teacher created a situation and students participated in the situations. They were excited by the use of pictures as it encouraged them use their faculty of imagination. Students came with varied description of the picture. They had a different description. Teacher's distribution of cake and water made them feel that they were not in the classroom rather they were enjoying a party with their friends. Teacher observed that they were using language to communicate the present situation as described in the picture. Students learnt the use of auxiliary verb is, are, am with verb first and 'ing'.

(https://pixabay.com/photos/coventry-garden-market-london-food-973852/)

As language is primarily used for speech, this principle was exploited to its most in the classroom. The classroom followed the natural hierarchy of language learning like listening, speaking, reading and writing.

However, it was teachers' perspective regarding the application of the Direct Method. Teacher followed the learner-centered approach and involved them in learning process. Students were encouraged to come up with new structures in target language. Teacher emphasized more on fluency. Teacher overlooked a few grammatical mistakes as it might have discouraged the students and broken their rhythm of speaking the target language. Though this method turned out to do well, success of this method cannot be truly measured until students, the target group, are given an opportunity to express their opinion and share their experiences. In order to record students' observation and experiences, a questionnaire set was given to them focusing on the key elements of the Direct Method especially on the contents, which were taught in the classroom. In addition to the questionnaire, students were also interviewed with a set of open-ended questions to assess whether they had any query, doubt or confusion, which were not the part of the questionnaire. The open-ended questions provided enough space to students to put forward their opinion frankly.

Analysis of Students' Feedback

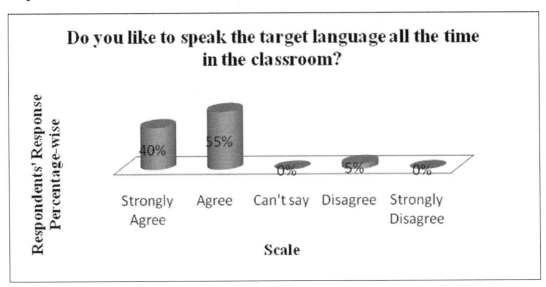

Figure 1

The first statement in the questionnaire if *students like to speak the target language all the time in the classroom* reveals that there are 40% participants who felt that *they liked to speak the target language all the time in the classroom* 55% of the participants admitted to it. 5% of the participants disagreed.

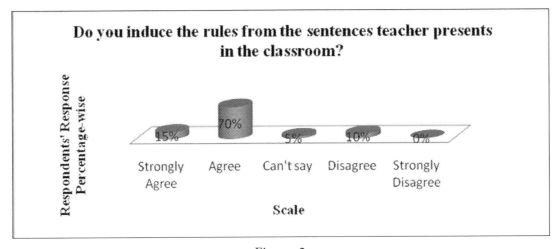

Figure 2

The second statement in the questionnaire if *they induce the rules from the sentences teacher presents in the classroom* displays that there are 15% of the participants who opined *they induced the rules from the sentences teacher presents in the classroom.* 70% of the participants agreed though (5%) of the participants had no idea. 10% of the participants did not accept the statement.

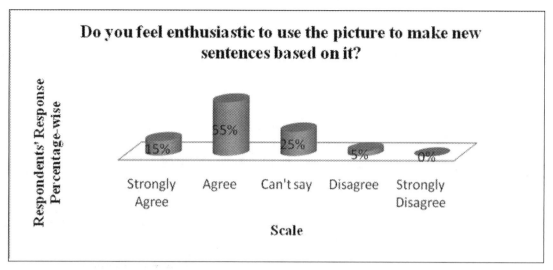

Figure 3

The third statement in the questionnaire if *they feel enthusiastic to use the picture to make new sentences based on it* shows that 15% of the participants are of the opinion that *they feel enthusiastic to use the picture to make new sentences based on it.* 55% of the participants agreed to the statement though 25% of the participants had no opinion. 5% of the participants dissented.

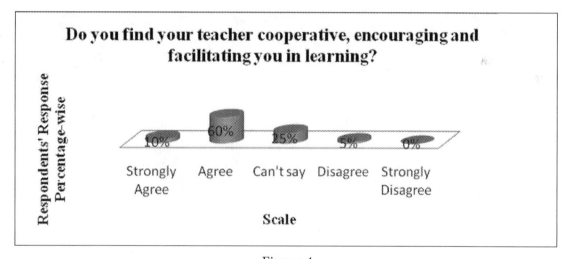

Figure 4

The fourth statement in the questionnaire if *they find their teacher cooperative, encouraging and facilitating them in learning* exhibits that there are 10% of the participants who strongly agreed that *they found their teacher cooperative, encouraging and facilitating them in learning.* 60% of the participants also admitted to it though 25% of the participants had no opinion. 5% of the participants disagreed to the statement.

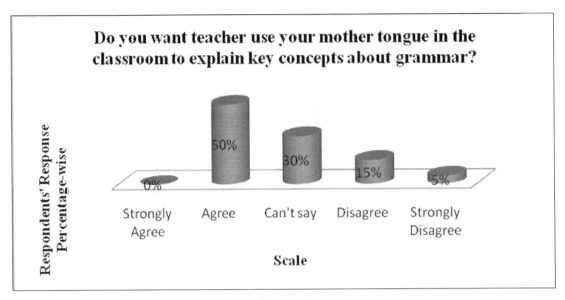

Figure 5

The fifth statement in the questionnaire whether *they want teacher use their mother tongue in the classroom to explain key concepts about grammar* divulges that there is none who strongly agreed to the statement. 50% of the participants agreed with the statement though (30%) of the participants did not express their opinion. 15% of the participants disapproved and 5% of the participants strongly disagreed with the statement.

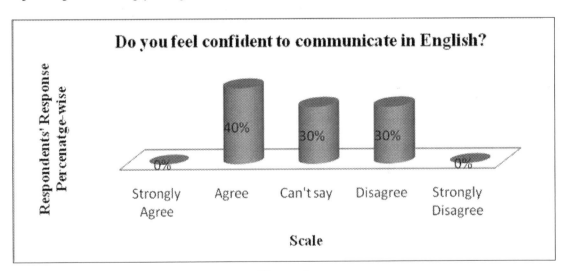

Figure 6

The sixth statement in the questionnaire if *they feel confident to communicate in English* discloses that there is none who strongly agreed to the statement. 40% of the participants concurred that *they felt confident to communicate in English.* 30% of the participants were not sure about it. 30% of the participant disagreed.

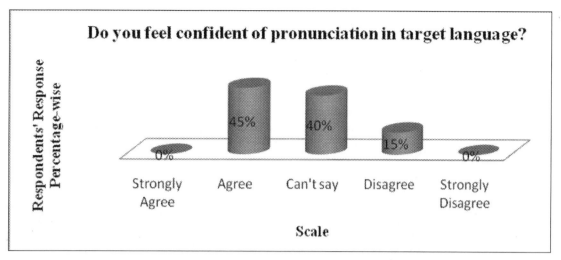

Figure 7

The seventh statement in the questionnaire if *they feel confident of pronunciation in target language* shows that there is none who strongly agreed to the statement. 45% of the participants concurred that *they felt confident of pronunciation in target language*. 40% of the participants were not sure about it. 15% of the participants disagreed.

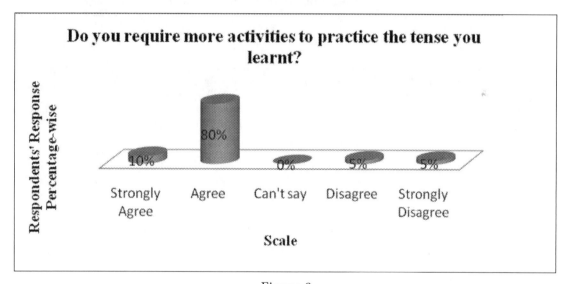

Figure 8

The eighth statement in the questionnaire if *they require more activities to practice the tense they learnt* unveils that 10% of the participants were in absolute agreement to the statement that *they required more activities to practice the tense they learnt*. A big no (80%) of the participants agreed while there was none who did not state an opinion. 5% of the participants did not agree with the statement and the same number (5%) of the participants had absolute disagreement.

Interview Questions

Twenty samples were selected out of 30 in which participants responded to the following questions in the interview:

1. Mention some difficulties faced in class:

2. Mention some confusions, doubts or queries you had:

Table-1: Results of Interview Question no.1

Q.1.	Number of participants	some difficulties faced in class
	5	Not able to communicate in English
	6	Could not understand everything what teacher said
	5	Mother tongue was completely banned so couldn't understand instructions and ask the questions as we did not know how to ask questions in English
	4	It was difficult to describe the picture completely

Table-2: Results of Interview Question no.2

Q.2.	Number of participants	some confusions, doubts or queries
	5	Why can we not use *is* with *I* if it is singular Why do we remove *e* from the verb *share* while adding 'ing' into it Why *you* is always treated as plural
	6	The focus was only on the pronouns like *they* and *I*
	5	Teacher did not provide any rule about how to use auxiliaries with different pronouns which led to confusion
	4	Still confusion among subject, verb and object

Discussion and Conclusion

The analysis of students' questionnaire proves that most of the students were satisfied with the implementation of the Direct Method of Teaching in the classroom. However, the data collected through questionnaire and interview questions show that not all of the students were satisfied with this method. This is the fact that most of the students (95%) wanted to speak the target language all the time in the classroom. However, as the interview question set displays that they were not able to communicate in the target language. It means their desire is to learn the language but they still do not know how to get command over the target language. This is a very important point as practicing a few sentences on a situation cannot make learners command the language. One needs to think, behave and act in the language if one really wants to acquire a language. This kind of approach to language teaching provides exposure to a particular situation, which not necessarily can provide a canvas to the learners' imagination. Kwambehar (2015) has rightly indicated towards another important criticism of this method in these words, "Another weakness of this method is that the mechanical repetitive drills which were outwardly done may not impart the thoughts of the learners" (p.30). It is considerable that these mechanical drillings in a language cannot ignite the spark of imagination, which could provide a platform to the language learners where they can form infinite sentences in the target language. One of the most important principles of language and discourse is to form the infinite number of well-formed sentences that could be generated with finite means. This principle of language and discourse is missing here. It is so because mechanical and context-specific situational drilling cannot pave the way for the learners to form the sentences and use language beyond situations. This type of teaching is like a body without soul.

One of the reasons for poor communication among students may be attributed to teacher's inability to pay individual attention on every child as the class is big. Here we agree to Rao and Ediger (2014) who opine about the Direct Method, "Method needs individual attention on pupils. So, it does not suit to our conditions in the class" (p.103). The classes at PY where this method was experimented are usually packed. It is not possible for a teacher to pay individual attention on each child. Moreover, the teachers also have to finish lengthy syllabus on time. This is another reason, which limits their creativity with the method. This study assures that students need more classes and exposure to target language before being able to communicate confidently in the target language. Direct Method requires a lot of practice and exposure to target language in order to enable students to speak target language fluently, accurately and confidently. Direct Method is criticized because it claims to learn the target language as one learns one's mother tongue. However, Direct Method of teaching neglects one very practical fact that the amount of time one spends learning first language can never be equal to the time spent in target language. A learner learns the first language from his cradle. He gets his family members, his friends, his neighbors as his unconscious teachers who always keep him teaching the first language especially listening and speaking skills. So, the quality and quantity of time is very important while learning a language. Kwambehar (2015) has rightly said:

> This method aims at enabling the learner to learn and acquire the L2 as he did the L1. This aim seems unrealistic because the time and the opportunity the learner has to learn the TL are too limited as compared to his L1 acquisition. Whereas the learner had all the time right from birth to his L1, he is faced with limited number of minutes on the school timetable to learn the L2, the rate of learning cannot be the same (p. 30).

In response to statement two, a majority of students (85%) admitted they were able to obtain the rules from the sentences they spoke in the classroom. However, 5% of the students did not express opinion and 10% disagreed to the statement. It is also clearly visible during the interview session, as many of the students confessed they were confused with the auxiliary verb rules. It shows that not all of the students were able to induce the rules from the sentences. It invites our attention to the fact why Direct Method declined in Europe by the 1920s. One of the prominent reasons might be lack of methodological basis of Direct Method. The British applied linguist Henry Sweet is also of the view that Direct Method of Teaching provided with many innovative techniques but it lacked a thorough methodological basis (Richards and Rodgers, 2001, p. 13). As students also expressed they needed some more activities to practice the tense, which stressed the need of grammatical activities, which are part of Grammar-Translation Method. Here too we require to include some portions from Grammar-Translation Method as was the need felt in France and Germany by the 1920s. Richards and Rodgers (2001) state about this method, "In France and Germany it was gradually modified into versions that combined some Direct Method techniques with more controlled grammar-based activities" (p.13).

The third statement in the questionnaire if they feel enthusiastic to use the picture to make new sentences based on it shows that a majority of students (55%+15%) agree that they feel enthusiastic to use the picture to make new sentences based on it. However, 25% of the students did not express their opinion. It shows they could not understand what to do with pictures. As during the interview session, in response to question one, around five students admitted that they could not understand instructions properly. It is one of the drawbacks of the Direct Method that sometimes students cannot understand instructions. As mother tongue is completely banned, neither teacher nor student can ask question or explain instructions in mother tongue. This study emphasizes on the inclusion of mother tongue in the classroom, at least, to understand instructions. However, teacher can solve this problem by improving his teaching techniques or changing classroom management. He can form the group of four students and make one brilliant student leader of the group who can help his friends in understanding the instructions. Nevertheless, teachers' efforts to use visual aids, contrary to common practices, are praiseworthy as there are many students who are motivated by visual aids and not by oral session in the class as Rao and Ediger (2014) state, "Emphasis is laid on oral approach, but there are many more who pay interest in visual things (p103)."

The fourth statement in the questionnaire if they find their teacher cooperative, encouraging and facilitating them in learning exhibits that a majority of students agreed to the statement. However, 25% of the participants had no opinion, which reflects the gap between the teacher and students. This percentage of students is also reflected during interview session, which confirms the assumption that some of the students maintained distance from teacher because of language barrier, as they did not know at all how to speak target language. One of the reasons of this gap may also be the overcrowded classroom as it is discussed above. In a crowded class, it is not possible for teachers to develop rapport with all students.

The fifth statement in the questionnaire whether students want teacher to use their mother tongue in the classroom to explain key concepts about grammar displays that 50% of the participants agreed to the statement. It means students wanted the mother tongue to be used to explain the key concepts in target language. Many of the students also admitted during the interview session that they could not understand the instructions in the target language. It stresses the need to use some chunks of mother tongue in the classroom.

The sixth statement in the questionnaire, if they feel confident to communicate in English discloses that none of them strongly agreed to the statement. 40% of the participants admitted that they felt confident to communicate in English. 30% of the participants did not express their opinion, which indicates their lack of confidence in the target language. 30% of the participant disagreed that shows students lacked communication skill in the target language. They also accepted it during the interview session.

The seventh statement in the questionnaire if they feel confident of pronunciation in target language shows that there is none who strongly agreed to the statement. 45% of the participants agreed that they feel confident of pronunciation in target language. 40% of the participants were not sure about it. It shows they are not confident whether they pronounce target language correctly or not. 15% of the participant disagreed. It again stresses the need of pronunciation training in a Direct Method of teaching. Moreover, it also indicates teachers' inefficiency, as not all the teachers are good at pronunciation. It also makes difficult for students to learn pronunciation as Rao and Ediger (2014) state, "Efficient teachers are not available. Their pronunciation is faulty. They hardly have good command and they cannot do justice to the language teaching" (p.103). This is true that Direct Method of teaching requires well-trained and competent teachers otherwise; the graph of success rate of this method goes down. Kwambehar (2015) has rightly remarked, "This kind of method requires a very competent teacher of the TL who is richly endowed with the fluency and proficiency of the TL otherwise teaching cannot be effectively done using this method" (p.30).

The eighth statement in the questionnaire, if they require more activities to practice the tense they learnt, unveils that 10% of the participants were in absolute agreement. A big number (80%) of the participants agreed to it, which shows the strong need to include some portion of the Grammar-Translation Method so that students can understand the basic concept of grammar and practice them well through exercises. The same is accepted during the interview session. Students admitted that they had doubts regarding subject verb agreement and use of auxiliaries. Rao and Ediger (2014) have rightly remarked, "This method mainly rests on functional grammar, but the knowledge of formal grammar is also necessary" (p.103).

CHAPTER 4

The Audio-Lingual Method

As in the previous chapter, we have read how Direct Method of Teaching lost ground and popularity in academic circles because of lack of solid methodological base. The linguist like Henry Sweet (an English philologist, phonetician and grammarian) felt this need and argued for the development of sound methodological principles, which could serve as the basis for teaching techniques. In the 1920s and 1930s, applied linguists again went over the principles suggested by the Reform Movement (to revolutionize methods of modern language instruction by teaching them as living languages. Before that date, school and university instruction had been strictly grammatical, philological and literary) and systematized the principles which laid foundation for what developed into the British approach to Teaching English as a foreign language. Subsequent developments led to audiolingualism in the United States and the Oral Approach or Situational Language teaching in Britain (Richards and Rodgers, 2001, p. 13-14). There is also no doubt in the fact that this method was developed during the World War Second especially to teach the army men. Kwambehar (2015) states, "This method was developed in the United States of America during the Second World War when the US government commissioned American university teachers to develop a foreign language program for military personnel" (p.29). As a result, The Army Specialized Training Program (ASTP) was established in 1942. The ASTP, the so-called Army method, had a significant impact on linguistic and the way foreign languages were taught.

It provided a kind of conceptual background to this method and paved way for the further development of this method. Like Grammar-Translation Method, this method was also product of war situation. It was based on Leonard Bloomfield's technique (informant method) of memorization and repetition in simple foreign language patterns. The goal of this method was to practice the target language with the native speaker/the informant who makes learners speak the language as well as acquire the basic structure of grammar (Richards and Rodgers, 1987). The second step towards audiolingual method became The Aural-Oral approach, which was invented by Charles Fries (an American structural linguist, a language teacher, and the creator of the Aural-Oral method). According to Fries, language should be taught by using intensive oral drilling of its basic patterns (Richards and Rodgers, 1987). This method had a particular emphasis on proper pronunciation and intonation. However, learners still struggled to overcome the confusions, which were born out of the contrastive analysis of two languages. As we read in the second chapter of the Grammar-Translation Method, learners were confused when they learned two languages at the same time. The same problem even persisted with the Direct Method of Teaching as the advocates of this method proposed to include some grammar based activities, which could provide a methodological basis for the learners. There was no book still published which could address these issues of contrastive analysis and point out the differences between the grammatical structures of two languages. Fries' book "Principles in Teaching and Learning English as a Foreign Language" published in 1945 addressed these issues. The idea of contrastive analysis (the systematic comparison of two or more languages, with the aim of describing their similarities and differences) refers to the problems of learning a foreign language rising out of the conflict of different structural systems like the difference between the grammatical and phonological patterns of the native and the target language. So, the idea of contrastive analysis of two languages was presented in this work, which prevented the potential problems in second language acquisition and provided the basis for a major branch of applied linguistics called systematic comparison providing a new perspective to Foreign Language Teaching. Here emerged Audio-linguistic Approach to language teaching. This method promoted the discipline of language teaching from an art to science. This method claimed to have transformed language teaching from an art to science, which would enable learners to achieve mastery of a foreign language effectively and efficiently (Richards & Rodgers, 1987).

Audio-lingual approach, as it inculcated the concept of contrastive analysis, suggests that students be taught phonology, morphology, and syntax of the language. It would be easier to learn these patterns through contrastive analysis of the differences between the native tongue and the target language as the identified differences between the two help students to acquire new language easier. In order to understand this method in a better way, one must be aware of the behaviorist psychology, which has a significant impact on the teaching and learning principles of audio-lingual method. Behaviorist psychology claimed that it knows the secrets of all human learning including language (Richards & Rodgers, 1987). Behaviorism is based on three main elements of learning: stimulus, response and reinforcement.

Audiolingualism utilizes this schema in a very positive way. If these three principles of behaviorist psychology are applied on foreign language learning we observe that the stimulus is the information about foreign language. The response is student's reaction on the presented material. The reinforcement is natural self-satisfaction of target language use (Richards & Rodgers, 1987).

Audiolingualism stresses on memorization and repetition of dialogues or other drill patterns, which minimizes the scope of making mistakes and increase the chances of producing a correct answer that leads to reinforcement of good habits. Second, Foreign language can be learned and taught more effectively if it is presented in spoken form before students will see written form. Aural-oral training is needed to provide the foundation for the development of other language skills (Richards & Rodgers, 1987). Third, the meaning of words and phrases of a second language should be learned and taught in a linguistic and cultural context. Rivers (1964) states, "Teaching a language thus involves teaching aspects of the cultural system of the people who speak the language" (p.19-22). Suryani (2012) rightly states:

Audio Lingual Method is a style of teaching used in teaching foreign language. It was derived from Skinner's Behaviorist Psychology. It is one of the methods in English teaching-learning process. Audio Lingual Method trains students in order to reach conversational proficiency in a variety of foreign language, and puts the emphasis on behavior (p.4).

Like Direct Method of teaching, this method also focuses on the use of language rather than memorizing the grammatical structures without context. It focuses on oral repetition of sentences in a particular situation, thus providing a context to language use. Like Direct Method of teaching, it stresses on the use of meaningful sentences. There is so much common between direct method and audio-lingual method. However, it is different from the direct method in the sense that it also stresses on the grammatical structures of the utterances though in context. Reading and writing skills are also taken into consideration but they are secondary to listening and speaking skills. Audiolingualism is a technique of foreign language instruction that emphasizes audio-lingual skills over reading and writing and is characterized by extensive use of pattern practice. Kwambehar (2015) states:

> This method advised that learners be taught a language directly without using the learner's native language to explain new words or grammar in the target language. This method didn't focus on teaching vocabulary; rather, the teacher drilled students in the case of grammar. It believed that learning a language means acquiring habits (p.28).

The Audio-lingual method is very firm to the zero use of target language in the classroom. There is no room for the mother tongue and it encourages use of only target language in the classroom. The language is practiced, most probably, in the dialogue form. There is use of audio in the classroom in order to listen to target language and practice it. There is a lot of audio drilling in this method. The audio-lingual teaching method is defined as a method, which emphasizes on repetition of the words to help students to be able to use the target language communicatively. The purpose of the repetition/drills is to break down the troublesome sentences into smaller part. Drilling is a key feature of audio-lingual approaches to language teaching which placed emphasis on repeating structural patterns through oral practice (Brown, 1998). Teacher practices particular dialogues from an excerpt of communication and makes learners memorize it. Communication is usually situation based. A particular situation is presented in the form of communication and then it is practiced. Abdul (2016) rightly states:

> Each level has its own distinctive patterns. Language learning is viewed as the acquisition of a practical set of communication skills. It entails language and learning the rules by which these elements are combined from phoneme to morpheme to word or phrase to sentence. Language is primarily spoken and only secondarily written (p.45).

There is no translation in an audiolingual classroom. Language is used in a particular context. Students guess the meaning of unknown words in the context they are used in. There is a lot of drilling and practice. Students memorize the dialogues with particular emphasis on form and pronunciation. Correct pronunciation is emphasized from the first day of language use. Pronunciation is improved through continuous practice and memorization.

However, like other methods, this method also began to decline. In the 1960s, many linguists criticized the theoretical foundation of Audiolingualism as students were found to be unable to use skills learned in the classroom in real communication (Richards & Rodgers, 1987).

A big bolt to this method came in 1966 when Chomsky criticized behaviorist theory, which was the main foundation of Audiolingualism. He claimed that this theory failed to provide a model of how humans learn languages. Chomsky introduced an alternative theory of language learning, explaining that languages are not acquired by repetition and imitation, but "generated from the learner's underlying competence" (Richards & Rodgers, 1987).

With the appearance of Chomsky's transformational grammar theory, Audiolingualism lost its ground that led to a crisis in the American language teaching system (Richards & Rodgers, 1987). Therefore, current teaching practices still use this method but merge it with traditional practices in order to make it more efficient. In order to understand the practical application of this method, one study is being shared here which was conducted at Princess Noora School at Najran University Campus, Najran, KSA.

Experience

It is a classroom at PY in Najran University It is a training session with Arab speakers. Students' level is poor. They do not use much of the target language and usually switch to their mother tongue. An Indian teacher who does not know Arabic at all is taking this class. So, teacher has to use only target language in the classroom. Twelve students in the classroom aim to develop their four skills in the target language. Teacher plays a recording that consists of a conversation between a dentist and a patient transcribed here:

> *Dentist: Good morning, Mr. What's the problem?*
> *Patient: I've got toothache. I think it's in this tooth.*
> *Dentist: How long have you been having toothache?*
> *Patient: I have been having toothache for last four days.*
> *Dentist: Yes, you've got some bad decay in there. I'm going to have to fill that tooth.*
> *Patient: Oh, OK, Can you do it now?*
> *Dentist: No, you'll need to book an appointment with the receptionist on the way out. You should do it as soon as possible.*
> *Patient: OK, I'll do that.*

Teacher asks the students to listen to recording and repeat each sentence. In the beginning, students are not able to pronounce the exact word. Teacher stops recording and asks students to repeat the same word until they are very close to the exact pronunciation of the word. Teacher practiced it for 10 minutes from the audiotape. After that teacher began to pronounce the sentences himself and asked students follow him. There were some students who were not able to speak the sentences correctly. However, teacher did not lose courage and continued with drill and practice. Mart (2013) rightly states:

> The Audio-Lingual Method aims to develop communicative competence of students using dialogues and drills. The use of dialogues and drills are effective in foreign language teaching as they lead the students to produce speech. Repetition of the dialogues and the drills will enable students to respond quickly and accurately in spoken language (p.64).

So, practicing the dialogues many times students learnt to say the dialogues on their own.

When the teacher realized that students were able to read the dialogue, he divided students in pair. One student was assigned the role of dentist and another one was assigned the role of a patient. They practiced the dialogue with each other while teacher took the round in the classroom and ensured that every student was involved in learning. Teacher supplied students with correct pronunciation wherever he realized students were not able to pronounce the word correctly. The class lasted for one hour and students were able to practice the dialogues successfully.

Observation

Students were very enthusiastic in the classroom as it engaged all of the learners. Teacher followed student-centered approach, which ensured involvement and participation of every student in the classroom. The classroom followed more natural presentation of skills like listening, speaking, reading and writing. There was no use of mother tongue, which created some kind of disinterest among students. As they participated, they enjoyed the class more. Teacher observed that students learnt dialogues of a particular situation, which prepared them for most of the situations, but not all the situations. There is a lot of motivation and encouragement in the classroom. Students memorized the dialogues and practiced them that taught them how to use language in proper context.

Analysis of Students' Feedback

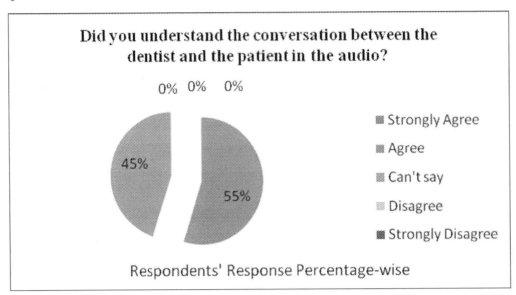

Figure 1

The first statement in the questionnaire *if* they understood the conversation between the dentist and the patient in the audio reveals that there is none who strongly agreed to the statement. 55% participants (a majority) felt that they understood the conversation between the dentist and the patient in the audio. 45% of the participants had no idea. There was none with disagreement.

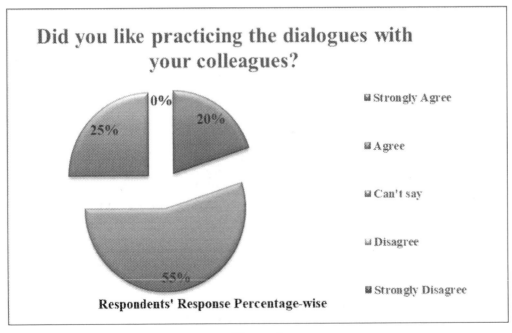

Figure 2

The second statement in the questionnaire *if they liked practicing the dialogues with their colleagues* displays 55% of the participants opined *that they liked practicing the dialogues with their colleagues.* 20% strongly agreed to the statement while 25% had no opinion. There was none with disagreement.

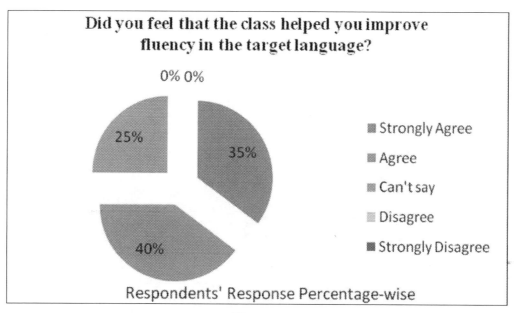

Figure 3

The third statement in the questionnaire if *they felt that the class helped them improve fluency in the target language* shows that there are 35% of the participants who strongly agreed to the statement. 40% of the participants are of the opinion that *the class helped them improve fluency in the target language.* 25% of the participants had no opinion.

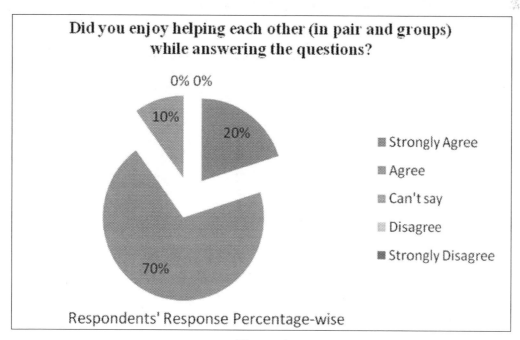

Figure 4

The forth statement in the questionnaire if *they enjoyed helping each other (in pair and groups) while answering the questions* exhibits that 70% of the participants agreed to the statement. There are 20% of the participants who agreed that *they enjoyed helping each other (in pair and groups) while answering the questions.* 15% of the participants had no opinion. There was none with disagreement.

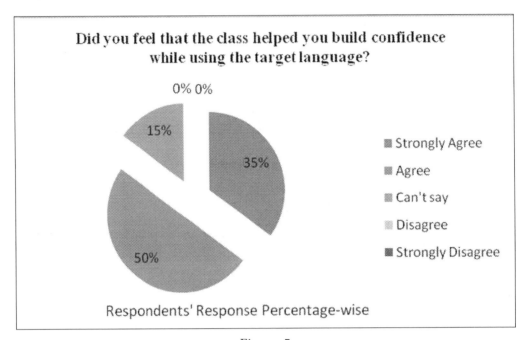

Figure 5

The fifth statement in the questionnaire if *they felt that the class helped them build confidence while using the target language* divulges that there are 85% (if strongly agree and agree are merged)of the participants who agreed to the statement that *they felt that the class helped them build confidence while using the target language.* 15% of the participants did not express their opinion. There was none with disagreement.

The sixth statement in the questionnaire if *they induced the rules of the tenses from the structures* discloses that there are 20% of the participants who strongly agreed to the statement. 50% of the participants concurred that *they induced the rules of the tenses from the structures.* 30% of the participants were not sure about it. There was none with disagreement.

The seventh statement in the questionnaire if *the class helped them acquire the language* shows that there are 20% of the participants who strongly agreed to the statement. 60% of the participants had no opinion. 15% participants concurred that *the class helped them acquire the language.* 5% of the participants were in strongly disagreement.

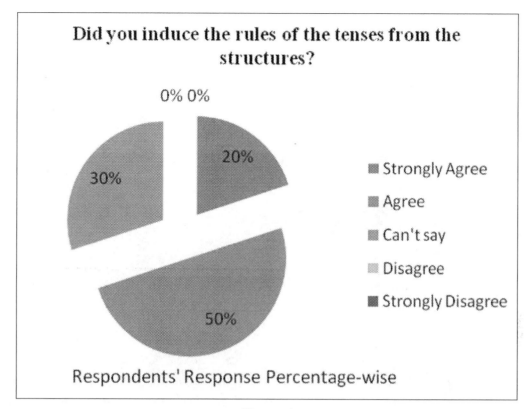

Figure 6

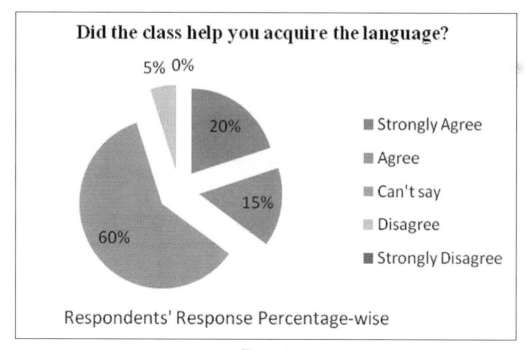

Figure 7

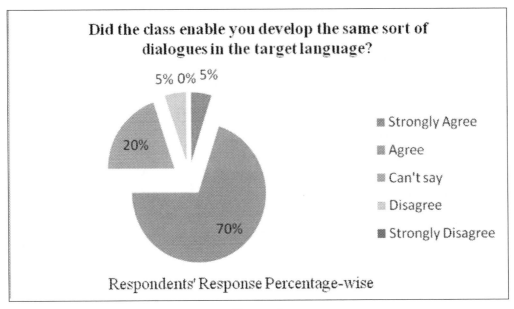

Figure 8

The eighth statement in the questionnaire, *if the class enabled them develop the same sort of dialogues in the target language,* unveils that there are 5% of the participants with absolute agreement to the statement that *the class enabled them develop the same sort of dialogues in the target language.* 70% of the participants agreed while there were 20% of the participants who did not state an opinion. 5% of the participants did not agree with the statement. There was no ne with disagreement.

Interview Questions

Twenty samples (filled in with complete information) were selected out of 30. Participants responded to the following questions in the interview:

1. Mention some difficulties faced in class:

2. Why did you like the class?

Table-1: Results of Interview Question no.1

Q.1.	Number of participants	Some difficulties faced in class:
	7	Not able to understand the accent of the different words in the audio.
	6	Could not understand everything what we listened to.
	7	The sound was too low for me.

As shown in Table 1, in response to question number 1, there were varied responses, only common responses were placed in the table here. Most of the students (7) agreed that they were not able to understand the accent of the different words in the audio. Six students said that they could not understand everything what they listened to. Seven students also admitted that the sound was too low for them.

Table-2: Results of Interview Question no.2

Q.2.	Number of participants	Why did you like the class?
	5	The classroom provided a good practice of the target language.
	6	The classroom was very encouraging and motivating.
	5	The dialogues were in easy language.
	4	There was a lot of enjoyment and fun in the classroom.

As shown in Table 2, in response to question number 2, there were varied responses, only common responses were placed in the table here. Most of the students (6) agreed that the classroom was very encouraging and motivating. 5 students admitted that the classroom provided a good practice of the target language. Another group of 5 students said that the dialogues were in easy language. 4 students said that there was a lot of enjoyment and fun in the classroom.

Discussion and Conclusion

The first statement in the questionnaire, if students understood the conversation between the dentist and the patient in the audio, shows that 55% of students agreed with the statement while 45% had no opinion. It is a matter of great concern, as a big percentage of students had no opinion. As a rule of the audio-lingual method, language is presented in spoken form before students see written form. The same rule has been applied here. However, a majority of students did not state their opinion. It seems they were simply practicing the dialogues without having an idea how to use them in the outside world. It invites our attention towards the most common criticism of this method as Wordsworth (1967) states:

> Probably the main disadvantage in this vehicle is extra demands it makes upon the ingenuity of the teacher and the greater danger of lapsing into artificial speech patterns in attempts to create various communication situations (p.35)

Nevertheless, there may be various reasons why students did not understand the conversation, as they were unable to comprehend the contents and understand the accent because of poor quality of audio etc. As this method is based on the use of audio, teachers have to ascertain the students easily understand that audio. During the interview, seven students admitted that they were not able to understand the accent of the different words in the audio. It is clear that students were not familiar with the accent. The same number also admitted that the sound was too low for them. It shows that teacher has to fix all the technical requirements before starting the class. Six students also admitted that they could not understand everything what they listened to. It may also be because of the contents and grammatical structures of the conversation that led students not to completely understand the dialogues as they might be above their level.

The second statement in the questionnaire if they liked practicing the dialogues with their colleagues exhibits that 75% of students agreed with the statement while 25% students had no opinion. It proves students liked this activity while practicing the dialogues with each other. It conforms to on one of the basic principles of audiolingual method of memorization and repetition, which lead to reinforcement.

Kwambehar (2015) states about this method, "It believed that learning a language means acquiring habits. There is much practice of dialogues on every situation. In this method, a new language is heard and extensively drilled before putting it in written form" (p.28). They like listening and speaking the same language. It reaffirms the main problem (as in statement one) lies with the accent in the audio. As students were not used to British accent, they could not understand the conversation. In this method, teachers have to make sure that students are well familiar with the accent they are going to use in the class. Teachers must provide them with accent training. Five students also admitted during the interview that the classroom provided a good practice of the target language.

The third statement in the questionnaire if they felt that the class helped them improve fluency in the target language fetches 75% positive responses from the students. They liked practicing the dialogues in the pair, which improved their fluency. This method succeeded here, as its one of the basic motives is to develop fluency among learners. Students repeat the dialogues. Through repetition, students can use the target language automatically and fluently as well. In this method, it is desirable that students form a habit to use the target language with ease, therefore, the more they repeat, and the easier they will speak the target language without making a conscious effort. This method not only assists in developing fluency but also in understanding the stress, rhythm, intonation, structure, etc. Tim Bowen (as qtd. in Mart, 2013) explains the contributions of this method to language learning as:

> Most teachers will at some point require learners to repeat examples of grammatical structures in context with number of aims in mind: stress, rhythm, intonation, 'consolidating the structure', enabling learners to use the

structure accurately through repetition, etc. Question and answer in open class or closed pairs to practice a particular form can also be argued to have its basis in the audio-lingual approach, as can, without doubt, any kind of drill (p.64).

The forth statement in the questionnaire if they felt that the class helped them build confidence while using the target language displays that 85% of the students agreed with the statement. Six students also admitted during the interview that the classroom was very encouraging and motivating. Teacher tried their best to build confidence among students, which is the first step in improving the communication. In this method, communication is usually situation based. A particular situation is presented in the form of dialogues and then it is practiced. Suryani (2012) states:

> In Audio Lingual Method, the teacher wants their students to be able to use the target language communicatively. Audio Lingual Method uses repetition, replacement, and question answer to drill speaking skill especially student's vocabulary. The teacher is easier to control the student's behavior and student's vocabulary (n.p.).

It shows that teacher has organized the classroom in a very interactive way so that students can communicate with each other and develop their confidence in the target language.

The fifth statement in the questionnaire if they enjoy helping each other (in pair and groups) while answering the questions shows that 90% of students agreed with the statement. They (four students) also admitted during the interview that there was a lot of enjoyment and fun in the classroom. It confirms that teacher has created a very cooperative and healthy environment in the classroom to use the target language as much as possible. Students practiced the structures (dialogues) with each other through repetition and drill, which is at the centre of behavioral theory. It is based on Leonard Bloomfield's technique (informant method) of memorization and repetition in simple foreign language pattern.

The sixth statement in the questionnaire if they induced the rules of the tenses from the structures shows that 70% students agreed with the statement while 30% of the students had no opinion. Teacher did not use grammar deductively rather grammar rules were presented in a context so that learners may induce the rules from the structures and understand them in proper context. This method also stresses that grammar can be learnt through habit formation. Kwambehar (2015) states:

> This method advised that learners be taught a language directly without using the learner's native language to explain new words or grammar in the target language. This method didn't focus on teaching vocabulary; rather, the teacher drilled students in the case of grammar. It believed that learning a language means acquiring habits (p.28).

As the focus of this method is on function and not the form, some students could not elicit the rules from the structures presented in the dialogue forms.

The seventh statement in the questionnaire if the class helped acquire the language shows that only 35% of students agreed with the statement while 60% had no idea. 5% students disagreed with the statement. Language acquisition is a natural phenomenon and it is not possible in a second language classroom for students to acquire a language rather they learn a language. Moreover, situations presented in audiolingual method are usually artificial ones and have no direct predictability with outer world. It is true that situational learning prepares learners for several situations but not for all situations. Sometimes learners have to face unpredictable situations where the memorized structures fail to develop communication.

The eighth statements in the questionnaire if the class enabled them develop the same sort of dialogues in the target language shows that 75% students agreed with the statement. 20% students had no opinion while 5% students disagreed with the statement. It shows that teacher succeeded in creating one situation for listening and speaking which might further help them create the same sort of situations. It is the real purpose of a language. However, there is no certainty that learners will develop the same sort of dialogues, as teacher has not assigned them any task. Until teacher assigns them a task and students successfully complete it, it is difficult to claim whether students learnt to write on the same sort of situations or not.

CHAPTER 5

The Silent Way

In the previous chapters, we have observed that teacher played an important role in the learning process. His presence was important and strongly felt in the classroom. He was all in all in the class and dominated the classroom through his speech and lecture. He usually adopted teacher-centered approach. Learners hardly got any chance to take the charge of their learning. They were the passive learners in the classroom, just listening to the teacher. For example, the Grammar-Translation Method was completely teacher-centered. However, learners got scope to participate in the Direct Method. However, the role of teacher was also essential in the Direct Method of Teaching. Teachers' Talk Time (TTT) was reduced a little bit in the Direct Method but it was not completely banished. In the Audiolingualism too, teacher played an important role in the classroom. In this method, students used to practice and memorize the structures of language in context, which they were supposed to use in practical lives. One of the problems with this method was of transferring the classroom learning to use it outside for communicative purposes. So, the basic purpose of this method, to enable people to communicate in target language, was not achieved. Here we agree with Chomsky that language acquisition cannot take place through habit formation. Habit is an experience of learners. Nevertheless, learners have to create many utterances, which they have neither experienced nor practiced before. That is where the creativity and novelty of a language lies. A learner creates innumerable utterances with the rules of structures he has learnt as per his needs to live and communicate in a society. Learners have to discover the rules of the language they are learning through their cognitive ability (Freeman, 2000). This particular emphasis on cognition led to the establishment of Cognitive Approach, which stresses that learners have to use their cognitive ability to learn a language rather than being stimuli to their environment. Learners had to shoulder the responsibility of their own learning. This approach covered both inductive and deductive grammar exercises so that learners can use their cognitive ability to learn the language. Although no teaching method developed directly from the cognitive approach, it had a remarkable contribution in the emergence of several innovative methods (Freeman, 2000).

The same is the case with Dr. Caleb Gattengo who invented *The Silent Way* in 1970s which follows the theory of constructivism (a theory of learning in which the learners are provided the opportunity to construct their own sense about what is being learnt by building the connection through experiencing things and reflecting on those experiences). Like other methods, it was not the product of the cognitive approach yet it shared one of the basic principles of this approach, that teaching should be subordinated to learning. In this method, Gattengo laid the principle that teachers have to assist the learning rather than dominate it. Teachers dominate the class with their speech and do not let students use their creative and imaginative faculty. That is why this method stressed that teachers should be silent so that students may get enough opportunity to learn in the class. There is almost no TTT except a few utterances in the Silent Way class. In the Silent Way, learning is transferred in a silent way; probably by sound or color charts, wall pictures, Fidel charts, Cuisenaire rods, etc. The resources have a very important role in learning through this method. The Silent Way encourages the learning of a foreign language through self-correction, problem solving, imagination, and teaching awareness over repetition.

The basic principle of the silent way is to motivate students to produce language as much as possible. The Silent Way believes in first producing sounds, then words and afterwards sentences are taught through colored rods of different shapes associated with different linguistic items. Teacher pronounces each element and asks for its repetition. Thus, teacher directs the classroom but has an indirect role, because he/she has to be silent most of the time, giving an active role to the learner. However, it also follows mentalist accounts, because self-correction and learner autonomy are promoted. Teacher has to keep silence so that he/she should not dominate the classroom. Stevick (1980) defines the Silent Way teacher's task as (a) to teach, (b) to test and (c) to get out of the way (p. 56). The resources are prime in this method, as the learners have to learn from them. There is silence so that students can focus more on what they learn. There is no focus on memorization or repetition rather on creativity and discovery. Learners are in themselves an autonomous body. They are not instructed, interfered or guided step by step by the instructor. The language is learnt through the silent awareness and then an active trial is given to the language.

The Silent Way, by Dr. Caleb Gattengo in the early 1970s, can be termed as discovery learning-based approach to second language acquisition. Students learn by authentic experiences, with minimal direct input by teacher. Teacher is merely a facilitator and hardly interferes with the learning styles of students. It lets students explore and learn by themselves. Gattegno, the inventor of the method, also believes that to teach language is just to serve learning process and not to dominate it. Students may learn with help of many ways/resources/realias, like:

1. Learning is facilitated through discovery and creation. There is no scope for memorization or repetition. Repetition, according to Gattengo, "consumes time and encourages a scattered mind to remain scattered." (Richards and Theodore, 2010)

2. The classroom is full of physical objects, which assist learning process. These objects are a source of physical stimuli, and supply visual aids and images that will abet in student recollection. (Richards and Theodore, 2010)

3. Problem solving is an exclusive way to facilitate learning, which must involve the material to be learned. In Gattengo's own words, this encourages students to develop

"inner criteria to allow them to monitor and self-correct their own production." (Richards and Theodore, 2010)

In a silent way class, teacher relies a lot on realia. They use different sorts of eye-catching materials, to attract students and keep them mentally engaged. Teachers use different sorts of materials in the classroom like:

Sound/color charts. Sound/color charts are very attractive and eye capturing for students as these charts match each phoneme with a specific color, or combination of colors. This way students associate sound to a particular color and correlate it. When teacher points to a particular phoneme, it gives students a clue about the name of the color.

Word charts. Word charts carry particular color that denotes to a specific color with the same color code as the rectangle chart. Different colors draw students' attention and they feel motivated to find new vocabulary supplied through the word charts.

'Fidel' charts. The main goal of these charts is to familiarize students with the complex spelling structure of English language. They show all the possible spellings for each phoneme, which use the same color code as the rectangle chart. Students can use a pointer and a Fidel chart to sound out and form new words, or existing vocabulary words.

Wall Pictures. Wall pictures are used as important visual aids to the learning process. These wall pictures contain an image of the physical representation of the word being learnt, as well as a color-coded version of the word itself. For example, when learning the word "cow," students will be presented with a picture of a cow, and the color-coded word "cow" below. This provides valuable contextual information about the meaning and usage of the word. So, students learn how language is contextualized.

Cuisenaire rods. These colored rods are used to create clear and visible situations for students to correlate between a concept and its expression. It also allows students physically construct words and sounds in a free-range, imaginative, play-based environment.

Experience

Let us share an experience here with the silent way to record students' observation about the success and limitations of this method. It was experimented at the PY unit of Najran University, KSA. Students' English is not very good. Most of the teachers use Arabic in the classroom. That is why, it was decided that in order to reduce TTT (Teachers' Talk Time) in the classroom, silent way must be introduced and experimented with the intermediate level learners. Teacher followed the steps of the silent way and had minimal interference with the learning styles of learners. Teacher first introduced the method and then directed the classroom with the help of wall pictures, etc.

Teacher aimed to teach the simple structure in present tense with the form 'be' verbs. He used the wall pictures to make students learn preposition and use of 'be' forms. Teacher pointed towards the picture and asked students different questions based on picture like: '*Where the train track is?*' Students responded that the train track is beside the platform. Teacher asked *what the passengers are doing.* Students responded they are waiting for train. Teacher denoted one road with the help of orange rod. He asked the students *where the tall and beautiful buildings are.* Students responded they are near the railway track. The following picture shows different objects donated by different color of rods.

Figure-1
(*https://pixabay.com/photos/chicago-illinois-city-urban-1804480/*)

In this way, teacher motivated students to answer questions. Teacher uses another picture to teach simple, comparative and superlative degrees. There are many buildings in the pictures, which are of different heights. Teacher asks many questions based on the building. For example, which is the tallest building, which building is taller, which is the shortest building etc.

Observations

Teacher remained silent most of the times and observed students faced difficulties in the beginning. However, they began to make slow but steady progress gradually. Teacher almost kept silence and only pointed to rods of colors without saying anything.

(https://pixabay.com/photos/nyc-new-york-city-america-usa-city-4854718/)

Teacher prefers to gesture with different sentences that motivate students actively use their brain and trigger their inner self in order to learn new structures. Students switch their roles in asking and answering the questions, which make them take interest in the classroom and enjoy learning by doing. As the learners' level is too low, teachers have to use a few words of their mother tongue, Arabic, in order to facilitate learning. Teacher motivates them to go ahead with the target language. This way learning took place in the classroom and students actively participated in it.

Teacher found that students were highly motivated. TTT was reduced to a great extent. Students took charge of their own learning. Students felt confident that triggered their interest in learning the language.

Silence is one of the learning tools in the classroom as it provides more scope to learners practice the target language. There is no interference of the teacher rather teacher seems to be invisible who only facilitate learning process. Meaning of a word is conveyed by focusing on students' perception and not by translation. It helps teachers avoid target language completely in the classroom. Learning is more object/concept based rather than translation based. Students learn from each other. This method motivated students more for group and collaborative learning. Teachers provide students many opportunities to learn from each other. Teachers only interfere when he feels no one in the group is able to provide correct answers. Here teacher breaks silence for a few minutes otherwise students would learn a wrong answer. Teacher observes that students are progressing though with some mistakes. Teacher focuses more on progress than perfection and slowly observes that students are improving their mistakes too. This method provides a great opportunity to teacher to listen to students attentively which otherwise is impossible in a classroom. As teacher speaks less, students pay close attention to what he says as teacher hardly repeats the word. There is no homework given so that students may learn naturally without taking 'learning' as a burden to them. Teacher observes that slowly students are able to use language for self-expression and they communicate to each other. Their background knowledge is exploited largely. Student- teacher talk time is almost zero in this method though teacher creates situation silently so that students can speak on them. Teaching and evaluation go hand in hand, as teacher has enough time to assess students on their performance and thus provides them feedback. Peer-correction is emphasized in this method as Nagaraj (1996) states, "Learners' errors are dealt through self-monitoring and peer-correction. No disapproval is indicated by the teacher" (p.59). Students learn better, when they correct each other's mistakes as it gives them not only a sense of authority but also a sense of responsibility. The realia used like rods and pictures can also be used for further teaching of advanced concepts like teacher can teach some difficult preposition with help of rod. More complex grammatical structures can also be approached through the rod and the pictures.

However, it was teachers' perspective regarding the application of the Silent Way. Teacher follows the learner-centered approach and involves them in learning process. Students are encouraged to come up with new structures in target language. Teacher emphasizes more on fluency. Teacher overlooks a few grammatical mistakes as it may discourage students and break their rhythm of speaking the target language. Though this method turned out to do well, success of this method cannot be truly measured until students, the target group, are given an opportunity to express their opinion and share their experiences. In order to record students' observation and experiences, a questionnaire set was given to them focusing on the key elements of the Silent Way especially on the contents, which were taught in the classroom. In addition to the questionnaire, students were also interviewed with a set of open-ended questions to assess whether they had any query, doubt or confusion, which were not asked in the questionnaire. The open-ended questions provided enough space to students to put forward their opinion frankly.

Analysis of Students' Feedback

Table 1

S. No.↓.	Scales → Statements ↓	5 Strongly agree	4 Agree	3 Can't say	2 Disagree	1 Strongly disagree	Mean
	Did you like the method of teaching?	0 0%	11 55%	9 45%	0 0%	0 0%	3.55
	Did you understand how to use the preposition?	0 0%	16 80%	4 20%	0 0%	0 0%	3.8
	Did you understand the rules and usage of degrees (simple, comparative and superlative) in English language?	7 35%	10 50%	3 15%	0 0%	0 0%	4.2
	Did you understand how and when to use verb 'be' (is, are, am) in English?	4 20%	14 70%	2 10%	0 0%	0 0%	4.1
	Did you understand the relationship between rods and the objects they represented?	4 20%	12 60%	3 15%	1 5%	0 0%	3.95
	Did you understand the body language and face expressions of the teacher?	1 5%	14 70%	4 20%	1 5%	0 0%	3.75

Reed (1989) is of the opinion that Likert-type rating scale should be used to generally gather data. Jung, Osterwalder and Wipf (2000) support the Likert scale: "this was the only assessment instrument I found that was practical for the classroom" (p.2). To interpret the level of means, the authors applied Siti Rahaya Ariffin and Salbiah Mohamad's (1996) model of explaining means. It is summarized in Table 2.

Table 2: Score category breakdown adopted from Siti Rahaya Ariffin and Salbiah Mohamad (1996)

Means	Corresponding level
1.0 - 1.80	Very low
1.81 - 2.60	Low
2.61 - 3.40	Moderate
3.41 - 4.20	High
4.21 - 5.0	Very high

The first statement in the questionnaire *if they liked the method of teaching* reveals that there is none who strongly agreed to the statement. 55% participants (a majority) felt *that they liked the method of teaching.* 45% of the participants had no idea. There was none with disagreement. The mean of the statement is 3.55 that lies in the category of 'High' as per the breakdown adopted from the scale of *Siti Rahaya Ariffin and Salbiah Mohamad* (1996).

The second statement in the questionnaire *if they understood how to use the preposition* displays that there is nobody who strongly agreed to the statement. However, 80% of the participants opined *that they understood how to use the preposition.* There was none with disagreement. The mean is categorized as high.

The third statement in the questionnaire *if they understood the rules and usage of degrees (simple, comparative and superlative) in English language* exhibits that 35% of the participants strongly agreed. There are 50% of the participants who agreed that *they understood the rules and usage of degrees (simple, comparative and superlative) in English language.* 15% of the participants had no opinion. There was none with disagreement. The mean is ranked as high.

The fourth statement in the questionnaire *if they understood how and when to use verb 'be' (is, are, am) in English* divulges that there are 20% of the participants who strongly agreed to the statement that *they understood how and when to use verb 'be' (is, are, am) in English.* 70% of the participants agreed with the statement. 10% of the participants did not express their opinion. There was none with disagreement. The mean is high.

The fifth statement in the questionnaire *if they understood the relationship between rods and the objects they represented* shows that there are 20% of the participants who strongly agreed to the statement. 60% of the participants concurred that *they understood the relationship between rods and the objects they represented.* 15% of the participants were not sure about it. There were 5% with disagreement. The mean is high.

The sixth statement in the questionnaire *if they understood the body language and face expressions of the teacher and followed the commands accordingly* unveils that there are 5% of the participants with absolute agreement to the statement. 70% of the participants agreed while there were 20% of the participants who did not state an opinion. 5% of the participants did not agree with the statement. There was none with disagreement. The mean is high.

Interview analysis

Another method used to collect the data was interview method. Twenty samples were selected out of 30, which were filled in with complete information. The participants responded to the following questions in the interview:

1. Students rate (on a scale of 1-5) the effectiveness of this method where 1 represents the lowest and 5 represents the highest value:

2. Mention some common learning difficulties faced in class:

3. Mention some confusions, doubts or queries you had:

Table-3: Results of Interview Question no. 1

Q. No	Number of students	Scale
1.	4	2
	10	3
	6	4

As shown in the table, in response to the first question, 4 students rated the effectiveness of the method as 2 on a scale of 1-5 as mentioned earlier. 10 students rated the effectiveness of the method as 3 and 6 other teachers rated as 4. The overall effectiveness of the method was rated 1-4s from students' point of view.

Table-4: Results of Interview Question no. 2

Q.2.	Number of participants	Some common learning difficulties faced in class:
	5	Not able to distinguish among different colored rods.
	8	Forgot what each color of the rod represented.
	7	Couldn't get a chance to speak English in the classroom

As shown in Table 4, in response to question number 2, there were varied responses, only common responses were placed in the table here. Most of the students (8) agreed that they forgot what each color of the rod represented. Some students (7) could not get a chance to speak English in the classroom. Five students said that they were not able to distinguish among different colored rods.

Table-5: Results of Interview Question no. 3

Q.3	Number of participants	Some confusions, doubts or queries you had:
	5	Couldn't understand instructions
	8	Didn't get chance to ask questions to teachers
	7	Couldn't understand the body language and face expressions of the teacher

As shown in Table 5, in response to question number 3, there were some common confusions, doubts or queries by the students. A majority of students (8) reported (as shown in responses) that they did not get chance to ask questions to teachers. Seven students said that they could not understand the body language and face expressions of the teacher. Five students said that they couldn't understand instructions.

Discussion and Conclusion

The overall analysis of the questionnaire exhibits that students liked the silent way of teaching English. However, there are some values assigned against the statement, which invite our attention and indicate towards the limitations of the method in some respects. In response to a direct question to students if they like method of teaching, 45% of the students had no opinion. It shows that they did not understand how this method facilitated learning in the classroom. The positive aspect about this method is that no value is assigned against 'disagree' and 'strongly disagree', which shows that students liked this method at large and it became success in the classroom. However, the values assigned against 'can't say' show that many students could not understand and comprehend this method. Students liked the method because it gave them chance to participate and speak in the classroom. The interview question set shows that the students on a scale of 1-5 supported the method.

However, students also stated some of the difficulties they faced during the implementation of this method like they were not able to distinguish among the different colored rods, though teacher explained in the classroom what each color represented. They could not remember it for a long time and it resulted into misunderstanding of the instructions. As the teacher neither spoke nor could encourage students to ask him questions, students did not dare to state the problems they had in-between the classroom teaching. It also shows that teacher's continuous assessment was not very effective, as he could not recognize those students who were lagging behind and could not address their issues. Here, it is understandable that teaching and assessment cannot go hand in hand in the silent way, as teacher has to keep silence throughout the classroom and could provide the feedback only at the end of the class.

Some students stated that they could not get a chance to speak English in the classroom, which indicates the teaching techniques, to teach through the Silent Way, need improvements. Teacher needs to improve his techniques and procedures in the classroom and ascertain that every student is participating in the classroom

Some students stated that they could not understand the instructions. As the teacher hesitated to speak more in the classroom, students could not ask him to explain the instructions again. It resulted into miscommunication and misunderstanding which ultimately affected students' learning in the classroom.

Some students might have questions during the classroom teaching but they could not dare to ask which resulted into a kind of confusions regarding the concepts teacher was teaching through the silent way.

Some students reported that they could not understand body language and face expressions of the teacher. It indicates to one of the disadvantages of this method, as not all the students might be trained in soft skills. They might not understand the messages that teacher tried to convey them through his body language.

Like other methods, the silent way also had some advantages and disadvantages. It requires well-trained teachers to implement the principles of the Silent way. Though it has so many characteristics, yet it cannot be categorized as a 'method' as Freeman, 2000 states, "We have avoided referring to the Silent Way as a method since Caleb Gattegno says it is not one". (p.70)

CHAPTER 6

Suggestopedia

In the previous chapters, we have read about different methods and approaches of teaching English. All of them have their particular characteristics, their advantages and disadvantages. These methods and approaches focused on how they could improve teaching and learning of English language. These methods and approaches suggested different ways, procedures, and techniques of teaching and learning the language. All of them dealt with the physical aspects of language teaching and learning. However, there has been no method, which could focus on the psychology of learners. As the ultimate goal of teaching and learning rests on learners, it is necessary to understand the psychological state of learners while they enter the classroom. Learning is only possible when learners are in a good state of mind and find the classroom environment non-threatening, enjoyable, easy and pleasant. Unless learners feel confident and comfortable in the classroom, they cannot participate wholeheartedly in the learning and teaching process in the classroom. This chapter is significant as it changes our overall perspective of how we perceive learning and teaching of a language as it focuses on the psychological aspects of learners, which no method previously has taken into consideration. The method, to be described in this chapter, focuses on the psychological aspects of learners: their fears whether real or imaginative, their doubts, their confusions, etc., which learners have as they enter the classroom. This particular method known as Suggestopedia is unique in the sense as it deals with the psychology of learners, their mental states, etc.

The Bulgarian psychiatrist and educator Georgi Lozanov developed Suggestopedia method. It is also known as Desuggestopedia, as it is the application of the study of suggestion to pedagogy which helps in desuggesting and eliminating the fears, doubts and confusions learners are supposed to come with in the classroom. Suggestopedia provides with certain learning recommendations derived from suggestology which Lozanov describes as a "science… concerned with the systematic study of the non-rational and/or non-conscious influences" that human beings are constantly responding to" (qtd. in Osman 2017, p. 1).

Richards and Rodgers (2001) state, "Suggestopedia tries to harness these influences and redirect them so as to optimize learning" (p.100). Therefore, the main objective of this method is to eradicate these negative influences so that they can positively corporate in the learning and teaching process. Teacher creates an atmosphere of joy and happiness in the classroom. He tries to bridge the psychological gap between a teacher and student so that learners feel comfortable in the classroom. This method stresses on the maximum use of mental capacities of learners. It attempts to change the negativism of students into the positivism so that they can remove the psychological fears related to learning and develop a positive attitude towards learning. Nagaraj (1996) remarks, "Suggestopaedia is the pedagogic application of suggestion; it aims to help learners to overcome the feelings that they cannot be successful, and so removes their mental barriers to learning. It helps learners reach the *hidden reserves* of the mind" (p.63). If these hidden reserves of the mind are used positively in language learning and teaching, learners can make incredible progress in language learning, as Lozanov (1978) claims, "a 1,000% increase in learning is possible with suggestopaedia" (as qtd. in Dipamo and Job 1991, p. 128)

Therefore, Suggestopedia is a method of teaching that takes into account the psychological aspects of language teaching and learning. It stresses on the fact that language can be acquired naturally in a comfortable environment. Most of the times, learners are passing through some psychological issues which hinder the acquisition of second language. For example, sometimes, it is observed that learners are scared of teachers. They hesitate to clear doubts with their teachers. They do not ask questions and even if they ask, teachers do not encourage them for this practice. Learners may also develop a negative attitude towards second language learning as they may find it difficult to learn. Suggestopedia provides a comfortable space to students where students can comfortably ask questions to teachers. Moreover, teachers also create a positive environment in the classroom by being attentive, patient and positive to students' questions. They motivate them to ask as many questions as possible. In a traditional classroom, students may be physically and mentally tired and feel indifferent to language learning. When the classroom environment is full of joy and positivism, students feel relaxed and learn better.

Suggestopedia is based on three key principles; first, principle of euphoria that refers to the ecstasy and absence of anxiety in a learning environment. In order to create an anxiety free environment in the classroom, teacher needs to start his / her lesson taking students into confidence that they can do well in the classroom and make progress in language learning as Dipamo and Job (1991) opine, "Each Suggestopedia lesson starts by creating an expectancy that learning will be easy and fun. Students are exposed to music, posters on the wall depicting scenes relevant to the task, given affirmations to do or reminded of how well they did last time" (p.128). This method believes in motivating and encouraging learners towards language learning by creating a pleasant atmosphere in the classroom, as Lozanov (1978) explained, "The creation of a pleasant learning atmosphere can help students to lower their levels of tension, fear, anxiety and all other emotions that produce a negative attitude towards learning in most conventional language classrooms. These feelings are normally aroused by a lack of confidence in one's ability to understand, memorize and utilize the material given in the lesson" (p. 264).

Suggestopeadia also helps learners relive from mental stress associated with traditional learning, which hampers the cognitive ability of learners. It helps learners use their brain as a whole and they are not deviated as Lozanov (1978) remarks, "The second principle is the unity of the conscious and the para-conscious and the integration of brain activity, which focus on the human being as an integrated whole" (p. 265).

The third key principle of this method is to supply a suggestive link, which refers to the extent of reverse of the mind that stresses on the requirement of creation of mutual relations within the method of instruction because it is the part of psychotherapeutic application. In alternative words, it will be same that this method inculcates combine and cluster learning, cooperative learning because it arouses potentials of learning. Lozanov (1978) suggests, "The level of the suggestive link is measured by the degree to which the reserves of the student have been tapped" (p. 266).

Students unconsciously bring a negative attitude to language in the classroom. They are afraid that they will not be able to learn a language. It is also one of the reasons that they use only 5-10 percent of their brain and the rest remains unused. This method focuses on using that portion of brain. Suggestopedia has two levels of performance; first, it desuggests their doubts, fears that occupy 90 percent of their brain, and then suggests them that they can do. Suggestopedia is a counter attack to all the negative emotions of learners that they are supposed to bring to classroom. In addition, suggestion can help activate intellectual and cognitive processes by deactivating negative suggestions in a process called de-suggestion (Lozanov, 1978). This method suggests the positive attitude to language learning. Therefore, this method focuses on the psychology of learners. In order to assess the practical application and outputs of this method, one study is shared here which was conducted at an intermediate level class at North Carolina State University, USA.

Experience

It is an intermediate level class at North Carolina State University, USA. Students belong to different nationalities like China, Russia, India, France, Italy, Pakistan, Afghanistan, etc. The classroom is decorated. It has colored pictures of different countries which make learners feel associated themselves to their countries. Learners are not fluent in English language. They attended the proficiency courses in English. As they come to USA for the first time, they have certain psychological fears like: they are not familiar with American accent; they do not have friends from native countries in the classroom, they do not understand languages of each other as their mother tongues vary from each other. All these factors lead to a kind of psychological fears among learners that they cannot do well. In order to desuggest and eliminate these fears, teacher uses the principles of joy and psycho-relaxation. Teacher arranges the chairs in a semicircle way so that learners can face and maintain eye contact with each other. Teacher believes it will encourage collaborative learning among students in the classroom.

In order to implement these principles in the classroom, teacher uses lyrics titled "Let me Love You" (DJ Snake ft. Justin Bieber – Let Me Love You, song) to teach in the classroom. He plays the lyrics in the classroom without assigning any task based on the lyrics. He asks students to close eyes and enjoy music. Students feel happy and relaxed in classroom. This way teacher creates a harmonious environment in the classroom. Teacher again plays the lyrics and asks them to repeat the words as they listen to them in the lyrics. Some of the students are not able to understand few words in the lyrics. Teacher pauses the audio and asks them to look at the transcript of the lyrics, which they read to understand the word they could not understand. Teacher asks them to pronounce the word as they listen to them in lyrics. The excerpts of the lyrics are written here:

I used to believe we were burning on the edge of something beautiful
Something beautiful
Driving the edge of a knife
I won't give up, nah-nah-nah
Let me love you
Don't you give up, nah-nah-nah
I won't give up, nah-nah-nah
I won't give up, nah-nah-nah
Let me love you
DJ Snake ft. Justin Bieber – Let Me Love You (Lyrics)

Teacher distributes handouts among students and asks them to categorize the adjectives, verbs and nouns as they listen to in the song.

Activity -1

Adjectives	Verbs	Nouns

Students listen to the lyrics and write five adjectives, verbs and nouns under each category. Teacher gave this activity in-group, so students were able to help each other. Most of the groups performed well.

Another activity teacher did in the classroom was to write a few sentences based on the grammatical structures as they listen to and read in the lyrics. Teacher asked them to form a few sentences with the structure. Following is the activity:

Activity 2

I used to _____

I will not _____

Do not you_____

Let me _____

Driving the_____

Students came up with various answers like:

*I used to play, eat, sleep, go, read, write etc.*_____

I won't call you, love you, hate you, believe you etc. _____

*Don't you give up, look up, look after etc.*_____

Let me love you, help you, teach you, catch you etc. _____

*Driving the car, bus, truck etc.*_____

Activity 3

Teacher asked one of the participants from the group to come up at the front and read the sentences and words in activity 1 and 2.

Observation

Teacher observed that students were very happy in the classroom. They were helping each other. The differences and distances among different nationalities had vanished. There was a lot of peer and group work. It was an integrated class so students developed all the four skills i.e., listening, speaking, reading and writing. When teacher played the lyrics, students were listening to it attentively. There was complete silence in the classroom except the sounds of the lyrics. Most of the students understood the lyrics though at the third or fourth time.

Playing music and lyrics was a good technique to improve listening. When the teacher supplied them with activity one, he motivated them to speak to each other and help each other. As they did not know the mother tongue of each other, they had to speak only target language. It improved their speaking skills. Teacher also gave them a handout containing the lyrics in written form, which they read repeatedly to complete activities. This improved their reading as well as writing skills. The class was interactive and learners had no fear while learning.

These observations and experiences include teacher's voice about the method. However, we do not know about the experiences and observations of learners. In order to include the observations and experiences of the learners in the study, teacher uses questionnaire (quantitative) and interview (qualitative) methods as tools to narrate learners' experiences and consider their feedback.

Analysis of Students' Feedback

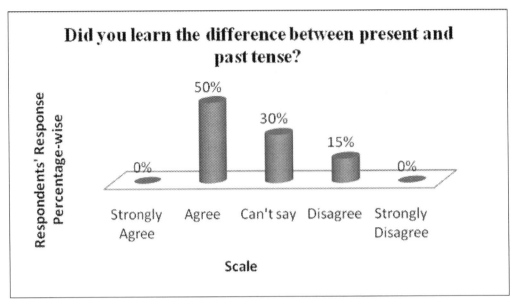

Figure 1

The first statement in the questionnaire *if they enjoyed the music and lyrics* reveals that there are 40% participants who felt that *they enjoyed the music and lyrics.* 55% of the participants admitted to it. 5% of the participants disagreed.

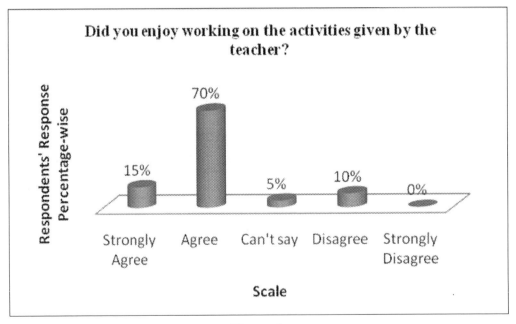

Figure 2

The second statement in the questionnaire if *they enjoyed working on the activities given by the teacher* displays that there are 15% of the participants who opined that *they enjoyed working on the activities given by the teacher.* 70% of the participants agreed though (5%) of the participants had no idea. 10% of the participants did not accept the statement.

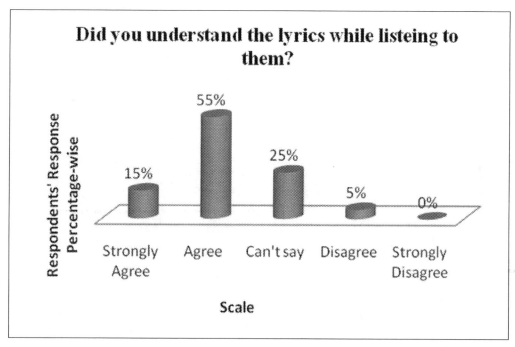

Figure 3

The third statement in the questionnaire if *they understood the lyrics while listening to them* shows that 15% of the participants are of the opinion that *they understood the lyrics.* 55% of the participants agreed to the statement though 25% of the participants had no opinion. 5% of the participants dissented.

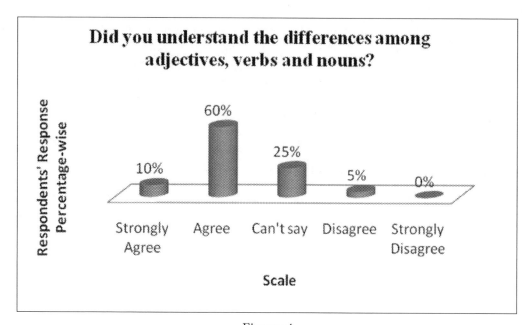

Figure 4

The fourth statement in the questionnaire if *they understood the differences among adjectives, verbs and nouns* exhibits that there are 10% of the participants who strongly agreed that *they understood the differences among adjectives, verbs and nouns.* 60% of the participants also admitted to it though 25% of the participants had no opinion. 5% of the participants disagreed to the statement.

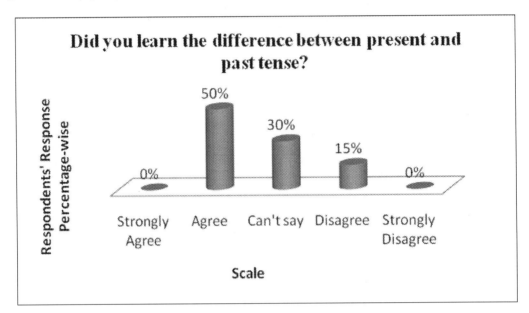

Figure 5

The fifth statement in the questionnaire *if they learnt the difference between present and past tense* divulges that there is none who strongly agreed to the statement that *they learnt the difference between present and past tense.* 50% of the participants agreed with the statement though 30% of the participants did not express their opinion. 15% of the participants disapproved and 5% of the participants strongly disagreed with the statement.

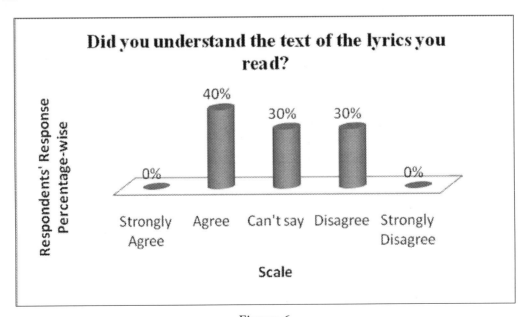

Figure 6

The sixth statement in the questionnaire if *they understood the text of the lyrics they read* discloses that there is none who strongly agreed to the statement. 40% of the participants concurred that *they understood the text of the lyrics they read.* 30% of the participants were not sure about it. 30% of the participants disagreed.

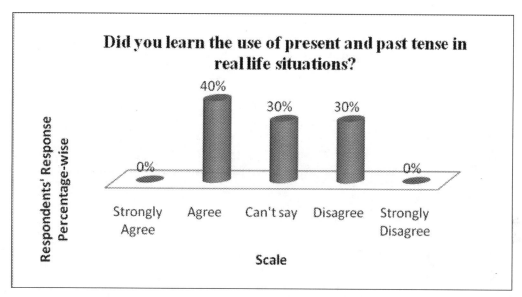

Figure 7

The seventh statement in the questionnaire if *they learnt the use of present and past tense in real life situations* shows that there is none who strongly agreed to the statement. 40% of the participants concurred that *they learnt the use of present and past tense in real life situations.* 30% of the participants were not sure about it. 30% of the participant disagreed.

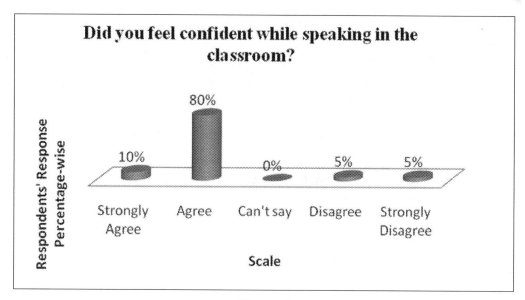

Figure 8

The eighth statement in the questionnaire *if they felt confident while speaking in the classroom* unveils that 10% of the participants were in absolute agreement to the statement that *they felt confident while speaking in the classroom*. A big no (80%) of the participants agreed. 5% of the participants did not agree with the statement and the same number (5%) of the participants had absolute disagreement.

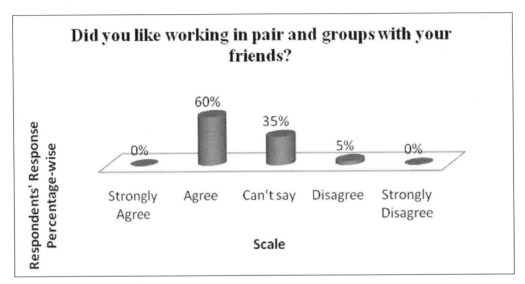

Figure 9

The ninth statement in the questionnaire if *they liked working in pair and groups with their friends* reveals no participant thought that *they liked working in pair and groups with their friends*. 60% of the participants agreed with the statement though 35% (a significant percentage) of the participants had no opinion. 5% of the participants disagreed with the statement.

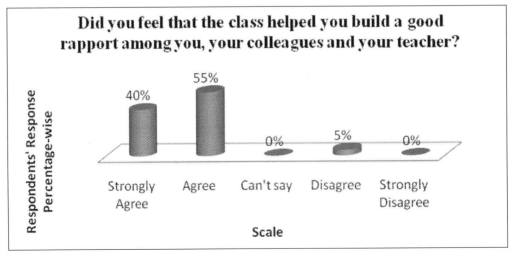

Figure 10

The tenth statement in the questionnaire if *they felt that the class helped them build a good rapport among them, their colleagues and their teacher* reveals that 40% of the participants strongly agreed with the statement that *they felt that the class helped them build a good rapport among them, their colleagues and their teacher.* 55% of the participants agreed to it. 5% of the participants did not agree with the statement.

Interview Questions

Twenty samples were selected out of 30, which were filled in with complete information. Students were asked the following questions in the interview:

1. Mention some difficulties faced in class.

2. Mention some confusions, doubts or queries they had.

3. Why did they like the class?

Table-1: Results of Interview Question no.1

Q.1.	Number of participants	Some difficulties faced in class:
	5	Not able to understand the accent of the different words in the lyrics.
	6	Could not understand everything what I watched and listened to.
	5	The sound was too low for me.
	4	These were not my favorite lyrics.

Table-2: Results of Interview Question no.2

Q.2.	Number of participants	Some confusions, doubts or queries:
	5	I was not able to understand the accent of my friends.
	6	I wanted to be the group leader and present the performance of my group.
	5	Time allotted to do the activity was short.
	4	Still confused among adjective, verb and noun.

Table-3: Results of Interview Question no.3

Q.3.	Number of participants	Why did you like the class?
	5	The music was very soothing and relaxing.
	6	The classroom was very encouraging and motivating.
	5	The classroom was full of positivism.
	4	There was a lot of enjoyment and fun in the classroom.

Discussion and Conclusion

The analysis of the questionnaire shows that students liked this method. The result of the first statement in the questionnaire displays that students (95%) like music and lyrics in the classroom. It helps teacher to eliminate the psychological fears of students, which create a barrier in second language acquisition. Students also admitted during the interview session that music was very soothing and relaxing. As the students found an environment of joy and easiness in the classroom, they tried to use their maximum mental capabilities.

Suggestopaedia aims to use the mental reserves of the students, teacher tried to use the mental reserve of students that usually remains unused and occupied by unnecessary fears, doubts and confusions. This result matches with the research reviews of a research on relaxation training that indicates that people learn more efficiently when relaxed. For example, results of Setterland (1983), in a research on the effects of relaxation training on 300 students after a strenuous activity, show a clear picture of recovery from strenuous activities. About 90% of students found that relaxation was pleasant and positive. Another study (Hansler, 1985) showed that relaxation training through suggestive techniques could enhance thinking and cognition matters related to general learning and academic progress.

Because of trying their level best, students enjoyed working on the activities (statement 2) given by the teachers. Therefore, here teacher exploited the first principle: principle of euphoria that refers to the ecstasy and absence of anxiety in a learning environment.

In response to statement three if they understood lyrics, around 70% students admitted that they understood the lyrics. However, 25% of the students had no idea and 5% disagreed. It stresses on the need of further repetition of the activities so that all the learners may comprehend the contents of the lyrics. It might also be because the students were not able to grasp American accent as they admitted during the interview session.

In response to statement four if they were able to comprehend the differences among adjectives, verbs and nouns, 70% of the students understood though 25% students had no opinion. 5% of the students disagreed with the statement. This is also success of this method as a majority of students was able to understand the differences between adjectives and nouns. Some of the students admitted that they were still confused among the three components of grammar. It may also be because the time given for the activity was short. 5 students also admitted the same during the interview.

In response to statement five if they were able to learn the differences between the present and past tense requires attention as only 50% of the students agreed that they understood the differences between the two. 30% of the students had no idea, which indicates they did not understand while 15% disagreed and 5% strongly disagreed to the statement. It shows that teacher needs to provide more practices to comprehend the differences between the two. Grammar-Translation Method differentiates between the two, which may be attributed to the very principle of suggestopaedia as it focuses more on contents than form. From the beginning, students learn to focus on the contents of the message rather than on its form. When students find themselves capable of speaking in a particular situation, their confidence increases and this, in turn, increases their capacity to learn (Freeman, 1986).

In response to the statement six, if they were able to understand the text of the lyrics they read shows the unanticipated results. Only 40% of the students were able to understand the text when they read it though they made a progress in understanding the text while they listened to it. It affirms our beliefs in the principle two of suggestopaedia as it helps learners relive from mental and physical stress so that they can use their cognitive abilities, which bring improvement in their learning and help in increasing psychomotor achievement of learners.

Another research (Carter, 1984) described the effects of relaxation training in improving handwriting. Carter could prove that relaxation training proved successful in increasing psychomotor achievement and cognitive abilities of the emotionally disturbed and learning-disabled children as opposed to the control group.

Suggestopaedia achieves this effect by starting the class with music, song, etc., to create a joyful mood. When students were listening to the lyrics, they understood well as music relieved them form stress and united their conscious and para- conscious and integrated their brain which focuses on the human being as an integrated whole. As a result, they enjoyed the music (as shown in statement one) and understood it (as shown in statement three). When the teacher stopped music and distributed the same text to read, they were not able to do well in absence of music and joyful environment. It may also be because they were not good in reading skills. So, they must be given some more practices in reading activities and should not stop music. Most of the students also admitted this during the interview session that they could not understand everything they listened to. It may also be because, as some students admitted, the sound was low or not every student liked the lyrics though the music was enjoyed by 95% of the students.

In response to statement seven, if they were able to understand the use of present and past tense in real life situations, shows that 45% agreed to it. 40% of students had no opinion while 15% of the students disagreed. It shows that suggestopeadia succeeded in eliminating the fears of learners though it did not get much success in connecting the classroom learning to the real life situations. They were not able to use the tenses in real life situations. May be because the environment outside the classroom is full of stress and does not provide joyful and pleasant mood which help learners in second language acquisition.

In response to statement eight if they felt confident while speaking in the classroom shows that 90% of the students agreed to it. It shows suggestopaedia is very successful in developing confidence as well as improving speaking skills of students. Students admitted this during the interview session that the classroom was very encouraging and motivating. It was full of positivism. Suggestopaedia succeeded in addressing their negative emotions and replacing them with positive ones. As a result, they regained their lost confidence and spoke well in the classroom and language was acquired in a natural way. Suggestopedia in language education settings is based on the assumption that language learning is as natural as breathing, and it is possible to be either inhibited by threat, anxiety and stress or counter-influenced by peace of mind, challenge, tedium, self-confidence and satisfaction (Holt, 1983).

In response to statement nine, if they liked working in pair and groups with their friends shows that 60% of the students agreed to the statement. As it was the first class, teacher expected students would improve and make progress with passage of time. Here teacher makes success with the third principle of suggestopaedia that it motivates for cluster and cooperative learning as it arouses potential learning.

In response to statement ten in the questionnaire, if students felt that the class helped them build a good rapport among them, their colleagues and their teacher confirms success of the principle three of suggestopaedia. As this method motivated for collaborative learning, it was quite helpful in building the rapport among students, their colleagues and their teacher. Although this method was successful, it has further scope of improvement. Moreover, this method is not very successful in a big classroom. In Third World countries, classrooms are over-crowded, and the classroom set-up may not be appropriate for using music and other tasks and techniques used in suggestopedia; according to Adamson (1997), this method suits a classroom of 12 students at maximum. (as qtd. in Zaid, 2014, p. 114)

CHAPTER 7

Community Language Learning

As the previous chapter – Suggestopaedia, affirms that learners have some sort of psychological fears, the fears prove as barriers in second language acquisition. In order to eliminate fears, teacher desuggests fears by adopting many techniques in the classroom like playing music, encouraging collaborative learning among learners and uniting conscious and unconscious mind of learners to integrate the brain as a whole to devote to language learning. Some of the principles of suggestopaedia are shared even by the Community Language Learning like: encouraging the collaborative learning, counseling the learners to eliminate fears and bridging distance between teacher and learners. This method was developed by Charles Curran, a Jesuit priest with background in Clinical Psychology and Counseling and exclusively focuses on adult learners. He studied adult language learning for several years and was greatly inclined to Carl Rogers' humanistic psychology (Rogers 1951; Brown 1994).

Richards and Rodgers (2001) state, "Community Language Learning draws on the counseling metaphor to redefine the roles of the teacher (the counselor) and learners (the clients) in the language classroom. The basic procedures of CLL can thus be seen as derived from the counselor-client relationship" (p.90). In this method teacher plays the role of a counselor who provides counseling to his clients, the learners, to remove the psychological fears they have regarding their success in acquiring second language. Freeman (2000) states, "Curran believes that a way to deal with the fears of learners is for teachers to become 'language counselor.' A language counselor does not mean someone trained in psychology, it means someone who is a skillful understander of the struggles learners face as they attempt to internalize another language" (p.89). It has its essence in the counselling learning between the priest and his clients, language learners. In this method, learners are treated as clients, and teachers are considered counselors. There is no particular technique employed in this method. It focusses on human relationships as a motivating factor between the client and the counsellor to learn the language. The clients are imparted complete freedom to decide what that they want to learn.

The Community Language Learning method relies on translation as a tool to facilitate second language learning in the beginning. This dependency on the mother tongue of learners is for a short time and teacher stops using it as soon as learners acquire the basic structure of target language and are able to comprehend the contents and message in the target language. Therefore, the basic purpose of this method is to enable learners to communicate in target language. The tape recorder is used for developing communication skills among learners.

The focus gradually shifts from aspects of grammar and phonetics to actual sharing of ideas, beliefs, opinions, wants and desires (Nagaraj 1996, p. 62).The clients are motivated to use the target language partially in order to convey their message. Unlike the Grammar-Translation Method, CLL focuses on communicative aspects of language learning. Language is used actively to communicate, not passively to practice in written form. Richards and Rodgers (2001) state, "Another language teaching tradition with which Community Language Learning is linked is a set of practices used in certain kinds of bilingual education programs" (p.90). It is referred to by Mackey (1972) as "Language alteration" (qtd. in Richards and Rodgers 2001, p.90).

Defining to language alteration, Richards and Rodgers (2001) further state, "In a language alteration, a message/lesson/class is presented first in the native language and then again in the second language. Learners know the meaning and flow of L2 message from their recall of the parallel meaning and flow of an L1 message" (p.90-91). In order to make this method more interactive and interesting, the counsellor can use tape recorder to record what the clients speak. The counselor plays the recording afterwards for the clients to listen their own recording and learn where they made a mistake regarding, structure, pronunciation etc.

Community Language Learning (CLL) was primarily designed for monolingual conversation classes where the teacher-counselor would be able to speak the learners' L1. The objective to integrate translation was to promote the idea that learners disassociate language learning from risk taking. Learners did not feel any anxiety or hesitation as teacher was well familiar with their mother tongue and accordingly could differentiate the language intricacies. It's a method solely based on English for communication and is extremely learner-focused. Although each course is unique and learner-dictated, there are certain criteria that should be applied to all CLL classrooms like learners must be motivated to practice the accurate pronunciation. Teacher also interfered to correct the learners though in a polite way. This method can be divided in to five stages for the ease of understanding about how to implement it in the classroom.

Stage 1- Translation

Learners form a small circle and ask teachers the message or word he wants to express in target language. Teacher provides the translation, which is repeated by the learners.

Stage 2- Group Work

Learners work in pair and groups to preparing small conversation or summary of a topic, which they subsequently present, to the teacher and rest of the class.

Stage 3 - Recorded conversation

Once learners are ready with their notes/ topics, teacher encourages them to come up with their sentences/ queries and teacher helps translate the language chunks into English, which learners could not. Learners practice the target language and let the teachers know they are ready. When they feel ready to speak, the learners take the microphone and record their sentences.

Stage 4 – Transcription

Next learners listen to the tape and transcribe their conversation. Teacher only intervenes when learners ask for help. He distances himself from the learning processes and motivates collaborative learning among learners so that they could take charge of their own learning.

Stage 5- Analysis

Learners analyze and study the sentences of the conversation/ transcription to focus on lexical items and application of grammatical rules inductively.

Stage 6- Reflection and Observation

At this stage, learners report and reflect on their experiences of working in pair and groups.

Stage 7- Listening

Learners listen to a monologue by the teacher, which includes the elements learners might have overheard in class interaction.

Stage 8 – Free conversation / Discussion

Next, the learners discuss with teachers how they felt about the activity. They also describe their experiences of talking to a microphone. Learner expressed how they felt speaking to a microphone. Some of them admitted they were hesitant though they overcame their hesitation with the passage of time in further classes. As it is a discussion part, there is no need for recording it (Richards and Rodgers, 2001, p.93-94).

Learners have well defined roles in CLL class. Learners with other learners and teachers form a community and prefer to work collaboratively. In this method, teacher-learner relationship is quite significant. It develops a holistic approach to language including both cognitive and affective aspects of language learning. The process of language learning is divided into five stages and compared to the ontogenetic development of the child. The first stage is termed as 'birth' in which feelings of safety and belongings are recognized. The second stage refers to learners' abilities to make them independent from the parent. The third stage refers to the development of speaking independently and establishing their own identity rejecting others' influences. The fourth stage enables learners to receive criticism and resultantly improve style and knowledge of linguistic appropriateness as the last stage. At the end of the process, the child has become adult. The process of learning a new language is like being reborn and developing a new persona (Richards and Rodgers 2001, p.92). The most important characteristics of this message is that learners get a new identity as they complete their course in CLL successfully acquiring second language.

In order to assess the practical application and outputs of this method, one study is shared here which was conducted with the adult learners at the community college of Najran University, KSA.

Experience

This method was used at the community college of Najran University, KSA. Teacher was an Indian who knew only basic Arabic. They were the adult learners who had a strong desire to learn English language. Most of them were either primary teachers or the clerks who did not know English at all. They wanted to learn English so that they could get a promotion. They used to join the class in the afternoon.

It was the first class so the teacher wanted to make it interactive as well as interesting for his learners. He made the leaners sit in a semicircle and greeted all of them in English one by one. The learners were able to say greetings like good afternoon, how are you, etc. Then the teacher asked them why they needed to learn English language. They explained their own reasons but most of them were regarding promotion in their respective jobs. As learners knew a little vocabulary, teacher started forming sentences. Teacher asked them what they wanted to speak English. They came up with different sentences in their mother tongue like, "ana Ahmed," the teacher translated it like my name is Ahmed and asked the learners to repeat it. As he said it first time, it was not very clear. When he said it three to four times, he improved the utterance of the sentences. Teacher formed the group and assigned them to form the dialogues of everyday usage. Teacher followed these stages (as described in the CLL method) to teach in the classroom.

Stage 1- Translation

Teacher helped learners with translation of few sentences, which they were not able to understand.

Stage 2- Group Work

Teacher formed group in the classroom and encouraged them for collaborative learning. Learners worked together to write some dialogues to which teacher provided correction wherever necessary.

Stage 3 - Recorded conversation

When the learners were ready with their dialogues, teacher went through them and made learners make some corrections. After this, the teacher assigned the role activity. He selected two learners form the class namely Abdul and Ahmed who were good in speaking the target language. Then teacher asked them to read their dialogues and record it.

Stage 4 – Transcription

When the recording activity was done, teacher played the recording one by one and asked learners to listen to it very carefully. They were enthusiastic to listen to each other's utterances in English. The teacher also asked them to note down their sentences and practice them at home. The following was the transcript (self-developed) learners practiced in the classroom.

Abdul: Hi

Ahmed: Hi

Abdul: How are you?

Ahmed: I am fine. How are you?

Abdul: I am also fine.

Ahmed: Where do you live?

Abdul: I live in Faisaliya, Najran,KSA.

Ahmed: Where do you live?

Abdul: I live in Sanaaya, Najran,KSA.

Ahmed: What is your favorite subject?

Abdul: My favorite subject is English.

Ahmed: What is your favorite subject?

Abdul: My favorite subject is also English.

Ahmed: Where do you work?

Abdul: I work at the Najran University.

Ahmed: Where do you work?

Abdul: I also work at the Najran University.

Ahmed: How do you go to university?

Abdul: I go by my car.

Ahmed: How do you go to university?

Abdul: I go by university bus.

Ahmed: Do you love your job?

Abdul: Yes, I love my job.

Ahmed: Do you love your job?

Abdul: Yes, I also love my job.

Ahmed: Which country do you like most?

Abdul: I like KSA most.

Ahmed: Which country is your favorite?

Abdul: My favorite country is KSA.

Ahmed: Nice to talk to you!

Abdul: Nice to talk to you!

Stage 5 – Analysis

After listening was over, teacher asked the learners to analyze the dialogues. The objective of this activity was to motivate learners to induce the grammatical rules from the linguistic structure. The conversation was based on the present tense so the learners were able to learn the structure of the present tense.

Stage 6- Reflection and Observation

Now teacher encouraged learners to reflect on their experiences. Learners had positive observations about the class.

Stage 7 – Discussion

At this stage, learners had discussion with teacher and other colleagues about their experiences. They shared the positive and negative aspects of the experiences of the classroom. Some of them admitted that they enjoyed recording their own voice while others admitted that they felt very hesitant and could not record their voice.

Observation

The teacher observed that learners enjoyed the class because they were not bound to follow any specific syllabus. They studied only what they required to study. Leaners designed their own syllabus as per their requirements. There was nothing imposed by the teachers rather teacher entertained different queries of learners. There was a strong emotional bond between teacher and learners. Teacher observed that learners learn better, when teachers teach them as per their needs, interest and requirements.

There were the feelings of community learning among learners as they belonged to a specific geographical setting of the city they lived in. Learners also continued their learning by exchanging a few utterances/expressions when they happened to meet each other outside the classroom. This method is highly leaner-centered as they are directly involved in the learning business. Learners' mother tongue is used as a tool in the classroom that facilitated language learning. As the teacher was a non-Arab, he was not very fluent in Arabic. He had to struggle while speaking Arabic to learners.

However, it was teachers' perspective regarding the application of Community Language Learning Method. Everything was narrated through the experience of the teachers. No voice of learners is heard during the implementation of the method. Teacher narrated the experiences of the learners as he felt them to be. However, the pros and cons of this method cannot be truly assessed until learners, the target group, are given an opportunity to express their opinion and share their experiences. In order to record learners' observation and experiences, a questionnaire set was given to them focusing on the key elements of Community Language Learning Method especially on the contents, which were taught in the classroom, and interpersonal relationship of learners and teachers. In addition to the questionnaire, learners were also interviewed with a set of open-ended questions to assess whether learners had any query, doubt or confusion, which were not part of questionnaire. The open-ended questions provided enough space to learners to put forward their opinion frankly.

Analysis of Students' Feedback

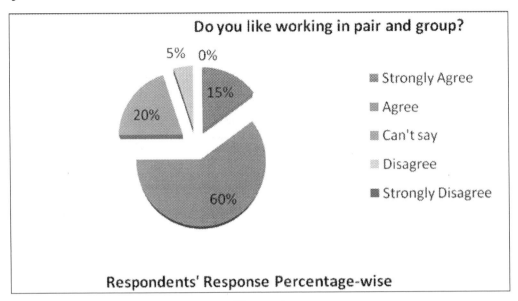

Figure 1

The first statement in the questionnaire if *they like working in pair and group* reveals that there are 15% participants who felt that *they liked working in pair and group*. 60% of the participants admitted to it though (20%) of the participants did not express their opinion. 5% of the participants disagreed.

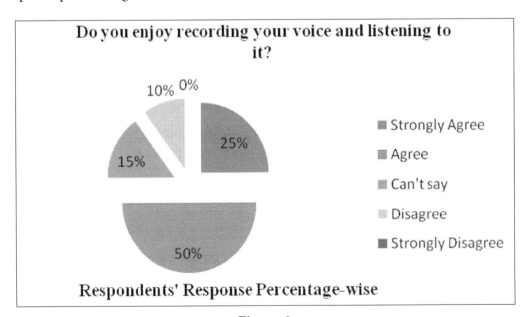

Figure 2

The second statement in the questionnaire if *they enjoy recording their voice and listening to it* displays that there are 25% of the participants who opined that *they enjoyed recording their voice and listening to it*. 50% of the participants agreed though (15%) of the participants had no idea. 10% of the participants did not accept the statement.

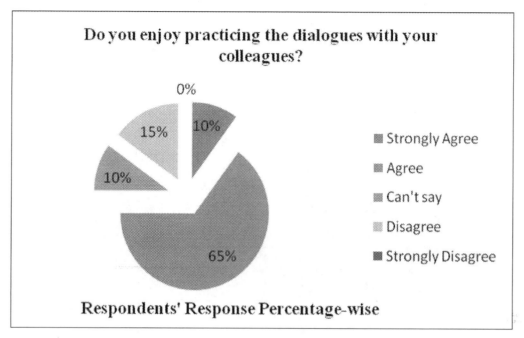

Figure 3

The third statement in the questionnaire if *they enjoy practicing the dialogues with their colleagues* shows that 10% of the participants are of the opinion that *they enjoy practicing the dialogues with their colleagues*. 65% of the participants agreed to the statement though 10% of the participants had no opinion. 15% of the participants dissented.

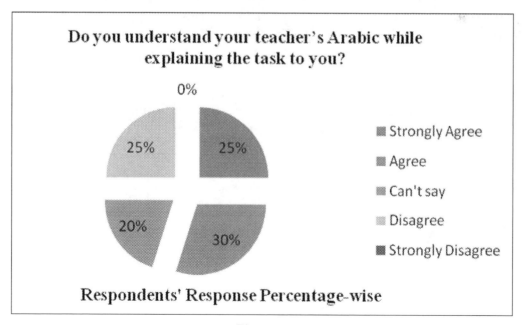

Figure 4

The fourth statement in the questionnaire if *they understand their teacher's Arabic while explaining the task to them* exhibits that there are 25% of the participants who strongly agreed that *they understood their teacher's Arabic while explaining the task to them.*30% of the participants also admitted to it.25% of the participants disagreed to the statement. 20% had no response while there was none who strongly disagreed.

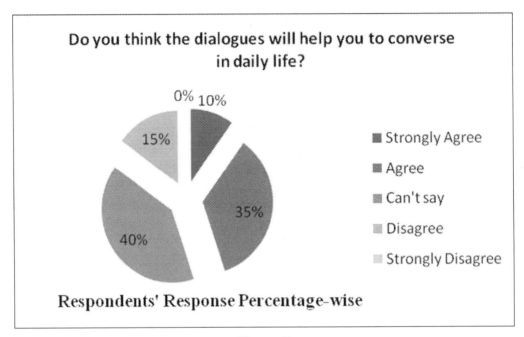

Figure 5

The fifth statement in the questionnaire if *they think the dialogues will help them to converse in daily life* divulges that there are 10% of the participants who strongly agreed to the statement. 35% of the participants agreed with the statement though (40%) of the participants did not express their opinion. 15% of the participants disapproved.

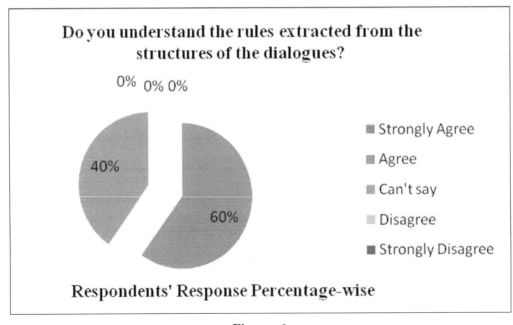

Figure 6

The sixth statement in the questionnaire if *they understand the rules extracted from the structures of the dialogues* discloses that there is none who strongly agreed to the statement. 60% of the participants concurred that *they understood the rules extracted from the structures of the dialogues.* 40% of the participants were not sure about it.

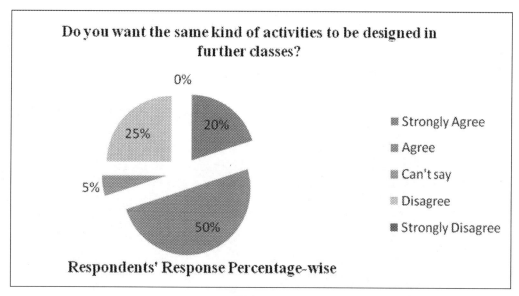

Figure 7

The seventh statement in the questionnaire if *they want the same kind of activities to be designed in further classes* shows that 20% of the participants stated that *they wanted the same kind of activities to be designed in further classes.* 50% of the participants accepted the statement and 5% of the participants had no opinion. 25% of the participants did not accept the statement.

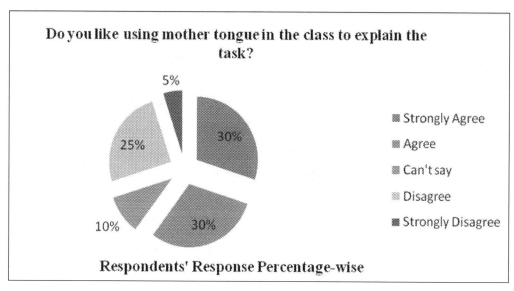

Figure 8

The eighth statement in the questionnaire if *they like using mother tongue in the class to explain the task* unveils that 30% of the participants were in absolute agreement to the statement that *they liked using mother tongue in the class to explain the task.* An equal no (30%) of the participants agreed while 10% of the participants did not state an opinion. 25% of the participants did not agree with the statement and 5% were in absolute disagreement.

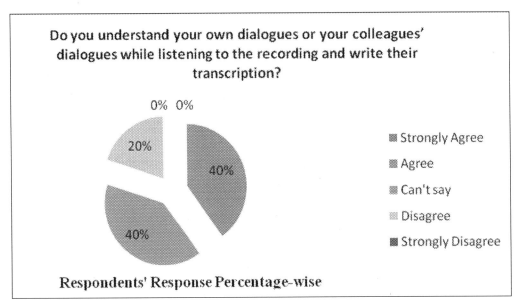

Figure 9

The ninth statement in the questionnaire if *they understand their own dialogues or their colleagues' dialogues while listening to the recording and write their transcription* reveals no participant thought that *they understood their own dialogues or their colleagues' dialogues while listening to the recording and write their transcription.* 40% of the participants agreed with the statement though the same number (40%, a significant percentage) of the participants had no opinion. 20% of the participants disagreed with the statement.

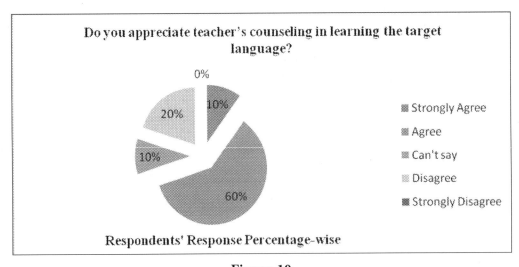

Figure 10

The tenth statement in the questionnaire if *they appreciate teacher's counselling in learning the target language* reveals that 10% of the participants strongly agreed with the statement. 60% of the participants agreed to it while 10% of the participants did not express their opinion. 20% of the participants did not agree with the statement.

Interview analysis

Another method used to collect the data was interview method. Twenty samples were selected out of 30, which were filled in with complete information. The participants responded to the following questions in the interview:

1. Learners rate (on a scale of 1-5) the effectiveness of this method where 1 represents the lowest and 5 represents the highest value:

2. Mention some common learning difficulties faced in class:

3. Mention some confusions, doubts or queries you had:

4. Why do you like this method?

Table 1: Results of Interview Question no. 1

Q. No	Number of learners	Scale
1.	4	2
	10	3
	6	4

As shown in the table, in response to the first question, 4 learners rated the effectiveness of the method as 2 on a scale of 1-5 as mentioned earlier. 10 learners rated the effectiveness of the method as 3 and 6 other teachers rated as 4. The overall effectiveness of the method was rated 1-4s from learners' point of view.

Table-2: Results of Interview Question no. 2

Q.2.	Number of participants	Some common learning difficulties faced in class:
	5	Not able to completely understand teacher's Arabic.
	8	My group leader dominated the group.
	7	We did not get a chance to record our voice.

As shown in Table 2, in response to question number 2, there were varied responses, only common responses were placed in the table here. Most of the learners (8) agreed that their group leader dominated the group. Some learners (7) could not get a chance to record their voice.

Table-3: Results of Interview Question no. 3

Q.3	Number of participants	Some confusions, doubts or queries you had:
	5	Couldn't understand instructions as teacher's accent in Arabic was not clear.
	8	Still had doubts about present tense as the rules were not clear.
	7	Couldn't understand accent of the colleagues while listening to and writing to transcript

As shown in Table 3, in response to question number 3, there were varied responses, only common responses were placed in the table here. Most of the learners (8) agreed that they still had doubts about present tense, as the rules were not clear. Some learners (7) said that they could not understand accent of the colleagues while listening to and writing to transcript. 5 learners said that they couldn't understand instructions as teacher's accent in Arabic was not clear

Table-4: Results of Interview Question no.4

Q.4	Number of participants	Why do you like this method?
	5	There was a feeling of facing the challenge together in a team.
	8	Knew so many colleagues we did not know before and loved to talk to them in mother tongue as well as target language.
	7	It was very different from traditional classes we attended in the university. There was a lot of freedom encouragement and motivation in the classroom.

As shown in Table 4, in response to question number 4, there were varied responses, only common responses were placed in the table here. Most of the learners (8) stated that they knew so many colleagues we did not know before and loved to talk to them in mother tongue as well as target language. Some learners (7) said that it was very different from traditional classes we attended in the university. There was a lot of freedom, encouragement and motivation in the classroom. 5 learners said that they there was a feeling of facing the challenge together in a team.

Discussion and Conclusion

The analysis of questionnaire reveals that learners in general liked this method. The values assigned against each statement affirm that there is still scope for further improvement to exploit this method to the interest of learners. In order to assess overall effectiveness of this method, two scales: 'agree' and 'strongly agree' are merged. In response to statement one, if they liked working in pair and group reveals that 75% (as the scales 'agree' and 'strongly agree' are merged) of the learners admitted that they liked working in pair and group work. It ultimately motivates for collaborative learning and comprehends one of the principles of CLL as Nagaraj (1996) states," CLL takes place in groups: they can be either small groups or large groups. These groups form the community"(p. 61). They also admitted during the interview that the classroom provided them with a spirit of teamwork and they enjoyed accepting challenges together. However, there were 20% of learners who had no opinion and 5% of Learners disagreed which affirms that this method is not 100% successful. It requires our attention to further modify either teaching techniques or the method itself.

In response to statement two, if learners enjoy recording their voice and listening to it displays that around 75% of the learners agreed to it. It proves that the classroom used another important principle (recording the conversation) of CLL and got success in it as Richards and Rodgers (2001) state, "Learners record conversations in the target language" (p.94). However, 15% of learners did not state an opinion, while 5% disagreed to it. It indicates that teacher did not swap the roles while recording the conversation. Teacher must ensure that every learner experiences recording their own voice.

In response to statement three if they enjoy practicing the dialogues with their colleagues shows that 75% of learners enjoy practicing the dialogues. They also admitted during the interview that they knew so many colleagues whom they had not known earlier and loved to talk to them. It shows that they formed their own community. Freeman (2000) states, "In groups, learners can begin to feel a sense of community and can learn from each other as well as the teacher. Cooperation, not competition, is encouraged" (p.97). Nevertheless, 10% had no comment while 15% of learners disagreed which shows that there is still scope for further improvement in order to get 100% success out of this method.

In response to statement four, if they understand teacher's Arabic while explaining the task to them shows that only 55% of learners agreed to it which is less than the values assigned to previous two statements. Here, it is a harsh criticism of this method related to CLL's use of mother tongue. If teacher does not know learners' mother tongue, he cannot be very successful in implementing this method. However, if teacher is a native speaker of Arabic language, he would hardly use English in the classroom. In both the ways, learners will suffer. It is unusual demand from teachers as Richards and Rodgers (2001) state, "Community Language Learning places unusual demands on language teachers. They must be highly proficient and sensitive to nuance in both L1 and L2" (p.97). If teacher is not well versed in learners' L1, learners would not understand his instructions as they admit they could not understand the instructions because of teacher's non-native accent in Arabic. Moreover, they also admitted during the interview that they could not understand accent of the colleagues while listening to and writing to transcript. It shows that learners were also unable to understand each other's accent in target language.

In response to statement five if they think the dialogues will help them to converse in daily life shows that only 45% of the learners admitted to it whereas 40% (a big majority) had no opinion. 15% of learners disagreed to it. It proves that learners were not able to connect their outer world with the classroom. It also fails the basic principle of CLL, the communication. It may be because CLL does not have a definite syllabus where communication may get a specific place. Richards and Rodgers (2001) have also criticized CLL on these grounds as they remark, "Since Linguistic and or communicative competence is specified only in social terms, explicit linguistic or communicative objectives are not defined in CLL. Most of what has been written about it describes its use in introductory conversation courses in a foreign language" (p.93).

In response to statement six if they understand the rules extracted from the structures of the dialogues displays that only 60% of the learners admitted that they understood the rules whereas 40% of the learners did not have an opinion which indicated that they were confused about whether they understood the rules or not. Eight learners (almost 40%) also admitted during the interview that they still had doubts about present tense, as the rules were not clear. It may also be because the focus of the lesson was on listening and speaking. Another important factor is that CLL lacks a particular syllabus, which might contribute to lack of practices for the same. Richards and Rodgers (2001) state, "Other concerns have been expressed regarding the lack of a syllabus, which makes objectives unclear and evaluation difficult to accomplish, and the focus on fluency rather than accuracy, which may lead to inadequate control of the grammatical system of the target language" (p.98).

In response to statement seven, if they want the same kind of activities to be designed in further classes, 70% agreed to the statement. However, 25% disagreed to it and 5% had nothing to say about. It shows that teacher needs to take into consideration the language requirements of other learners as well by taking their feedback and suggestions to improve the next class' activities. It emphasizes on the fact that activities in CLL classroom need to be designed very carefully as there is no syllabus. That is why a fine balance among method, teaching techniques, and activities is very essential.

The response to statement eight if they like using mother tongue in the class to explain the task exhibits that only 60% learners agree to the statement. 25% disagreed while 5% strongly disagreed to the statement. 10% did not state their opinion. It shows that learners have a strong will to use target language in the classroom. However, the beginning classes cannot guarantee success, as learners do not target language at all. CLL also aims to use mother tongue in the beginning as a tool and discards its use as soon as learners acquire the basic proficiency in target language. Freeman (2000) states, "In later stages, of course, more and more of the target language can be used. By the time learners are in Stages (iii) or (iv), their conversations have few native language words or phrases" (p.102).

The response to statement nine, if they understand their own dialogues or their colleagues' dialogues while listening to the recording and write their transcription, shows that only 40% learners agree to it; whereas, 40% (an equal number) learners did not state their opinion. It clearly states that they do not understand the listening properly. During the interview session, around seven learners admitted that they could not understand accent of the colleagues while listening to and writing to transcript. It means learners require a lot of practice in listening before they could understand each other. If the learners belong to different nationalities, it becomes more difficult to understand each other as their accents are influenced by their mother tongues. Therefore, CLL is successful with homogenous group of learners and not the heterogeneous groups of learners. It is the biggest drawback of CLL that it cannot be universalized.

The response to statement ten, if they appreciate teacher's counseling in learning the target language, shows that 70% learners agree to it. It proves that teacher's counseling was effective for learners. However, it cannot guarantee 100% success because not all the teachers are trained in counseling learners. They require special psychological training in order to be more effective. Richards and Rodgers (2001) have raised the same concern as they opine, "Critics of Community Language Learning question the appropriateness of the counseling metaphor on which it is predicted. Questions also arise about whether teachers should attempt counseling without special training" (p.98).

CHAPTER 8

Total Physical Response

Total Physical Response (TPR) is a method of teaching which was developed by James Asher, Professor of psychology, at San Jose State University, California. It borrows a lot from developmental psychology, learning theory and humanistic pedagogy, as well as language teaching procedures proposed by Harold and Dorothy Palmer in 1925 (Richards & Rodgers, 2001). In the 1960s and 1970s many researches stressed that language learning should start first with understanding and then producing (Winitz, 1981). This method inculcates the principles of Comprehension Approach as it heavily relies on listening comprehension. A new method, called the Lexical Approach, also fits within the comprehension approach. Developed by Michael Lewis, the Lexical Approach is less concerned with student production and more concerned that students receive abundant comprehension input. It deals with the concept that the child first listens to the language around him as part of receptive skill. Then the child starts producing / speaking their mother tongue as part of productive skill (Freeman, 2000). Asher shared the same notion when he reasoned that the quickest and less stressful way to learn the target language is to follow the commands of teachers with zero use of the mother tongue. Gradually, learners will acquire the second language as a child acquires his or her first language.

TPR is a method of teaching where teachers engage students not only mentally but also physically. Their whole body is active while they learn a language. Actions become a vehicle to convey the meaning of the target language, as Nagaraj (1996) states, "Meaning in the target language can be conveyed best through actions (p.67)". The most important quality of this method is that even the laziest student seems to be active in the classroom. When the learners move in the classroom, it circulates blood in their whole body; specially brain, which is a very important part for learning. TPR makes the learners take the charge of their leaning themselves. Students are engaged and thus feel motivated. When learners move in the classroom and follow the command of teachers, they feel energetic. It helps them relive their anxiety during learning. Distance between a teacher and a student is bridged as teachers make students feel closed and they bridge not only physical but also mental distance between students and teachers in the classroom. Teacher is no more treated like a sage whose teaching is taken like a sermon and a distance of reverence is maintained. Here Asher attacks the traditional concept of teacher and teaching. The formality between a teacher and students has no place in this method as Asher stresses on bridging the distance with students to understand their issues. Teacher loses his authority and becomes one of the students and he behaves like that so that students stay motivated to share their problems with teacher. Students find them playing or acting or making movements with them that triggers their confidence, which plays a vital role in learning second language. TPR is very encouraging for shy learners. They can also actively participate in learning through this method. The most important feature of this method is that learners learn language naturally without being stressed.

A similar research by Furuhata (1999) examined the TPR approach that included many features of the natural approach along with the learning of words and sentences linked to physical actions. In addition, students were not forced to speak before they were ready. It helped students to become more comfortable in the classroom and feel less pressure to speak the second language. (qtd. in Holleny 2012, p.13)

Therefore, the fear of leaning is vanished by the systematic presentation and implementation of this method. The psychological boundaries of the classroom are broken in this method. Learning becomes fun rather than a mental stress. Students play and learn the language. One of the best parts of this method is that teachers do not need even special resources to carry out learning activities in the classroom. It is very effective for teenagers and young learners; is appropriate for kinesthetic learners to be active in class. It is effective in making students memorize phrases and words and works well with mixed ability class (Sophaktra, 2009).

The most important ability required on the part of the teacher is being creative and having a desire to experiment new strategies of learning with learners. The challenge with teacher is to adopt innovative techniques in the classroom as per the requirements of learners.

At the core of this method lies the principle that physical actions provide a mental stimulus to students. Brain plays a vital role in language acquisition. In order to understand how second language or language learning is facilitated by brain; one must know the function and role of different parts of brain in language acquisition. Asher describes how some part of brain facilitates learning of a foreign language. For this dimension of his learning theory, he presents three influential learning hypotheses:

1. There is a specific innate bio-program for language learning which defines the best path for first and second language development.

2. Brain lateralization defines different learning functions in the left-and right –brain hemispheres.

3. Stress (an affective filter) intervenes between the act of learning and what is to be learned; the lower the stress, the greater the learning (Richards & Rodgers, 2001, p. 74).

Having studied the role of brain in language acquisition, Asher proposes that second language learning should be less stressful. It must be learnt in a way as a child learns his first language. When learners consciously make efforts to learn a second language, the natural phenomenon of language acquisition is reverted. The natural way of stress free learning is replaced by stressful artificial way of learning. At this stage, the problem of learning a second language starts, as it becomes language learning rather than language acquisition. Asher might have closely studied these issues in language learning. That is why he proposed the idea of language acquisition rather than language learning. Language learning may be stressful as it is conscious effort of learning a language but language acquisition cannot be stressful as learners unconsciously acquire it. In order to create an environment of natural way of acquisition, Asher stresses on removing learners' fear and stress before attempting to acquire second language. In order to eliminate learners' fear, Asher presented Total Physical Response, which stresses on the coordination of speech and action. Here it is necessary that natural sequence of language learning must be followed like listening, speaking, reading and writing. In this way, Asher proposes a Natural Method for language learning. Asher (1977) states, "A reasonable hypothesis is that the brain and nervous system are biologically programmed to acquire language...in a particular sequence and in a particular mode. The sequence is listening before speaking and the mode is to synchronize language with individual's body". (p.4)

In a way, it can be said that Asher provides a more systematic approach to language teaching as it focuses on the function of brain in language learning. If teacher understands the concept (the function of brain in language learning) which is the basic foundation of TPR, it would be easier for teacher to figure out how to make language acquisition easier for learners. Asher believes that TPR is directed to right brain learning whereas most language learning methods are directed to left-brain learning. Inspired by Jean Piager (A Swiss psychologist known for his work on child development, his theory of cognitive development and epistemological view are together called "genetic epistemology"), Asher states that the child acquires language through motor movement, a right hemisphere activity. It is necessary that right-hemisphere activities must take place before the left hemisphere can process language for production. In the same way, adult language learning should start from right hemisphere motor activities while the left hemisphere watches and learns. When there is sufficient amount of learning with right-hemisphere, the left-hemisphere will be activated to produce language and to start other, more abstract language processes (Richards and Rodgers 2001, p. 75).

In this way, Asher advocated a neurolinguistics approach (an approach to second language teaching) conceptualized by Joan Netten and Claude Germain primarily based on the research of Paradis (1994, 2004, 2009), N. Ellis (2011) and Segalowitz (2010), and is also influenced by the research on social interaction by Vygotsky (1962). His approach to language learning is more systematized and based on neuro-programming of language learning. His approach to language leaning seems to be more authentic and medically inspired as it specifically focuses on the functioning of particular parts of brain, which play key role in language acquisition, and learning.

Asher (1997) stated that the process of acquiring a language happens on the right side of a brain, which promotes visualization, and movements that aims to achieve comprehension literacy. In his keynote address at a conference in Calgary, Canada, stated that the right side of the brain is non-verbal (mute), non-critical and pattern seeking. According to him, the brain will try to communicate by whispering faintly and use body language such as gestures. When the pattern seekers find cause-effect relationship, they will store them in long-term memory (qtd. in Ghani & Ghous 2014, p. 4).

However, these are the theoretical assumptions about Total Physical Response. In order to assess the true potential of this method in language learning, one study is shared here which was conducted at Academic Staff College, Aligarh, India with intermediate level learners.

Experience

This experience is based on an intermediate level class at Academic Staff College, Aligarh, India. Students do not know much of the target language when they join English Access Micro scholarship Program (a program sponsored by the US Embassy to Human Resource Development Centre, India) to AMU (Aligarh Muslim University) through which 200 underprivileged AMU school children in the age-group of 12-16 years receive English proficiency and personality development training during off-school hours. Teacher experiments TPR method in the classroom to facilitate the target language. Teacher starts the class in a very jolly mood. He, first, takes attendance and then greets students in their native language. He explains students the method he is going to use in the classroom. He tells students that they have to follow only his commands with their physical movements and without speaking or uttering anything. The classroom is quite big so they have enough space to make movements in the classroom. In the first class, teacher starts with some basic commands in the target language as he asks students to stand up, sit down and students physically perform the command. Teacher repeats the same command for about ten minutes in order to make sure that every student understands the command and follows it. Then teacher goes ahead and commands students with some big chunks of language like switch on the tube light, switch off the tube light, etc. First, students seem to be confused what to do that indicates teacher that they did not understand the command. Therefore, teacher himself 'switched on' and 'switched off' the tube light. Here, teacher exploited a very important principle of TPR of combining language instruction with motor activities, as Holleny (2012) states, "The underlying belief of TPR is that by combining language instruction with motor activities, students are able to learn quicker, more effectively, and in a stimulating atmosphere" (p.8). Students then understood what teacher wanted them to do in the classroom. Then students followed the command exactly the way teacher wanted them to do. Teacher repeated the same activity for ten minutes. Now teacher asked four volunteers to come on the front. They were especially the ones who could speak the command with simple sentences. The volunteers spoke with teacher and the rest of the students followed the same commands, which were given by the teacher before, like: sit down, stand up, switch off the tube light, switch on the tube light, etc. After that, teacher asked the volunteers to speak some more sentences in order to give command to students like open the door, shut the door, etc., and the students followed them. Now teacher took a back seat and observed what students were doing. Teacher observed that volunteers were full of confidence in giving command to their colleagues. They were behaving as if they were the teachers. In the next class, teachers switched the role of the volunteers. In every class, teacher used to change the group of volunteers to ensure that every student gets a chance to give and follow the commands. Moreover, teacher realized that students fed up and deviated from learning if they are given the same kind of roles repeatedly.

Observation

Teacher observed that it was an effective way of teaching a foreign language. Students felt involved in learning process. The best thing about the method is that student gradually grabbed the language like their mother tongue. They induced the rules form the structure they were using in the classroom. In the beginning, they were not able to understand teacher and their colleagues but they comprehended body language of the teacher. There was more emphasis on conveying the message rather than stressing on the correct form as Richards and Rodgers (2001) state, "Physical Response requires initial attention to meaning rather than to the form of items. Grammar is thus taught inductively" (p.76). Students felt stress free throughout the class as it is the basic norm of Total Physical Response. They were not punished for anything rather they were imparted complete freedom in the classroom, which added to their confidence of learning a language. The role of shifting of the volunteers filled students with confidence and took the fear out. They did their best to imitate teacher and commanded the same way as teacher did. In the beginning, students did not speak much as they were listening to target language, which was being conveyed to them along with physical action. Here, teacher follows Asher's fundamental principle of TPR as directed to right-brain learning unlike other methods which direct to left-brain learning. Teacher makes the right-hemisphere activities to occur in the form of the input of target language especially through listening comprehension. It took some time for students to form sentences in the target language but they did which indicates the successful implementation of TPR with immediate and incredible results. In TPR, when there is sufficient amount of right-hemisphere learning in the form of listening to target language, the left hemisphere is triggered to produce language. (Richards and Rodgers 2001, p. 75) Students learnt better through observing action of teacher, their own action and their fellow students' action. It is also based on an important principle of TPR: learning by doing. The volunteers developed a feeling of being successful in delivering language chunks to their friends in the form of commands which added to their motivation that play a vital role in language acquisition. Here teacher succeeded in implementing the very basic principle of TPR as Nagaraj (1996) states, "A feeling of success aids language learning. Total Physical Response allows learners to achieve a high degree of success". (p.67) Teacher changes routine so that students should not be addicted to a set command of instructions. Teacher changes his command from time to time and injects new chunks of language to students, which they slowly understood and then tried to speak them as they acquired them. Teachers asked them to jump on and off the desk, which made them laugh and enjoy the commands. Teacher also asked them to shake hands with each other that promoted fraternity among students. The method had the following characteristics:

1. Group learning, collaborative learning
2. Practical use of language
3. Better student-teacher interaction
4. Better student-student interaction
5. Accuracy in grammatical structures and vocabulary inputs, spoken language is emphasized over written, understanding pronunciation of words.
6. Little help from the mother tongue in the beginning.
7. Teaching and evaluation go hand in hand.
8. Using commands to direct behavior
9. Role reversal
10. Action sequence
11. Helps slow learners with low achievements.
12. As Asher says, "it uses verbal discourse as an instructional strategy on left hemisphere of the brain", it seemed to work here.
13. Teaching words with gesture

However, it was teachers' perspective regarding the application of TPR as it followed the learner-centered approach and involved them in learning process physically as well mentally. Students were encouraged to come up with new structures in target language following the physical command of teacher as well as their colleagues through nonverbal clues. Teacher emphasized more on fluency and less on accuracy. Form was less important than meaning. Teacher overlooked a few grammatical mistakes as it might have discouraged students and broken their rhythm and enthusiasm of speaking a few chunks in the target language. Though this method turned out to do well, success of this method cannot be truly assessed until students, the target group, are given an opportunity to express their opinion and share their experiences. In order to obtain students' feedback, a questionnaire set was given to them focusing on the key elements of TPR especially on the contents, which were taught in the classroom. In addition to the questionnaire, students were also interviewed with a set of open-ended questions to assess whether they had any query, doubt or confusion, which were not part of the questionnaire. The open-ended questions provided enough space to students to put forward their opinion frankly. Students were described the contents of questionnaire and interview both in mother tongue and target language.

Analysis of Students' Feedback

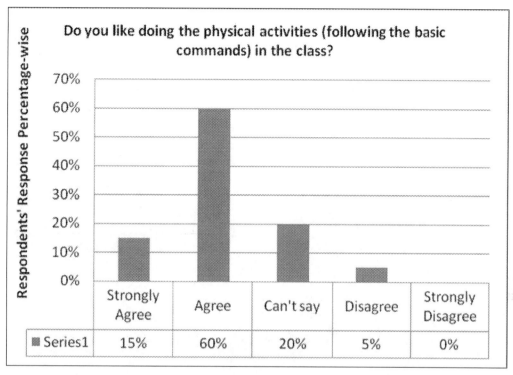

Figure 1

The first statement in the questionnaire if *they like doing the physical activities (following the basic commands) in the class* reveals that there are 75% participants who felt that *they liked doing the physical activities (following the basic commands) in the class.* 20% of the participants did not express their opinion. 5% of the participants disagreed.

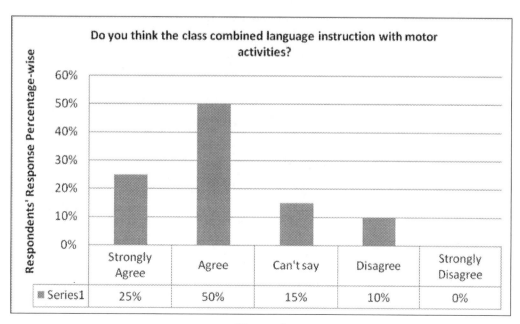

Figure 2

The second statement in the questionnaire if *they think the class combined language instruction with motor activities* displays that there are 75% of the participants who *think the class combined language instruction with motor activities.* 15% of the participants had no idea. 10% of the participants did not accept the statement.

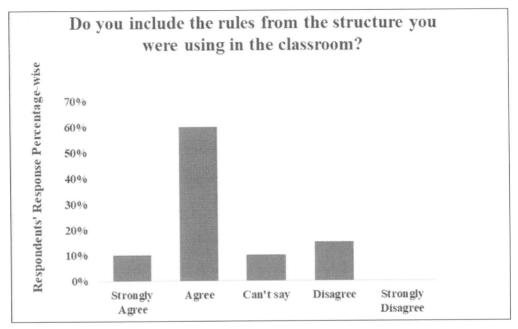

Figure 3

The third statement in the questionnaire if *they induced the rules from the structures they were using in the classroom* shows that 75% of the participants are of the opinion that *they induced the rules from the structures they were using in the classroom.* 10% of the participants had no opinion. 15% of the participants dissented.

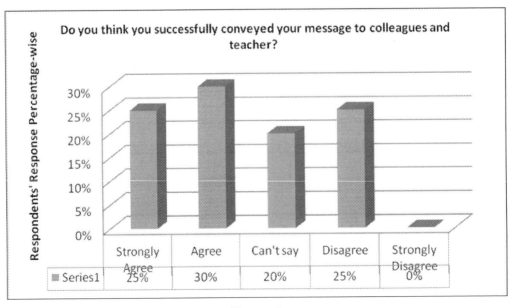

Figure 4

The fourth statement in the questionnaire if *they think they successfully conveyed their message to colleagues and teacher* exhibits that there are 55% of the participants who strongly agreed that *they successfully conveyed their message to colleagues and teacher.* 25% of the participants disagreed to the statement. 20% had no response while there was none who strongly disagreed.

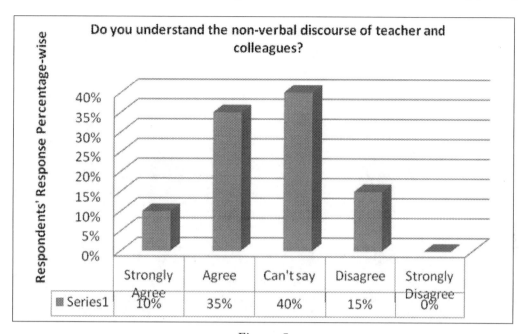

Figure 5

The fifth statement in the questionnaire if *they understand the non-verbal discourse of teacher and colleagues* divulges that there are 45% of the participants who strongly agreed to the statement that *they understood the non-verbal discourse of teacher and colleagues.* 40% of the participants did not express their opinion. 15% of the participants disapproved.

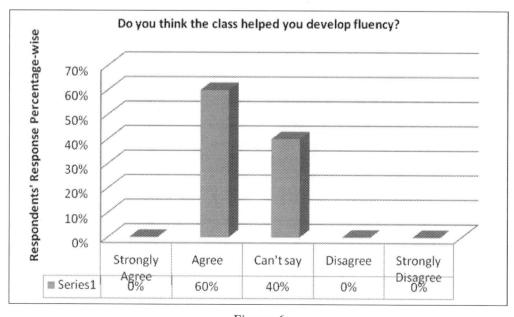

Figure 6

The sixth statement in the questionnaire if *they think the class helped them develop fluency* discloses that there is none who strongly agreed to the statement. 60% of the participants concurred that *the class helped them develop fluency*. 40% of the participants were not sure about it. There is none with disagreement.

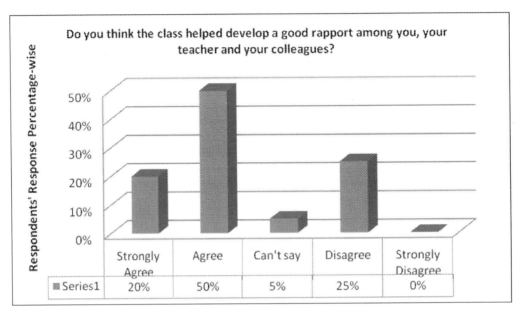

Figure7

The seventh statement in the questionnaire if *they think the class helped develop a good rapport among them, their teacher and their colleagues* shows that 70% of the participants stated that *the class helped develop a good rapport among them, their teacher and their colleagues*. 5% of the participants had no opinion. 25% of the participants did not accept the statement.

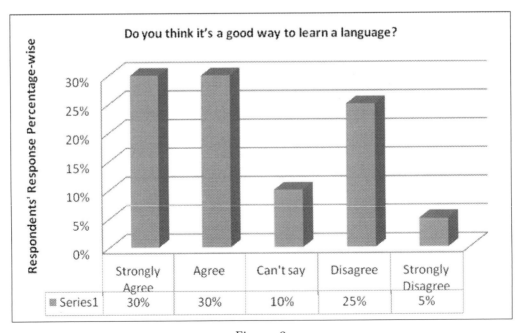

Figure 8

The eighth statement in the questionnaire if *they think it is a good way to learn a language* unveils that 60% of the participants were in absolute agreement to the statement that *it is a good way to learn a language.* 10% of the participants did not state an opinion. 25% of the participants did not agree with the statement and 5% were in absolute disagreement.

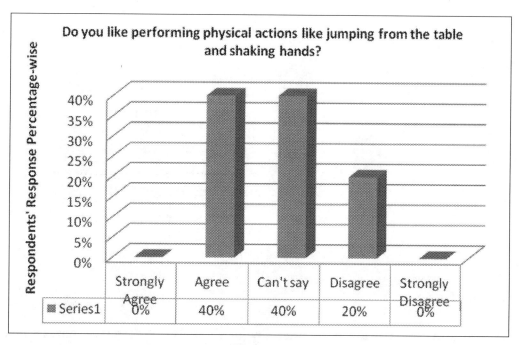

Figure 9

The ninth statement in the questionnaire if *they like performing physical actions like jumping from the table and shaking hands* reveals no participant thought that *they like performing physical actions like jumping from the table and shaking hands.* 40% of the participants agreed with the statement though the same number (40%, a significant percentage) of the participants had no opinion. 20% of the participants disagreed with the statement

The tenth statement in the questionnaire if *they feel the classroom learning was stress free, amusing and they enjoyed it* reveals that 70% of the participants strongly agreed with the statement. 10% of the participants did not express their opinion. 20% of the participants did not agree with the statement.

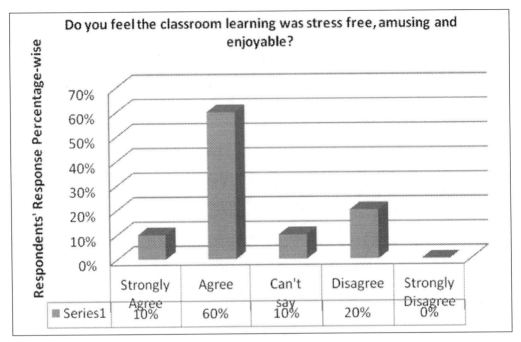

Figure10

Interview analysis

The data was also collected using the interview method. Twenty samples were selected out of 30, which were filled in with complete information. The participants responded to the following questions in the interview:

1. Learners rate (on a scale of 1-5) the effectiveness of this method where 1 represents the lowest and 5 represents the highest value:

2. Mention some common learning difficulties faced in class:

3. Mention some confusions, doubts or queries you had:

4. Why do you like this method?

Table 1: Results of Interview Question no. 1

Q. No	Number of learners	Scale
1.	4	2
	6	3
	10	4

As shown in table 1, in response to the first question, 4 learners rated the effectiveness of the method as 2 on a scale of 1-5 as mentioned earlier. 10 learners rated the effectiveness of the method as 4 and 6 other teachers rated as 3. The overall effectiveness of the method was rated 2-4s from learners' point of view.

Table-2: Results of Interview Question no. 2

Q.2.	Number of participants	Some common learning difficulties faced in class:
	5	We were tired, so did not like to continue class.
	8	Not able to communicate in target language.
	7	We were scared to jump.

As shown in Table 2, in response to question number 2, there were varied responses, only common responses were placed in the table here. Most of the learners (8) agreed that they were not able to communicate in target language. Some learners (7) said that they were scared to jump. Some learners (5) said that they were tired, so did not like to continue class.

Table-3: Results of Interview Question no. 3

Q.3	Number of participants	Some confusions, doubts or queries you had:
	5	Not able to completely understand teacher's commands.
	8	Still confused about how to give commands as we lack vocabulary.
	7	Could not comprehend relationship between physical action and commands.

As shown in Table 3, in response to question number 3, there were varied responses, only common responses were placed in the table here. Most of the learners (8) agreed that they were still confused about how to give commands as they lack vocabulary. Some learners (7) said that they could not comprehend relationship between physical action and commands. Some learners (5) said that they were not able to understand teacher's commands.

Table-4: Results of Interview Question no.4

Q.4	Number of participants	Why do you like this method?
	5	It was very encouraging as we had the feeling of participating in a game.

	8	It was easy to memorize the small sentences and then reproducing them.
	7	It was totally different from traditional classes as we had a lot of fun, friends and physical exercises and activities.

As shown in Table 4, in response to question number 4, there were varied responses, only common responses were placed in the table here. Most of the learners (8) agreed that it was easy to memorize the small sentences and then reproduce them. Some learners (7) said that it was very different from traditional classes as they had a lot of fun, friends and physical exercises and activities. Some learners (5) said that it was very encouraging as they had the feeling of participating in a game.

Discussion and Conclusion

Analysis of students' questionnaire and interview statements reveals that students usually liked TPR. They had a lot of fun while learning the language. Teacher succeeded to eliminate the fear of students to a great extent. As in response to statement one in questionnaire, 75% students like doing the physical activities (following the basic commands) in the class. It shows the natural inclination of students while learning the second language. During interview session, students admitted that it was easier for them to memorize the structures and then reproduce them. It indicates the successful implementation of TPR's principle of directing learning to the right-hemisphere of brain subsequently being reproduced by the left-hemisphere after sufficient input of reception of language chunks, items and structures. Nevertheless, 20% students had no opinion and 5% disagreed which indicates either they shirked doing the physical exercises in the class or they could not comprehend the commands in target language. It may also be as some students admitted during interview session that physical exertion obstructed them from learning the language.

In response to statement two, 75% students agree with the success of fundamental principle of TPR, as it claims to combine language instruction with motor activities. However, there are 15% of the participants who did not state an opinion and 10% disagreed to it. It shows students need further practice before they could finally comprehend the principle of combining language instruction with motor activities. Singh (2011) states, "Total Physical Response (TPR) is a language teaching method which establishes a link between speech, a primary mode of language and action. The mode of teaching language here is a motor activity" (p.20). During the interview session too, some students admitted they feared jumping off the table as teachers asked them to do. It stresses on the need that teacher has to be careful while giving commands to students.

The third statement if they were able to induce the rules form the structures they were using in the classroom fetches a good response from learners as 75% of them agreed to the statement. 10% did not state any opinion and 15% disagreed which shows teacher needs to provide some more practices of the same nature especially to slow learners. In the interview also students were confused about how to give command in target language and they lacked vocabulary. Teacher must supply the vocabulary with physical actions so that words may be engraved on learners' minds. TPR stresses on learning of verbs as this method is based on physical actions. Qiu (2016) states, "The TPR approach encourages students to learn English by actions, so words taught in class are mainly verbs or verb phrases by combining the pictures of words and physical actions. During the teaching process, students were asked to imitate actions until they could do actions by themselves. Gradually students turned to be more active in class". (p. 24)

The forth statement if they successfully conveyed their message to colleagues and teacher displays that only 55% of students admitted to it. 20% had no opinion and 25% disagreed. It shows that the message was not conveyed properly. There may be several reasons attributed to it. May be students could not understand the language sufficiently before they could produce it. There was less reception than production of target language in the classroom. Interview session further confirmed it as students admitted they had problem in communication. Teacher needs to provide more exercises to students and communication must be in focus while following the physical commands of teachers and students.

The fifth statement in the questionnaire if students understand the non-verbal discourse of teacher and colleagues exhibits that only 45% of learners agreed to it though 40% (a big number) of students had no opinion. 15% of learners disagreed which clearly indicates that they did not understand the non-verbal discourse of teacher and colleagues. It means students need more practice so that they can understand the gestures and expressions and exploit them for language learning. 5 students also admitted during the interview that they could not completely understand teachers' commands. Teacher must be patient while implementing TPR. He should not jump to speaking or ask learners to give and receive commands as Nagaraj (1996) states, "Later, learners give commands and the rest of the class performs actions" (p.67).

The sixth statement in the questionnaire if students think that the class helped them develop fluency unveils that only 60% of students admitted to it, whereas 40% had no opinion. As students practiced only a few commanding expressions or sentences, it was difficult for them to develop fluency. They needed to practice more before they could develop fluency in target language.

The seventh statement in the questionnaire, if the class helped develop a good rapport among them, their teacher and their colleagues, fetches a very positive response from students as 70% of students admitted to it. 5% had no opinion while 25% disagreed. TPR develops the spirit of teamwork, which is one of the most important principles of this method. Language cannot be learnt in isolation. Therefore, developing a good rapport is very essential.

The eighth statement in the questionnaire, if they think it is a good way to learn a language, shows that 60% of learners agreed to it. 10% had no opinion. 25% disagreed while 5% strongly disagreed. It stresses on the need that TPR alone is not sufficient for successful language learning. It must be accompanied by other methods so that learners may be greatly benefitted with this method.

The ninth statement in the questionnaire, if they like performing physical action like jumping from the table and shaking hands, displays only 40% agreed while 40% (an equal number) had no opinion. 20% disagreed to it. It emphasizes that teacher needs to be very careful while selecting the activities to be performed in the TPR classroom. Not all the students like jumping off the table. Moreover, they may also be hurt while jumping. It is also seen that shaking hands is more a cultural phenomenon than showing reverence through greetings. In some countries like Sudan, people do not like to shake hands. They greet each other by touching or patting their shoulders. Seven students also admitted that they were scared. Five students stated that they were tired so they did not want to continue. It stresses on the need that teacher needs to select the activities which require less physical exertion on part of students. As far as teaching materials are concerned, teacher should use other supporting materials also as Richards and Rodgers (2001) advise, "These may include pictures, realia, slides and word charts".(p.77)

The tenth statement in the questionnaire if they feel that classroom learning was stress free and they enjoyed it shows that 70% of students agreed to it. It shows the class exploited the most fundamental principle of TPR as Richards and Rodgers (2001) state, "An important condition for successful language learning is absence of stress". (p.75) 10% of the participants had no opinion while 20% disagreed to it. It stresses on the need of taking special care or providing remedial classes to slow learners so that they can also keep pace with the rest of the students of the class.

CHAPTER 9

Communicative Language Teaching

As we go through the previous chapters on different methods and approaches to language teaching, we realize that the goal of most of the methods was to develop linguistic and communicative competence among learners. Different methods and approaches served different purposes and goals at different times and were the favorite of their period. Undoubtedly, all of them had an impact on their learners in the beginning and slowly declined and disappeared from the stage of language learning and teaching as others, more innovative and effective, replaced them. Methods and approaches observed many innovations, modifications and changes from time to time but the goal of developing linguistic and communicative competence among learners through teaching has never changed and would probably never change. Language teachers and scholars have always been trying to invent innovative methods, techniques and approaches, which could help in achieving the goal of language teaching. This goal always lets them work exhaustively and rejects the obsolete ones as well as replaces them with new ones. There have been many methods and approaches before CLT, which did well, but the scholars and teachers' motivation to do something better every time had been providing many opportunities to language learners to be benefitted. This idea of innovation in language teaching has always made them realize that they need to reconsider whether they are going to achieve this goal or not. Behind this conscious realization was the unavoidable fact that students learnt to produce sentences accurately but they failed to communicate. So the real purpose of language learning, the communication, was lacking and that is what compelled linguists, scholars and language teachers to invent a method or approach which could motivate learners to connect their language learning to the outer world fluffing the real purpose of language teaching and learning all over the world. It never means that linguistic competence was not required as Jin (2008) states:

> The relation between linguistic competence and communicative competence is also important. At the fundamental stage, linguistic competence is the spontaneous, flexible, and correct manipulation of the language system. Communicative competence involves principles of appropriateness and a readiness on the part of the learner to use relevant strategies in coping with certain language situations. Linguistic competence, then, is the basis of communicative competence. Without linguistic competence, there is no communicative competence. But communicative competence does not automatically result from linguistic competence. Forms of classroom activities

such as role playing, simulations and real-life interactions should be used to provide as much practice as possible for students to develop communicative competence while practicing linguistic competence" (p.85).

Teachers apply CLT in the classroom since they realize that many students do not achieve communicative competence. In addition, many teachers consider that CLT focuses on communicative language for four English skills. CLT is different from other methods, for example; direct method and natural approach. Laili (2015) states, "CLT emphasizes fluency and accuracy in using language and teachers work just as facilitators and guides in the classroom. There are many important factors leading to its emergence in English language teaching such as; promoting social interaction, creating authentic language, making communicative language teaching in teaching four English skills and building learner-centered instruction" (p.6).

It made scholars apprehend that communicative competence required more attention than mere linguistic competence as communicative competence is not being developed among students. Students may know the rules of linguistic usage, but be unable to use the language (Widdowson, 1975). It was necessary for students to practice those rules in real life communication otherwise language learning was incomplete. Students must be able to communicate in different social, professional and academic setting where language is used as a tool for communication. Such observations led an important role to bring a shift from linguistic structure-centered approach to a Communicative Approach in the late 1970s and early 1980s. (Widdowson, 1975). Communication proficiency was more important than linguistic proficiency. The advocates of CLT wanted to teach the language and not about the language as Richards and Rodgers (2001) state, "They saw the need to focus in language teaching on communicative proficiency rather than language" (p.153).

According to this theory, the aim of language learning is to acquire communicative competence. In order to achieve this goal, some principles have been proposed by Richards and Rodgers (2001) with regard to language learning: "Communication principle: Activities that involve real communication promote learning…task principle: Activities in which language is used for carrying out meaningful tasks promote learning…meaningfulness principle: Language that is meaningful to the learner supports the learning process" (p.161). Consequently, language-learning activities are supposed to be developed and fulfilled around these principles. The "desired outcome", as Knight (2001) states, "is that the learner can communicate successfully in the target language in real situations, rather than have a conscious understanding of the rules governing that language." (p.155)

If we take a cursory glance on the development of this approach, we realize that the birth of Communicative Language Teaching may be historically attributed to the changes in the British language teaching tradition dating from the late 1960s. Jin (2008)remarks, "The Communicative Approach, also called Communicative Language Teaching or Functional

Approach, was the British version of the movement in the early 1960s in reaction to the structuralism and behaviorism embodied in the audio-linguistics"(p.81). In the late sixties, the current situational approach was questioned. British applied linguists began to consider the fundamental dimension of language teaching at that time—the functional and communicative potential of language which was missing in the language classroom. Scholars like Christopher Candlin and Henry Widdowson were inspired by the works of British functional linguists such as John Firth, and Halliday and American work in socio-linguistics like Dell Hymes as well as work in philosophy. They emphasize that language teaching must focus on communicative proficiency rather than on mere mastery of structures. The impact from the European Common Market constituted another impetus for Communicative Approach (Jin 2008, p.81).

One of the basic ideas, which inspired the origin of Communicative Language Teaching Approach, was the rejection of mastery of syntactical structures for the sake of mastery only. It came as a reaction to structural approach to teaching. Communicative Language Teaching can be comprehended in a better way if we take into account certain aspects to structural approach to teaching. Structural approach to teaching focuses primarily on forms, structures, and its practice in isolation without even considering its practical use in real life situations. Language is live. In other words, it is not dead so it cannot be learnt through ways, which make it 'dead'. The term 'dead' refers to language learning without context. If language has no context, it is dead. It has no life because it is not used in real life situations. One might be good at grammatical structures of a language but it is useless unless one knows how to use them in real life for practical purposes. In my understanding, to bring language to the threshold of everyday practical usage is likely to give it a soul that makes the language work in real life. If we consider a few questions before going ahead with this approach, it will make us easier to understand this approach. Why do we need a language? What is the primary function of a language? Can there be a substitute of language? Is there any other practical and lively way to convey our message without relying on language? Do we need language or does language need us? The same questions can be applied to second language learning.

If we consider first question why we need a language, we will realize that language is our everyday need. One cannot do anything without language. One cannot go to shopping, job, business, and doctors without language. Our everyday life is hampered if we do not know language. Therefore, language is our need and it is true that we need different situations, settings and contexts to contextualize language. Language can never have only one context, setting, or situation. The same is the fact even with the second language that we do not learn until we need it. Therefore, our necessity compels us to learn the language. There may be various motivations to learn a second language like to get a good job, to be able to work in a multilingual environment, to go abroad etc. English is an international language and one can easily connect to the rest of the world through the medium of English language. 'Need' is the key word for what we aspire to learn a language. Communicative Language Teaching focuses on why we need a language. Obviously, we need language for communication in different settings, contexts, situations etc. CLT focuses here and prepares learners to use language in real life by creating real life situations. So communicative language teaching focuses more on communication than the individual sentences (without context) to practice structure. Therefore, CLT provides a context to language to use it communicatively in everyday life as a lingua franca. It provides language various situations, which could provide it a context. Teacher deliberately creates various mock situations/ settings in the class so that students must know how to communicate differently in different situations.

The next question we are going to deal with is what the primary function of a language is. As we discussed above, the most basic function of a language is to make humans communicate to each other. In context of second language like English, the function is the same either in a monolingual or multilingual setting. The learners may be motivated to get a good job either in their native country or abroad.

The next question is if there can be a substitute of language. In my understanding, there is no substitute of language. One might adopt non-verbal ways to communicate one's message but that is not the practical solution to manage the linguistic needs of everyday life.

The next question addresses the concern if there is any other channel, more practical and lively way, to convey our message without relying on language. I do not find there is any other vehicle except language to code and decode messages. As it is the only way to convey the message, the language teaching must focus on how to convey the message in the best possible manner. CLT very effectively addresses this issue. To address the last question if humans need language or language needs humans. I understand both are complementary to each other. One cannot live without other.

Therefore, language is necessary to survive in the society. A child naturally acquires first language while the second language needs efforts on their part. One needs a systematic study of second language in order to master it. However, English is an international language and is a lingua franca in multiple language settings. It is also necessary because no message can be conveyed without knowing at least functional use of language. CLT provides a good solution to learn a second language by adopting the approach and providing techniques, which can be best used to teach and learn a second language.

Brown (2001) offered six characteristics of CLT: the first, classroom goals apply the component of communicative competence, the second, language technique is used to motivate students to use language for meaningful purposes, the third, complementary principles are fluency and accuracy even though fluency is more crucial in language use. The fourth, students are obligated to use the language productively and receptively in the classroom, the fifth, teachers give many opportunities to students to focus on their learning process and the sixth, teachers as facilitators guide students by keeping interaction between teachers and students or students and students (qtd in Laili, 2015, p.2-3). A good CLT class must inculcate these characteristics in the classroom.

In order to assess the practical application and outputs of this method, one study is shared here which was conducted at an intermediate level class in India where CLT was used in the classroom.

Experience

It is an experience with intermediate level of learners who have been studying English for last eight years but cannot communicate in target language. They are good in translating sentences from mother tongue to English language as they have been taught through Grammar-Translation method. Their main problem is that they cannot use the memorized structures in day-to-day life. It means they have linguistic competence but lack communicative competence. Moreover, they lack developing the fundamental characteristics of language like creativity and uniqueness. Learners were not able to form infinite number of sentences with the structure they learnt. Chomsky has criticized the structural linguistic theory for the same reasons in his book *Syntactic Structures (1957)*. Richards and Rodgers (2001) state, "Chomsky had demonstrated the current standard structural theories of language were incapable of accounting for the fundamental characteristics of language- the creativity and uniqueness of individual sentence" (p.153). The same issues, as indicated by Chomsky in the above quote, were observed in this class. Whatever they learnt was confined to the structural practices of translating sentences from mother tongue to target language. The challenge before a teacher in such classes is to motivate students to use their linguistic competence for communicative competence. As they were good at forming structural sentences, they needed to invent situations and provide context where they could exploit their linguistic competence to achieve communicative competence.

In order to achieve this goal, teacher changed the setting of the classroom and made them sit in groups and pairs, which was obviously a novice experience to them as they had been used to a traditional teacher-centered classroom. Nagaraj (1996) states about group work/pair work, "It forms an important part of any communicative activity; for peer interaction is an effective means of acquiring some language features which are not available in a formal teacher-fronted class"(p.45). Most of the students never faced each other and thus lacked interaction and communication. The first difficulty teacher countered with these students was a psychological distance between a teacher and student. They took teacher in high esteem as a sage. In the academic setting in India, pupils are supposed to listen and follow commands and not to question the authority of teacher. Because of their cultural orientation, it was difficult for teacher to break their hesitation and make them feel to ask teacher anything related to academic.

Teacher is sharing one of his experiences in the class after teaching practices of one month. It was Monday. Students had to complete two activities based on Communicative Language Teaching in an hour assigned by teacher. Teacher started this particular class by greeting all students one by one, noted their names, and tried to call them by their names, which was unusual for them. Teacher created a situation for them as if they are in a bank. In pair, one was manager and the other was a customer. They had to predict the situation themselves and accordingly write the conversation.

It was difficult for them. However, in order to facilitate the learning process, teacher allowed them to brainstorm and translate their ideas. This technique was used to facilitate communication among students. Teacher was flexible in his approach to teaching as Nagaraj (1996) states, "The development of language learning or teaching from form-based to a meaning-based approach: the move towards an eclectic approach from a rigid method: the shift from teacher-fronted to learner-centered classes: are all subsumed under the broad term COMMUNICATIVE APPRAOCH" (p.41). Rather than forming independent sentences, teacher asked students to write sentences in a dialogue form. They wrote a short conversation varying in nature from pair to pair. Teacher gave them role of bank manager and customer. One of the conversations is being shared here:

Activity 1

> *Manager: How are you?*
> *Customer: I am fine.*
> *Manager: How can I help you?*
> *Customer: I want to open a saving account.*
> *Manager: Do you have your identity and address proof with you?*
> *Customer: No, I do not have.*
> *Manager: Please bring your identity and address proof.*
> *Customer: OK, I will bring it tomorrow.*

(Self-developed conversation)

Teacher observed they did not lack the contents though there were some issues related to mechanics of writing which teacher overlooked in the beginning classes. The next problem teacher faced was their inability to read their own sentences because of hesitation and shyness. There were also some pronunciation inaccuracies which teacher also avoided in the classroom. It needed a few days for them before they could use the contents in real life situation as they did in *Activity 1* above. Teacher tried here to motivate learners to use language in social and professional context as Laili (2015) states, "There are many important factors leading to its emergence in English language teaching such as; promoting social interaction, creating authentic language, making communicative language teaching in teaching four English skills and building learner-centered instruction"(p.6).

Teacher motivated students for peer-correction in the classroom. Teacher also made their videos of conversation, which he played in the classroom to motivate them to speak.

Activity 2

Teacher shares a picture (image with three kids) with students and asks them to describe it.

Image 1 (self-developed)

Students came up with various descriptions of the picture like:

1. There are three kids in the picture.
2. There are two girls and one boy.
3. They are running after each other.
4. One girl is wearing red frock.
5. Another girl is wearing blue frock.
6. The boy is wearing red T-shirt and yellow short.

7. It is the picture of a park.
8. There is many small and big trees.
9. There is a tree with pink flower.
10. There is one footpath with black-white color.
11. There is one hut also in the park.
12. There is a lot of grass in the park.
13. The kids are running on a narrow passage.
14. The kids is very exciting.
15. They are very cute.
16. The kids are enjoying.
17. The kids are very happy.
18. One girl is wearing pink shoes.
19. Another girl is wearing blue floaters.
20. The boy is wearing brown floaters.

Students came up with around twenty sentences based on the pictures. They made some mistakes in sentences (8 and 14) related to the correct 'be' form. Teacher did not correct students while speaking. He preferred fluency to accuracy. Later, he corrected mistakes by repeating the correct sentences three to four times and students followed him.

In the succeeding classes, teacher used other techniques of CLT like card, game activities, role-play etc. and students slowly improved their performance.

Observation

Teacher realized that the classroom needed a lot of motivation in order to give life to students' dead sentences. Both the activities motivated students to communicate in target language in real life situations. Once they gained confidence, they were able to perform better and proved to be good communicator. Teacher observed they did not need much input in improving grammatical structures as they had already had much practice of that earlier. They needed to learn how to use their learnt structures in real life situations. For that, they needed to contextualize the language, which was to provide them different situations where they could use those structures. Teacher experienced that students who are taught through Grammar-Translation Method are speakers that are more accurate. This is also a fact that they were not fluent speakers of English language. In order to create fluency among students, it took several weeks. Some of the students improved faster than others improve, though by the end of 10 months course, students were able to communicate in target language and could easily convey their messages. The lesson implemented the principles of Communicative Language Teaching Approach largely as Richards and Rodgers (2001) state about the characteristics of this approach, "Pair and group work is suggested to encourage students to use and practice functions and forms". (p.171) The methodological procedures underlying these texts reflect a sequence of activities represented in Littlewood (1981) as follows:

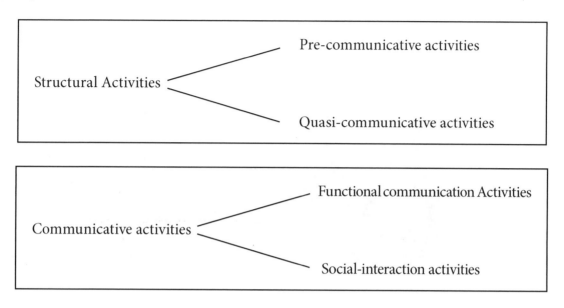

(qtd. in Richards and Rodgers 2001, p.171)

The following procedure was adopted by the teacher while implementing CLT in the classroom. First, teacher asked students to form dialogues in pair and group, which can be referred as structural activities. Then teacher gave students role-play of a bank manager and customer. Later, they described the picture of a park, which indicates to other functional and social-interaction activities.

However, it was teachers' perspective regarding the application of CLT approach. Teacher followed the learner-centered approach and involved them in learning process. Students were encouraged to come up with new structures in target language. Teacher emphasized more on fluency and overlooked accuracy related issues as it might have discouraged students and broken their rhythm of speaking. Though this method turned out to do well, success of this method cannot be truly assessed until students, the target group, are given an opportunity to express their opinion and share their experiences. In order to record students' observations and experiences, a questionnaire set was given to them focusing on the key elements of CLT approach especially on the contents, which were taught in the classroom. In addition to the questionnaire, students were also interviewed with a set of open-ended questions to assess whether they had any query, doubt or confusion, which were not the part of the questionnaire. The open-ended questions provided enough space to students to put forward their opinion in a more descriptive way.

Analysis of Students' Feedback

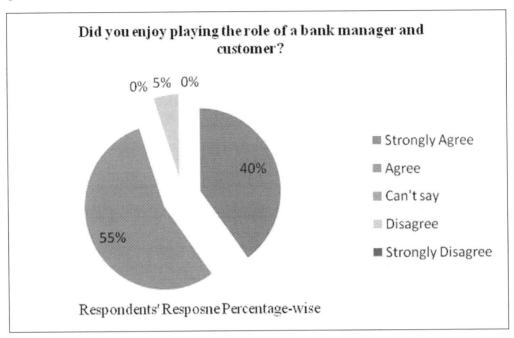

Figure 1

The first statement in the questionnaire *if they enjoyed playing the role of a bank manager and customer* reveals that there are 40% participants who felt that *they enjoyed playing the role of a bank manager and customer.* 55% of the participants admitted to it. 5% of the participants disagreed.

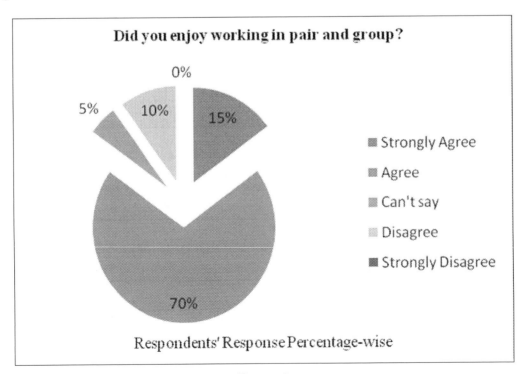

Figure 2

The second statement in the questionnaire *if they enjoyed working in pair and group* displays that there are 15% of the participants who opined that *they enjoyed working in pair and group.* 70% of the participants agreed though (5%) of the participants had no idea. 10% of the participants did not accept the statement.

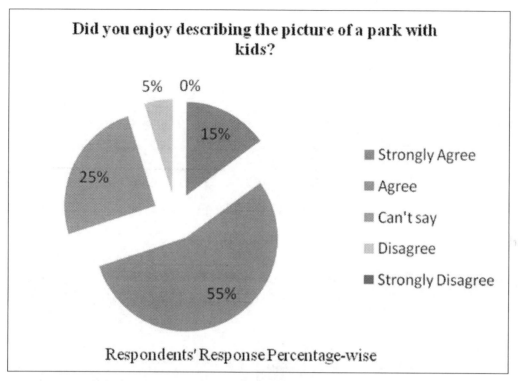

Figure 3

The third statement in the questionnaire if *they enjoyed describing the picture of a park with kids* shows that 15% of the participants are of the opinion that *they enjoyed describing the picture of a park with kids.* 55% of the participants agreed to the statement though 25% of the participants had no opinion. 5% of the participants dissented.

The fourth statement in the questionnaire if they *liked interacting and communicating with their colleagues in pair and group* exhibits that there are 10% of the participants who strongly agreed that they *liked interacting and communicating with their colleagues in pair and group.* 60% of the participants also admitted to it though 25% of the participants had no opinion. 5% of the participants disagreed to the statement.

The fifth statement in the questionnaire if *they liked correcting each other's mistakes in peer correction* divulges that there is none who strongly agreed to the statement that *they liked correcting each other's mistakes in peer correction.* 50% of the participants agreed with the statement though (30%) of the participants did not express their opinion. 15% of the participants disapproved and 5% of the participants strongly disagreed with the statement

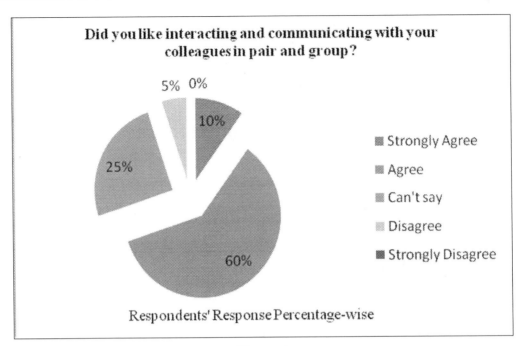

Did you like interacting and communicating with your colleagues in pair and group?

- Strongly Agree
- Agree
- Can't say
- Disagree
- Strongly Disagree

Respondents' Response Percentage-wise

Figure 4

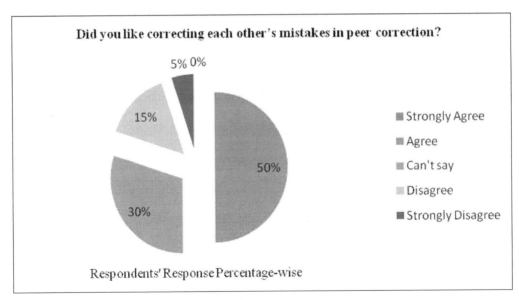

Did you like correcting each other's mistakes in peer correction?

- Strongly Agree
- Agree
- Can't say
- Disagree
- Strongly Disagree

Respondents' Response Percentage-wise

Figure 5

The sixth statement in the questionnaire if *they understood the rules and usage of the present tense and future tense through the activities* unveils that 10% of the participants were in absolute agreement to the statement that *they understood the rules and usage of the present tense and future tense through the activities*. A big no (80%) of the participants agreed while there was none who did not state an opinion. 5% of the participants did not agree with the statement and the same number (5%) of the participants had absolute disagreement.

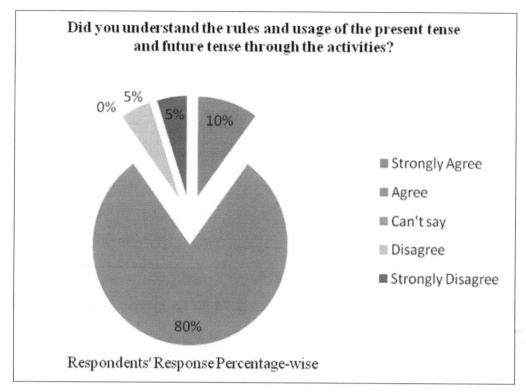

Figure 6

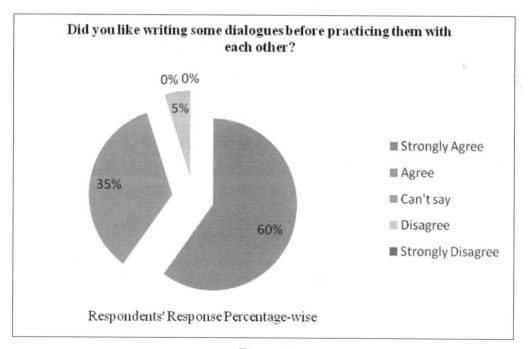

Figure 7

The seventh statement in the questionnaire if *they liked writing some dialogues before practicing them with each other* reveals no participant thought that *they liked writing some dialogues before practicing them with each other*. 60% of the participants agreed with the statement though 35%

(a significant percentage) of the participants had no opinion. 5% of the participants disagreed with the statement.

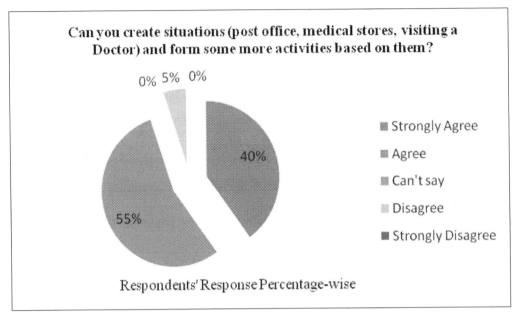

Figure 8

The eighth statement in the questionnaire if *they could create situations (post office, medical stores, visiting a Doctor) and form some more activities based on them* reveals that 40% of the participants strongly agreed with the statement that *they could create situations (post office, medical stores, visiting a Doctor) and form some more activities based on them.* 55% of the participants agreed to it. 5% of the participants did not agree with the statement.

Interview analysis

Another method used to collect the data was interview method. Twenty samples were selected out of 30, which were filled in with complete information. The participants responded to the following questions in the interview:

1. Learners rate (on a scale of 1-5) the effectiveness of this method where 1 represents the lowest and 5 represents the highest value:

2. Mention some common learning difficulties faced in class:

3. Mention some confusions, doubts or queries you had:

4. Why do you like this method?

Table 1: Results of Interview Question no. 1

Q. No	Number of learners	Scale
1.	15	4
	5	5

As shown in the table 1, in response to the first question, 15 learners rated the effectiveness of the method as 4 on a scale of 1-5 as mentioned earlier. 5 learners rated the effectiveness of the method as 5. The overall effectiveness of the method was rated 1-5s from learners' point of view.

Table-2: Results of Interview Question no. 2

Q.2.	Number of participants	Some common learning difficulties faced in class:
	5	Had a lot of hesitation while reading the dialogues.
	8	Could not understand the pronunciation of some of the colleagues. Could not understand the handwriting of colleagues and structures so could not correct the mistakes.
	7	My group was not very supportive.

As shown in Table 2, in response to question number 2, there were varied responses, only common responses were placed in the table here. Most of the learners (8) agreed that they could not understand the pronunciation of some of the colleagues. They also could not understand the handwriting of colleagues and structures so could not correct the mistakes. 5 students said that they had a lot of hesitation while reading the dialogues. Some learners (7) said that their group was supportive.

Table-3: Results of Interview Question no. 3

Q.3	Number of participants	Some confusions, doubts or queries you had:
	5	Could not form sentences on some of the scenes in the picture.
	8	Some of the objects were vague in the picture like hut.
	7	Could not fluently describe the picture.

As shown in Table 3, in response to question number 3, there were varied responses, only common responses were placed in the table here. Most of the learners (8) complained that some of the objects were vague in the picture like hut. 5 students said that they couldn't form sentences on some of the scenes in the picture. Some learners (7) said that they could not fluently describe the picture.

Table-4: Results of Interview Question no.4

Q.4	Number of participants	Why do you like this method?
	5	The materials used in the class were very mesmerizing like the picture of the park with kids.
	8	The class was stress free. Teacher was very friendly and cooperative.
	7	It was very different from traditional classes. We had a lot of fun, freedom lively interaction with colleagues and teacher.

As shown in Table 4, in response to question number 4, there were varied responses, only common responses were placed in the table here. Most of the learners (8) appreciated that the class was stress free. Teacher was very friendly and cooperative. 5 students said the materials used in the class were very mesmerizing like the picture of the park with kids. Some learners (7) said that it was very different from traditional classes, they had a lot of fun, freedom lively interaction with colleagues and teacher.

Discussion and Conclusion

The analysis of the questionnaire and the interview shows that students liked this method. For the ease of interpretation, the scales 'agree' and 'strongly agree' are merged. In response to statement one in the questionnaire if they enjoy playing the role of a bank manager and customer, 95% of students agreed to the statement. It proves that role-playing, as one of the principles of Communicative Language Teaching, had a great impact on students and they enjoyed it a lot. 5% of the students disagreed with the statement. Teacher needs to find out these students. 5 students during the interview session admitted that they had a lot of hesitation while reading the dialogues. It shows that students need more practices in dialogues reading to gain confidence and overcome hesitation.

In response to statement two in the questionnaire, if they enjoy working in pair and group displays that 85% of students enjoyed working in pair and group. It affirms that teacher successfully exploited the principle of collaborative learning of Communicative Language Teaching. 5% students had no opinion while 10% students disagreed to it. It invites our attention towards the interview as 7 of the students admitted that their group was not supportive. Teacher needs to ensure that every student is cooperating with each other in pair and group.

Teacher must change the members of group if they find the group members have not developed a good rapport with each other. It is mandatory for teacher to practice some more innovative techniques in the class to engage students. For example, teacher can use games in the class as it encourages more participation in the class as some students learn better, when they feel involved in learning process as Jin (2008) states, "Language learning is a hard task that can sometimes be frustrating. Constant effort is required to understand, produce and manipulate the target language. Well-chosen games are invaluable as they give students a break and at the same time allow students to practice language skills. Games are highly motivating since they are amusing and at the same time challenging. Furthermore, they employ meaningful and useful language in real contexts. They also encourage and increase cooperation."(p.83)

In response to statement three in the questionnaire, if they enjoy describing the picture of a park with kids shows that 70% of students enjoyed describing the picture of the park with kids. Teacher positively used the principle of using pictures in the classroom. Students came up with twenty different formations which prove using pictures ignited their faculty of imagination and they used it positively to improve communicative competence. 25% of students had no idea while 5% disagreed. 8 students, during the interview, admitted that some of the objects were vague in the picture like 'hut'. Teacher must use pictures with clear visibility of objects. If they use photocopy, it must be clear. If the objects are not clear, it would lead to lack of fluency as 7 students admitted to it. It would take time to come up with sentence formation as 5 students agreed they couldn't form sentences on some of the scenes in the picture. If the pictures are not clear, it would hamper language production. So, in this principle, teacher has to be very careful while using learning materials. The material should be authentic as well as clear otherwise; the success rate of this approach will be affected. Moreover, teacher training is must for successful implementation of CLT approach in the class. Ahmad and Rao (2013) state, "The identified impediments in applying the communicative approach are teacher training, students' hesitation in the use of target language, over-crowded class rooms, grammar-based examinations, and the lack of appropriate materials" (p. 202).

In response to the statement four in the questionnaire, if they like interacting and communicating with their colleagues in pair and group reveals that 70% students agreed to it. Teacher successfully used one of the principles of communication and mutual interaction of this approach. 25% of students had no opinion while 5% disagreed to the statement. Teacher must try to figure out why 25% had no opinion. May be they did not understand each other. 8 students admitted that they couldn't understand the pronunciation of some of the colleagues. As students did not understand pronunciation of each other, it might have led to lack of communication or miscommunication among students. The analysis reveals that teacher must work on the pronunciation of students. As communication is the fundamental principle of this approach, no communication can occur without eligible pronunciation. One of the significant reasons of inaccurate pronunciation may be attributed to the unavailability of native speakers. The institution cannot hire the native speakers for financial reasons. Teachers also lack training sessions, which will help in improving their teaching practices, and update their knowledge regarding innovative methods, approaches and techniques as Ju (2013) states:

> Teacher training is another big problem in the countries where real information exchange and authentic communications situation are insufficient. The lack of communication in a real situation with foreigners causes problems for both teachers and learners. Theoretically, CLT emphasizes communicative competence and encourages the fulfillment of successful interaction in dealing with real tasks. The idealist teachers of CLT should be fully competent in language competence, and a good command of the knowledge of linguistics and teaching methodologies. But practically, foreign language users, both teachers and learners, in these countries are unable to receive enough input of communicative practices since they have little chance to meet with native speakers. This kind of language environment is by no means good for the sustainable development of foreign language teaching and learning in these countries. (p.1581)

In response to statement five in the questionnaire, if they like correcting each other's mistakes in peer-correction reveals that only 50% of students agreed to the statement. It shows that teacher could not implement this principle of CLT successfully. 8 students also accepted that they couldn't understand the handwriting of colleagues and structures so couldn't correct the mistakes. While implementing this principle, teacher has to make students write properly. Their structures should also make sense. However, the principle of peer-correction must be applied on advanced level of learners.

In response to statement six in the questionnaire, if they understand the rules and usage of the present tense and future tense through the activities shows that 90% students agreed to the statement. It is a big success of this principle of CLT. Teacher provided the situations to students where they could use the structures of present and future tense. Teacher used language in real life situations as CLT advocates. It made the classroom lively, interactive and inspired students for real life communication, which is the basic motive of language. However, 5% students disagreed and 5% strongly disagreed which shows that these students need more guidance and practice. 5 students also admitted during interview that they were not able to form sentences. It also confirms our basic belief that no method or approach can guarantee 100% success.

In response to statement seven in the questionnaire, if they like writing dialogues before practicing with each other shows that only 60% students agreed to it. 35% had no idea whereas 5% disagreed to it. As it is the communication-based class, students could not be oriented to writing task in the class. It is better if teacher provides students written dialogues and ask them to practice it. In a communication class, teacher should focus only on communication.

In response to statement eight in the questionnaire, if they can create situations (post office, medical stores, visiting a Doctor) and form some more activities based on them, shows that 95% of students agreed to it. It confirms that teacher got a big success in the principle of language learning. Students learnt to use their creative mind to come up with similar kind of structures in different situations. It proves that students could, as Chomsky opined, form infinite number of sentences with similar structures.

This approach had a great success in the class as 5 students admitted in the interview that the materials used in the class were very mesmerizing like the picture of the park with kids. 8 students accepted that the class was stress free. Teacher was very friendly and cooperative. 7 students agreed that it was totally different from traditional classes as they had a lot of fun, freedom, lively interaction with colleagues and teacher. Teacher did not correct a few grammatical mistakes in the beginning, as it would have hampered their fluency. Nevertheless, students successfully conveyed the message. For example, during the role-play, students made some mistakes in sentences (8 and 14) related to the correct 'be' form. Teacher did not correct students while speaking. He emphasized more on accuracy as Ju (2013) states, "The insufficient and unsystematic learning of grammar may result in inaccurate expressions, which brings about another issue concerning language learning: fluency and accuracy. CLT focuses on fluent interaction with others, even at the expense of accuracy. Errors are tolerable since they do not interfere with the successful transformation of information". (p. 1580)

An overall analysis shows that this approach was very successful in the class. However, one cannot deny the fact that there are many impediments in implementing CLT approach in developing countries like India. To implement CLT successfully in the classroom requires many facilities like computer, internet, audio-visual aids, constant teacher training etc. In absence of these resources, CLT approach cannot be implemented in the country as a whole.

One of the problems is that many teachers are not very proficient in teaching English. They need competence skills, knowledge in using this approach and must be a proficient user of English. English teachers do no stop learning, because knowledge develops quickly and governments have responsibility to facilitate education need. (qtd in Laili, 2015, p.7)

CHAPTER 10

Content-based Language Teaching Approach

In the previous chapter, we learnt about Communicative Language Teaching Approach. This chapter focuses on Content-Based Language Teaching Approach. It is considered as an extension of CLT Approach as it borrows most of the principles from CLT Approach. Content-Based Language Teaching involves students to take charge of their own learning. Villalobos (2014) states, "Content-Based Instruction is an approach in which the teaching is organized around the content. Likewise, the principles of Content-Based Instruction are heavily rooted on the principles of communicative language teaching since they involve an active participation of students in the exchange of content" (p.71). Teacher may take subject matter from any subject but that must be in English, the target language. It is better if contents suit to learners' interest, as it will encourage their curiosity and hard work. Brinton (2003) states, "Content-based instruction is the teaching of language through exposure to content that is interesting and relevant to learners" (p. 201).

Teacher may help students by describing some of the key terms associated with the subject matter that might be unknown to students. The goal of the teacher is to enable students understand subject matter in English. English is used as a medium to study different disciplines. There is no predetermined linguistic content. The focus is more on procedure rather than the product. In CBLT, contents are very important and language is a medium to comprehend the contents. Howatt (1984) stresses, "In these approaches rather than 'learning to use English,' students 'use English to learn it' (qtd in Freeman, 2000, p.137).The main difference among CBLT and other approaches is that other approaches comprehend the language through contents while CBLT comprehends contents through language. In either case, knowledge of language is inevitable. As materials are used in form of contents, the selection of materials must be made carefully. In absence of authentic contents, learning would not take place as CBLT completely relies on contents. The same material must bear certain characteristics like (1) Materials must contain the subject matter of the content course. 2 Materials must be authentic – like the ones used in native language instruction. 3 Examples must be drawn from realia and real life experience and contemporary issues from newspapers, magazines, radio and TV. (4) Material must bear linguistic simplification to adopt texts and promote comprehensibility (Stryker and Leaver, 1997).

Though this approach completely relies on contents, it cannot guarantee success without sound knowledge of language. One cannot even comprehend the contents completely without a sound knowledge of language that includes various components of language like syntactic and semantic use of language, lexical, phonological, morphological and contextual aspects of language. However, one remarkable difference lies in the fact that CBLT is not usually based on linguistic and language oriented syllabus. Richards and Rodgers (2001) state, "Content-Based Instruction (CBI) refers to an approach to second language teaching in which teaching is organized around the content or information that students will acquire, rather than around a linguistic or other type of syllabus".(p.204)

CBLT builds a strong relationship between language and content as it stresses that both are complementary to each other. Contents cannot survive without language and language has no existence without contents. Krahnke (1987) emphasizes, "It is the teaching of content or information in the language being learned with little or no direct explicit effort to teach the language itself separately from the content being taught". (as qtd. in Richards and Rodgers, 2001, p. 204)

In CBLT, comprehensible input is very important. Contents must be relevant, authentic as they provide ample scope to understand and comprehend the language as Omoto and Nyongesa (2013) state:

> If comprehensible input is provided and the pupils feel excited then language acquisition takes place. Content across the curriculum as envisaged in CBI provides multiple opportunities for language input, to understanding and use of the language. Furthermore, this content is meaningful and understandable since it is drawn from the context relevant and appropriate to the age, interest and cognitive level of the learners. That is what Krashen considers as comprehensible input (p.237).

In CBLT, as the name suggests, contents are very important as the teaching and comprehension of language depend on the contents. That is why CBLT stresses on the selection of authentic materials and contents. Snow (2001) said, "Content… is the use of subject matter for second/ foreign language teaching purposes. Subject matter may consist of topics or themes based interest or need in an adult EFL setting, or it may be very specific, such as the subjects that students are currently studying in their elementary school classes". (p. 303)

Mostly the contents are based on other academic streams like biology, history, geography etc. as Freeman (2000) remarks, "The special contribution of content-based instruction is that it integrates the learning of language with the learning of some other content, often academic subject matter". (p.137)

In order to assess the practical implications of this approach, an experience with the students of English Access Micro scholarship Program (sponsored by the US Embassy to Human Resource Development Centre) at UGC (University Grant Commission) Academic Staff College, AMU, Aligarh is being shared here. They are intermediate level of learners who come for evening classes to improve English proficiency exclusively belonging to the underprivileged section of society.

Experience

Let us step into a classroom where teacher is using content-based instruction to teach in the classroom. It is a grade 12th class where teacher uses history subject contents in order to teach English language. Teacher provides students with handouts based on history. It is a reading comprehension paragraph about the Taj Mahal, a famous historical building. It also contains the picture of the Taj. Students have to look at the picture and google the information about the Taj Mahal. They were asked some very basic questions about the Taj Mahal.

Having distributed the handouts, teacher asked students meaning of each object they see in the picture. They described each word in their mother tongue. Then teacher gave them an activity based on reading comprehension.

https://pixabay.com/photos/taj-mahal-ivory-white-marble-agra-3132348/

Activity 1 (Basic information)

Who built the Taj Mahal?

_____

Who is Mumtaz Mahal?

_____

Taj Mohammad and Soada Idris

When was Mumtaz Mahal born?

_____

Why was Shahjahan in deep sorrow?

_____

Why did Shahjahan decide to build the Taj?

_____

Where was Shahjahan buried after his death?

_____

Activity 2

Write the antonyms/opposites of these words:

*Queen*_____
Emperor _____
*Niece*_____
*Birth*_____
Before _____
Love _____

Activity 3

Speak at least five sentences about the Taj Mahal

Teacher made a group of four students and let them help each other. Students helped each other while answering the questions. Teacher facilitated the learning process in the classroom and went to every group to mark they are properly using the smart phone to search information about the Taj Mahal. After 30 minutes, teacher called one student from each group as group leader and he read the answers. There were some minor mistakes which teacher corrected during the feedback session.

Students came with different answers. It shows that materials used in the classroom expanded their horizon of imagination. In a CBLT class, materials must encourage creativity among learners as materials make lessons interesting and real. They enhance communicative language teaching, capture the learner's concentration, widen their scope of creative thinking and make language learning powerful and meaningful (Stryker and Leaver, 1997).

Though the materials in the class ignited imagination of students, they could not completely convey their ideas, as they were not very competent in language use. Most of the answers were in one, two or three words. Students avoided writing complete sentences in response to each questions. It shows they were hesitant in writing. There were some words, which did not have their antonyms in the text as searched by them. Teacher allowed students to use online or offline dictionaries to find out the antonyms. Most of them had pocket dictionary, which helped them find out the opposites of the words given in activity two.

One of the group leaders came and presented five sentences from each group. They came with incredible structures. Some common ones are presented here for analysis.

> *The Taj Mahal is beautiful.*
> *Shahjahan loved his wife very much.*
> *Mumtaz die in 1631.*
> *Mumtaz los her life in Burahnpur city.*
> *Taj Mahal is made of marble.*

Observation

It was observed that the classroom was well organized. Students had enough material to learn the target language. Students were very excited to see the picture of the Taj. Most of them had seen the Taj as it is not very far from Aligarh, their native place. Students learnt many structures as given above. There were some mistakes which teacher did not correct while speaking and addressed them during feedback session.

Before distributing handouts, teachers asked them what they knew about emperor, empress, king, queen etc. He also asked how many of them had visited the Taj. It activated their background knowledge so that they could connect it with present lesson. As constructivism plays an important role in a CBLT class, teacher implemented this principle in the classroom. This principle encourages learners to build a connection between what they already knew and what they need to know. Constructivism as a learning theory, simply speaking, is to make learning meaningful. The core constructivist perspectives are as follows: (a) learning is a self-directed process—knowledge is constructed rather than directly received; (b) instructor as facilitator; (c) learning as a socio-cultural process (Tobin and Tippins, 1993).

Omoto and Nyongesa (2013) share another view about this important principle:

> Constructivists build on the concepts of scaffolding, whereby learners constantly use their existing knowledge to help to bridge between known and unknown information. This method allows learners to grasp information that may be slightly above their current ability level by using what they know to inform what they need to know... Learners' consciousness is achieved by internalization of shared social behavior. The learner picks up observable social behavior which is built into his or her consciousness and is carried on into later

life. Constructivism has no fixed rules other than offering an alternative to the traditional, teacher-centered lessons. Constructivism is applied in a practical, real-life context just the way CBI is applied" (p.238).

This principle was very successfully applied in the class as students used their existing knowledge in order to learn something new. The contents and structures were also slightly above their level so they had to struggle with the text in order to learn something new. Teacher also gave homework to students based on the picture. Students were assigned to categorize the verbs, nouns used in the text.

Analysis of Students' Feedback

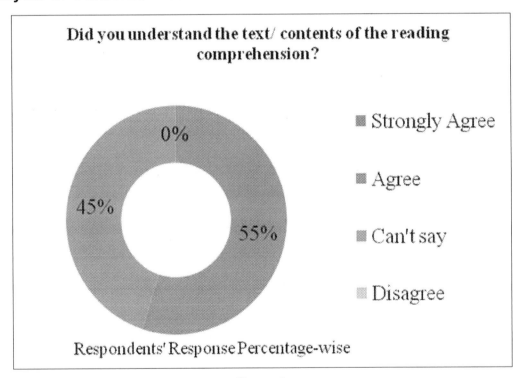

Figure 1

The first statement in the questionnaire if *they understand the text or contents of the reading comprehension* reveals that there is none who strongly agreed to the statement. 55% participants (a majority) felt that *they understood the text or contents of the reading comprehension*. 45% of the participants had no idea. There was none with disagreement.

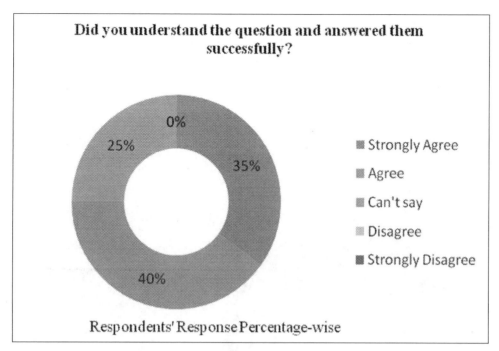

Figure 2

The second statement in the questionnaire if *they understood the question and answered them successfully* shows that there are 35% of the participants who strongly agreed to the statement. 40% of the participants are of the opinion that *they understood the question and answered them successfully.* 25% of the participants had no opinion. There was none with disagreement.

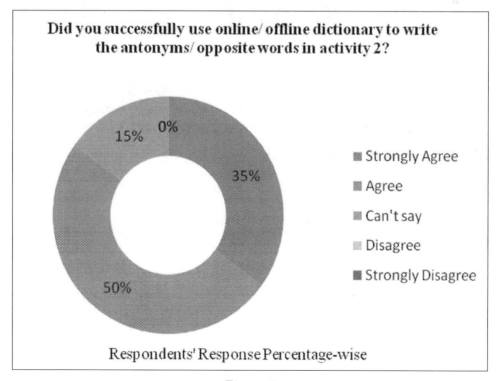

Figure 3

The third statement in the questionnaire if *they successfully used online/ offline dictionary to write the antonyms/ opposite words in activity 2* exhibits that 35% of the participants strongly agreed. There are 50% of the participants who agreed that *they successfully used online/ offline dictionary to write the antonyms/ opposite words in activity two.* 15% of the participants had no opinion. There was none with disagreement.

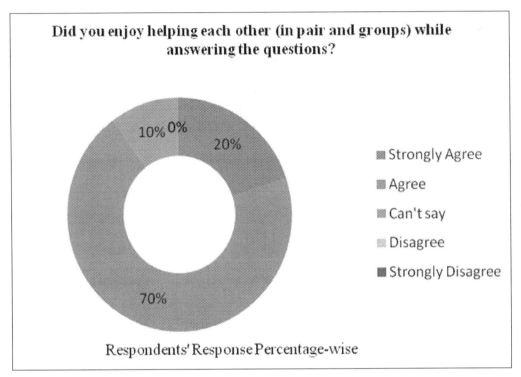

Figure 4

The forth statement in the questionnaire *if they enjoyed helping each other (in pair and groups) while answering the questions* divulges that there are 20% of the participants who strongly agreed to the statement that *they enjoyed helping each other (in pair and groups) while answering the questions.* 70% of the participants agreed with the statement. 10% of the participants did not express their opinion. There was none with disagreement.

The fifth statement in the questionnaire if *they enjoyed and felt confident about the speaking activity in the classroom* discloses that there are 20% of the participants who strongly agreed to the statement. 50% of the participants concurred *they enjoyed and felt confident about the speaking activity in the classroom.* 30% of the participants were not sure about it. There was none with disagreement.

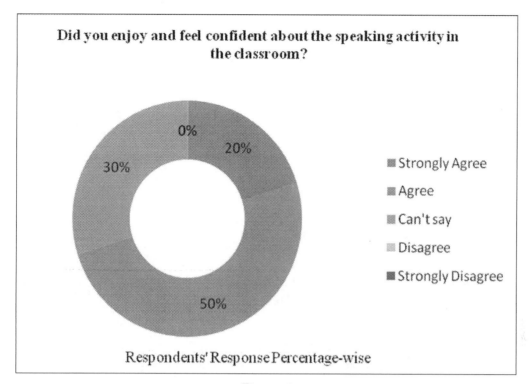

Figure 5

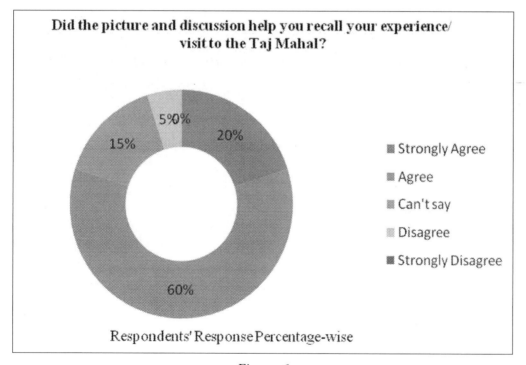

Figure 6

The sixth statement in the questionnaire if *the picture and discussion helped them recall their experience/ visit to the Taj Mahal* shows that there are 20% of the participants who strongly agreed to the statement. 60% of the participants concurred that *the picture and discussion helped them recall their experience/ visit to the Taj Mahal.* 15% of the participants were not sure about it. There were 5% with disagreement.

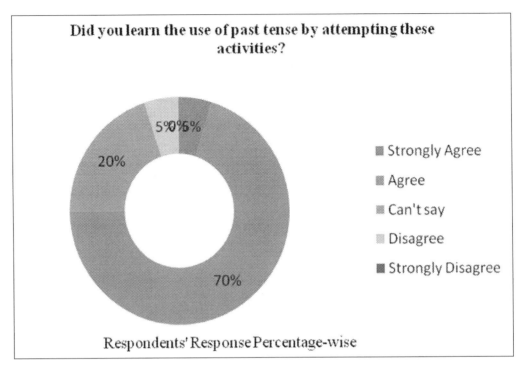

Figure 7

The seventh statement in the questionnaire if *they learnt the use of past tense by attempting these activities* unveils that there are 5% of the participants with absolute agreement to the statement that *they learnt the use of past tense by attempting these activities.* 70% of the participants agreed while there are 20% of the participants who did not state an opinion. 5% of the participants did not agree with the statement. There was none with disagreement.

Interview analysis

Another method used to collect the data was interview method. Twenty samples were selected out of 30, which were filled in with complete information. The participants responded to the following questions in the interview:

1. Learners rate (on a scale of 1-5) the effectiveness of this method where 1 represents the lowest and 5 represents the highest value:

2. Mention some common learning difficulties faced in class:

3. Mention some confusions, doubts or queries you had:

4. Why do you like this method?

Table 1: Results of Interview Question no. 1

Q. No	Number of learners	Scale
1.	4	2
	6	3
	10	4

As shown in the table 1, in response to the first question, 4 learners rated the effectiveness of the method as 2 on a scale of 1-5 as mentioned above. 10 learners rated the effectiveness of the method as 4 and 6 other teachers rated as 3. The overall effectiveness of the method was rated 2-4s from learners' point of view.

Table-2: Results of Interview Question no. 2

Q.2.	Number of participants	Some common learning difficulties faced in class:
	5	Did not visit the Taj Mahal. Therefore, we were unable to come up with more creative ideas about this mausoleum.
	8	Time was too short for three activities.
	7	Did not get a chance to be group leader. So, could not get chance to present the performance of my group.

As shown in Table 2, in response to question number 2, there were varied responses, only common responses were placed in the table here. Most of the learners (8) agreed that time was too short for three activities. Some learners (7) did not get a chance to be group leader. So, could not get chance to present the performance of their group. 5 learners said that they didn't visit the Taj Mahal. So, they were unable to come up with more creative ideas about this mausoleum.

Table-3: Results of Interview Question no. 3

Q.3	Number of participants	Some confusions, doubts or queries you had:
	5	Not able to completely understand past tense.
	8	Unable to understand the passive voice in past tense.
	7	Confusion with the first and second form of verbs.

As shown in Table 3, in response to question number 3, there were varied responses, only common responses were placed in the table here. Most of the learners (8) agreed that they were unable to understand the passive voice in past tense. Some learners (7) said that they were confused with the first and second form of verbs. 5 learners said that they were not able to completely understand past tense.

Table-4: Results of Interview Question no.4

Q.4	Number of participants	Why do you like this approach?
	5	The picture was a great source of learning, which helped a lot in understanding the text also.
	8	It was very easy to read, analyze and speak on the same topic.
	7	The class did not only improve communicative and linguistic competence but also general knowledge.

As shown in Table 4, in response to question number 4, there were varied responses, only common responses were placed in the table here. Most of the learners (8) stated that it was very easy to read, analyze and speak on the same topic. Some learners (7) said that the class did not only improve communicative and linguistic competence but also general knowledge. 5 learners said that that the picture was a great source of learning which helped a lot in understanding the text also. Richards and Rodgers (2001) state, "People learn a second language more successfully when they use the language as a means of acquiring information, rather than as an end in itself" (p.207).

Discussion and Conclusion

The analysis of the first statement if they understand the text/ contents of the reading comprehension shows that 55% students agreed with the statement while 45% had no idea. It shows that students could not completely comprehend the contents of the text. They were more interested in looking at the picture rather than searching information about. 5 students said that they were not able to completely understand past tense. 8 students said that they were unable to understand the passive voice in past tense. 7 students said that they had confusion with the first and second form of verbs. The results of questionnaire and the interview sessions match each other and prove that students did not know about past tense. They were unable to understand the structures of past tense: active and passive, which led to confusions and comprehension of the text. However, they performed better while they answered the questions based on the past tense. It proves that they understood the contents but could not use past tense properly. They needed more practices in past tense. Omoto and Nyongesa (2013) rightly state:

> CBI is not explicitly focused on language learning. Therefore, some students may feel confused or may even feel that they are not improving their language skills.

The teacher should deal with this by including some form of language focused follow-up exercises to help draw attention to linguistic features within the materials and consolidate any difficult vocabulary or grammar points (p.238).

The second statement in the questionnaire if they understood the question and answered them successfully reveals that 75% of students agreed with the statement. However, 25% students had no opinion. This percentage specially refers to those students who did not understand the past tense.

The third statement in the questionnaire if they successfully used online or offline dictionaries to write the opposite words in activity 2 reveals that 85% students agreed to it. Students liked to use the dictionary in their mobile, as they are obsessed with mobile. Teacher successfully used this obsession for language learning.

The forth statement in the questionnaire if they enjoyed helping each other (in pair and groups) while answering the questions exhibits that 90% students enjoyed pair and group learning. It shows that students had a good understanding with each other and helped each other in collaborative learning. However, 10% students had no opinion. This percentage refers to those students who admitted during the interview that they did not get a chance to be group leader. So, they couldn't get chance to present the performance of their group. Teacher needs to make sure that every student gets a chance to be group leader so that they could develop the skills of presentation in the target language.

The fifth statement in the questionnaire if they enjoyed and felt confident about the speaking activity in the classroom reveals that 70% students agreed to the statement. It shows a majority of students got benefitted with this approach. Students liked the description of the Taj Mahal as it is a historical monument famous all over the world. They also showed interest because the contents in the language classroom were different from the traditional ones. Omoto and Nyongesa (2013) state, "Content of other subjects offers opportunities for teachers to match the learners' interest and schemata with meaningful content thus facilitating the learning of language" (p.243). 30% students did not have any opinion, which refers to those students who were shy in speaking. They did not like to be group leader. They need further practices to develop their confidence so that they can perform as group leaders in successive classes.

The sixth statement in the questionnaire if the picture and discussion helped them recall their experience or visit to the Taj Mahal displays that 80% students agreed to it. It shows that teacher successfully applied the principle of constructivism. Students were able to use their previous knowledge in order to appreciate the present knowledge. CBLT (with contents from different subject matter) also plays an important role in the development of cognitive abilities of students as Omoto and Nyongesa (2013) state, "The use of content from other subjects makes English language sneak into the learners' cognition without pain" (p.243). However, 15% had no opinion whereas 5% disagreed to statement. It refers to those 5 students who admitted during the interview that they didn't visit the Taj Mahal. So, they were unable to come up with more creative ideas about this mausoleum. Teacher must use the videos in the classroom so that students may have a visual experience.

The seventh statement in the questionnaire if they learnt the use of past tense by attempting these activities shows that 75% students agreed to it. However, 20% had no opinion while 5% disagreed. It stresses on the need to address the issues of slow learners through remedial classes so that they could cope with the pace of the class.

The analysis reveals that CBLT played an important role in the language development of students except a few ones who need remedial classes. It was observed during the implementation of CBLT that it was both rewarding and challenging. However, it is also observed that CBLT may be more effective if it is combined with other approaches like TBLT, CLT etc. Villalobos (2014) states, "I strongly believe that CBI can be both challenging and rewarding. If students, the administration, and professors are positively involved in the process, this approach could be successful. Personally, I would join CBI with other CLT approach like task-based teaching (in order to provide more meaning) as part of the curriculum in order to help learners to acquire the target language" (p.81).

CHAPTER 11

Task-Based Approach

Task-based Language Teaching (TBLT) also known as Task-based Instruction proponed by Prabhu (1987a) advocates real life situations for language learning. The appearance of the Task-Based Approach (TBA) is associated to what became known as the 'Bangalore Project' (Prabhu 1987a) started in 1979 and completed in 1984. The word 'task' here denotes to the particular activities completed in the classroom. Such activities put a strong emphasis on meaning and the importance is assigned to the process of doing things (how) vs. the prevailing role given to content (what) in the teaching practice of that decade. (Sanchez, 2004, p.41) In a TBLT class, learners are given real life situation task, like visiting a doctor, bank, railway, etc. TBLT encourages group and pair learning. Teacher gives a particular task to students to complete it. The focus is more on completion of tasks and less on grammatical structures and accuracy. As the preoccupation with accuracy leads learners to focus more on form rather than function, TBLT focuses more on function rather than form. Richards and Rodgers (2001) state:

> Engaging learners in task work provides a better context for the activation of learning processes than form-focused activities, and hence ultimately provides better opportunities for language learning to take place. Language learning is believed to depend on immersing students not merely in "comprehensible input" but in tasks that require them to negotiate meaning and engage in naturalistic and meaningful communication"(p.223-224).

TBLT here differs from Content-Based Language Teaching (CBLT) as TBLT stresses that only engaging students in "comprehensible input" is not sufficient. CBLT emphasizes that teachers must activate students' previous knowledge in order to comprehend the present one. TBLT goes one-step ahead and emphasizes that students must be assigned to complete tasks in the classroom for the real learning to take place. When students are engaged in tasks as pair and groups, they learn better because of cooperation. Language cannot be detached from people or from society as the basic function of language is communication. Richards and Rodgers have rightly emphasized on learning processes rather than form-based activities, as Sanchez (2004) also opines:

> If the way we teach has an effect on learning, process syllabuses have a role to play in language teaching. Contrary to the 'propositional syllabuses' (based on the definition of structures, rules and vocabulary to learn); 'process syllabuses' face the teaching situation from the opposite side: they focus not on what has to be taught, but on how things are done or how goals are achieved. Goals to

be achieved are still there, but the means and skills to reach them are given priority in the analysis of the situation. It is assumed that if we perform the task adequately, the goals will be achieved more efficiently. (p.46)

When students form group, they exchange their views (using target language communicatively) on a task and face the challenges of the task in order to achieve a goal. Communicative Language Teaching (CLT) stresses on the same communicative aspects of language. It might have led Prabhu (1987 b) to develop TBLT, which revolutionized language teaching as he, states:

a strongly felt pedagogic intuition, arising from experience generally but made concrete in the course of professional debate in India. This was that the development of competence in second language requires no systematization of language inputs or maximization of planned practice, but rather the creation of conditions in which learners engage in an effort to cope with communication (p.1).

As Prabhu (1987 b) states, there is no maximization of the planned practice, learners must rather be engaged in an effort to cope with communication. It is the very essence of CLT as coping with communication is the real purpose of language. In order to let learners cope with communication, teacher must assign them the task which might encourage them to communicate as much as possible and they learn how to cope with different sorts of communication.

In a TBLT class, teacher takes a back seat and does not interfere much in the class. His role only confines to be a facilitator in the classroom rather than being a dominator in the classroom. TBLT has redefined the language teaching in terms of putting special emphasis on learners, which are usually neglected in learning process though the learning ultimately aims to enrich learners' learning experiences. Breen (1987) concludes that the TBA is a result of:

i) New views on language, ii) New views on teaching methodology, iii) New views on the contribution of the learners to the learning process, and iv) New views on how to plan teaching and learning.

Here points iii) and iv) deserve some comments. The role of learner has been systematically left aside for centuries. In addition, that has not only been the case in language teaching, but in all educational fields. Traditional education centered on the transmission of content which were well defined and laid down by teachers or by authorities. Not much else was added or considered regarding other elements also present in the teaching and learning situation. Research in language acquisition, among other reasons, has recently demonstrated what nowadays seems obvious: the most important element in the teaching-learning situation is the learner (qtd. in Sanchez 2004, p.45).

Task not only engages a learner in learning process rather provides a purpose to students. They realize they have to achieve a goal. The goal usually refers to the task provided by the teacher. Feez (1998) summarizes the task-based instructions in the following way:

1. The focus is on process rather than product.

2. Basis elements are purposeful activities and tasks that emphasize communication and meaning.

3. Learners learn language by interacting communicatively and purposefully while engaged in the activities and tasks.

4. Activities and tasks can be either those that learners might need to achieve in real life or those that have a pedagogical purpose specific to the classroom.

5. Activities and tasks of a task-based syllabus are sequenced according to difficulty.

6. The difficulty of a task depends on a range of factors including the previous experiences of learner, the complexity of the task, the language required to undertake the task, and the degree of support available (p.17).

In order to achieve success in a TBLT class, teacher may divide his class into different stages in order to complete the task. For example, teacher starts the class with pre-task. At this stage, teacher supplies students with some key vocabulary and grammatical structures. Vocabulary and grammatical structures are related with the task given to students. For example, teacher gives students a picture of village-marina-yachts. They have to look at the picture and name different objects in it. Teacher provides students with some basic vocabulary related to the picture.

During the second stage where students have to complete the task, teacher divides the students in pair and groups and assigns them further tasks.

Experience

Here we share a related experience of a TBLT classroom at Najran University where learners are supposed to be of advanced level, but in fact, they possess beginner level of proficiency in the language. Teacher provides them with a picture of marina-yachts in order to brainstorm the ideas of the yachts, ocean etc.

Task 1

Teacher first asks students what they see in the picture. Students come up with different words like yachts, sea, water, cars, road, trees etc. However, they are familiar with some words related to picture and teacher gives them some vocabulary related to picture in the pre-task activity like steamer, boat, buildings, people etc.

Task 2

Now teacher divides students in pairs and groups and gives them the same picture to describe it. Teacher facilitates the class and observes that students are not able to form sentences. Teacher supplies them with simple be form like 'there is a yacht', 'there is a boat', etc. Students come up with different descriptions like:

1. There is an island.
2. There are many boats.
3. There are beautiful roads.
4. Men women is sitting in steamers.
5. There is many street lights at both the sides of the road.
6. There is many cars on the road.

https://pixabay.com/photos/yacht-marina-sailing-ships-4638447/\

Task 3

Task 3 is based on writing. Teacher divides students in pairs and groups. Teacher assigns students to form some sentences with the help of form 'be'. Teachers ask them to write a few sentences based on the picture provided by the teacher. He asks them to use vocabulary provided to them in *Task 1* like steamer, boat, buildings, people, etc. Students come with the following descriptions:

1. This is a beautiful island.
2. It have many yachts.
3. There are many boats.
4. There are many steamers.
5. There are beautiful cars.
6. The roads are clean.
7. There are many homes.
8. There are many beautiful buildings.

Task 4

Teacher asks students to google about a similar picture. They google village-marina-yachts and collect some more information. Teacher asks them to jot down some more information about village-marina-yachts. Students come with some new information this time like:

1. It is in the USA.
2. It closes at 4:30 pm.
3. There are many yachts and boats for sale.
4. World class facilities are available here.

Observation

Teacher observed that students were enthusiastic in the class. As they were given a colored picture about the marina-yachts, they were attracted towards the picture. Some students named the picture in their mother tongue though some of the students were familiar with English names of different parts of pictures. As teacher formed groups in the classroom, students translated the different parts of the pictures in their mother tongue and vice-versa. Teacher observed all this and did not interfere with their learning styles. Teacher observed there was a lot of cooperation among students. The task was completely learner-centered and teacher was mere a facilitator. Students learnt from each other and teacher helped them only when they needed help. Students learnt the vocabulary related to the marina-yachts and simple grammatical structures. Students learnt the vocabulary and structures based on picture as provided to them. The pre-task stage provided them with ample time and opportunities to brainstorm the picture. Teacher observes that students enjoy pair and group learning as in *Task 2*. They made some mistakes related to is, are, am and Verb I + ing form while speaking about the picture as shown in sentences 4,5 and 6. However, they did not make the same mistakes while writing about the picture (Task 3) except sentence 2 where 'have' is used instead of 'has'. It may be because they got enough time to correct each other's mistakes. Students enjoyed *Task 4* too as teacher allowed them to use smart phones to google more information about the picture. They formed 4 correct sentences. Here collaborative learning played an important role in the completion of the tasks.

Analysis of Students' Feedback

However, it was teachers' perspective regarding the application of TBLT approach. Teacher followed the learner-centered approach and involved them in learning process. Students were encouraged to come up with new structures in target language. Teacher emphasized more on fluency and overlooked accuracy related issues as it might have discouraged the students and broken their rhythm of speaking. Though this approach did well, success of this approach cannot be truly assessed until students, the target group, are given an opportunity to express their opinion and share their experiences. In order to record students' observations and experiences, a questionnaire set was given to them focusing on the key elements of TBLT approach especially on the contents, which were taught in the classroom. In addition to the questionnaire, students were also interviewed with a set of open-ended questions to assess whether they had any query, doubt or confusion, which were not the part of the questionnaire. The open-ended questions provided enough space to students to put forward their opinion in a more descriptive way.

Analysis of Students' Questionnaire

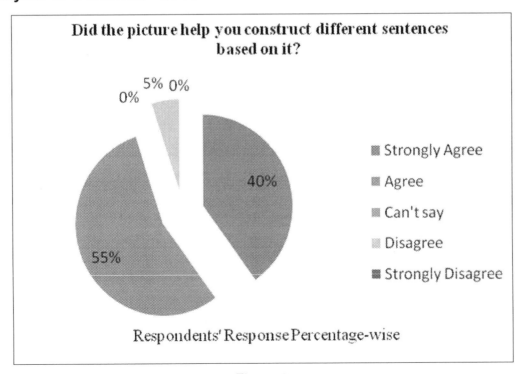

Figure 1

The first statement in the questionnaire, *if the picture helped them construct different sentences based on it*, reveals that there are 40% participants who *felt the picture helped them construct different sentences based on it*. 55% of the participants admitted to it. 5% of the participants disagreed.

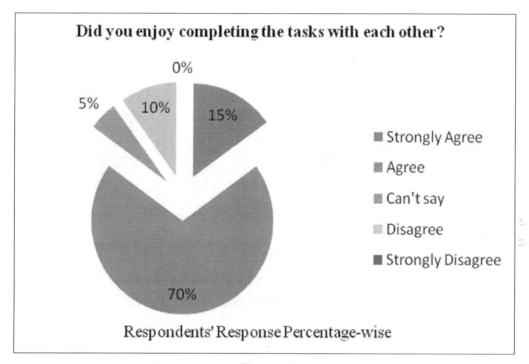

Figure 2

The second statement, *if they enjoyed completing the tasks with each other*, displays that there are 15% of the participants who opined that *they enjoyed completing the tasks with each other*. 70% of the participants agreed though (5%) of the participants had no idea. 10% of the participants did not accept the statement.

The third statement, *if the vocabulary provided by the teacher helped them form some new structures*, shows that 15% of the participants are of the opinion that *the vocabulary provided by the teacher helped them form some new structures*. 55% of the participants agreed to the statement, though 25% of the participants had no opinion. 5% of the participants dissented.

The forth statement in the questionnaire, *if they understood the use of 'be' forms*, divulges that there is none who strongly agreed to the statement that *they understood the use of 'be' forms*. 50% of the participants agreed with the statement, though (30%) of the participants did not express their opinion. 15% of the participants disapproved and 5% of the participants strongly disagreed with the statement.

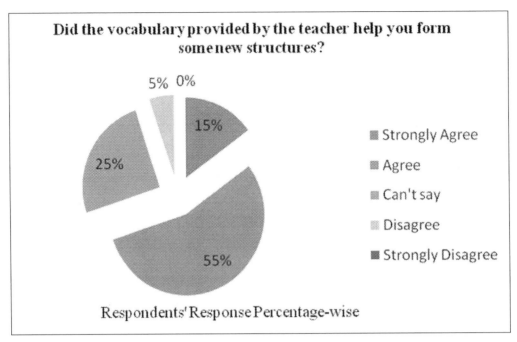

Figure 3

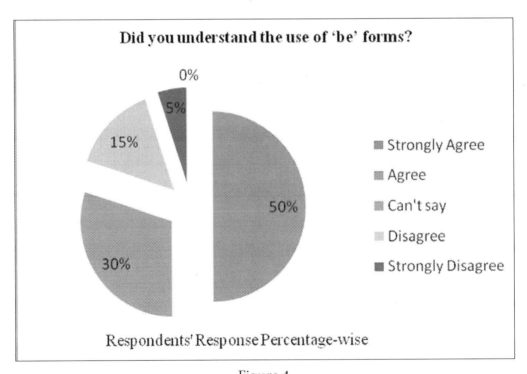

Figure 4

The fifth statement in the questionnaire, if *the activity provided them real-life situation to practice the language for communicative purposes*, unveils that 10% of the participants were in absolute agreement to the statement that *the activity provided them real-life situation to practice the language for communicative purposes*. A big no (80%) of the participants agreed while 'can't say' had no value. 5% of the participants did not agree with the statement and the same number (5%) of the participants had absolute disagreement.

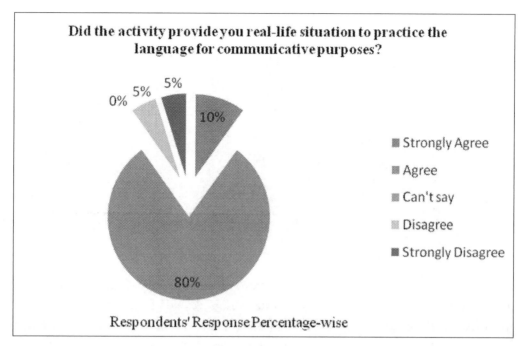

Figure 5

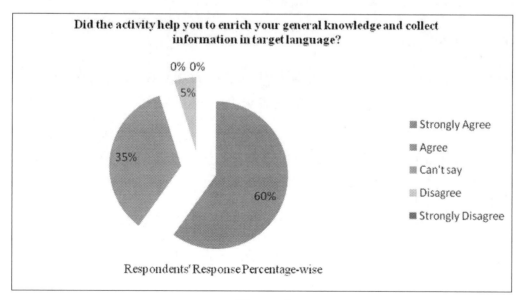

Figure 6

The sixth statement, if *the activity helped them to enrich their general knowledge and collect information in target language*, reveals no participant thought that *the activity helped them to enrich their general knowledge and collect information in target language*. 60% of the participants agreed with the statement though 35% (a significant percentage) of the participants had no opinion. 5% of the participants disagreed with the statement.

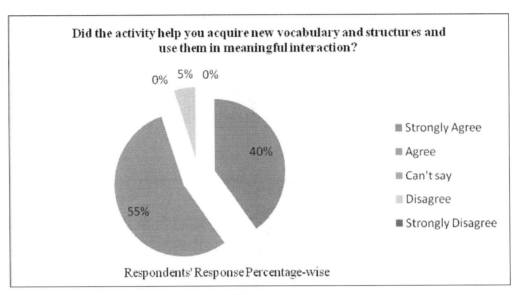

Figure 7

The seventh statement in the questionnaire, if *the activity helped them acquire new vocabulary and structures and use them in meaningful interaction*, reveals that 40% of the participants strongly agreed with the statement that *the activity helped them acquire new vocabulary and structures and use them in meaningful interaction*. 55% of the participants agreed to it. 5% of the participants did not agree with the statement.

Interview analysis

Another method used to collect the data was interview method. Twenty samples were selected out of 30, which were filled in with complete information. The participants responded to the following questions in the interview:

1. Learners rate (on a scale of 1-5) the effectiveness of this method where 1 represents the lowest and 5 represents the highest value.

2. Mention some common learning difficulties faced in class.

3. Mention some confusions, doubts or queries you had.

4. Why do you like this method?

Table 1: Results of Interview Question no. 1

Q. No	Number of learners	Scale
1.	15	4
	5	5

As shown in the table 1, in response to the first question, 15 learners rated the effectiveness of the method as 4 on a scale of 1-5 as mentioned earlier. 5 learners rated the effectiveness of the method as 5. The overall effectiveness of the method was rated 1-5s from learners' point of view.

Table-2: Results of Interview Question no. 2

Q.2.	Number of participants	Some common learning difficulties faced in class:
	5	It was difficult to form grammatically correct sentences.
	8	It was difficult to distinguish between male and female in the picture, as it was not very clear.
	7	Did not know anything about the village-marina-yachts.

As shown in Table 2, in response to question number 2, there were varied responses, only common responses were placed in the table here. Most of the learners (8) agreed that it was difficult to distinguish between male and female in the picture, as it was not very clear. 5 students said that it was difficult to form grammatically correct sentences. Some students (7) said that they did not know anything about the village-marina-yachts, which hampered their communication.

Table-3: Results of Interview Question no. 3

Q.3	Number of participants	Some confusions, doubts or queries you had:
	5	Confused about what is yacht and what is steamer.
	8	Had doubts about whether the background has cars or busses.
	7	Could not fluently describe the picture.

As shown in Table 3, in response to question number 3, there were varied responses, only common responses were placed in the table here. Most of the students (8) complained that they had doubts about whether the background had cars or busses. 5 students said that they were confused about what is yacht and what is steamer. Some learners (7) said that they could not fluently describe the picture.

Table-4: Results of Interview Question no.4

Q.4	Number of participants	Why do you like this method?
	5	The picture used in the class was very motivating.
	8	Learnt many new words about the village-marina-yachts.
	7	It increased general knowledge about the village-marina-yachts. Using smart phone in the class was very exciting.

As shown in Table 4, in response to question number 4, there were varied responses, only common responses were placed in the table here. Most of the learners (8) admitted that they learnt many new words about the village-marina-yachts. 5 students admitted that the picture, used in the class, was very motivating. Some learners (7) said that it added to their general knowledge about the village-marina-yachts. They also accepted that using smart phone in the class was very exciting.

Discussion and Conclusion

The analysis of students' questionnaire and interview shows that students liked this approach.15 rated it as 4 and 5 rated it as 5 on a scale 1-5. The analysis of the first statement shows that 95% students admitted that the picture helped them construct different sentences, which is a big success for this method. 5% students disagreed which is a minor percentage but needs attention. Teacher needs to start some remedial classes for these students, as the problem is not with approach rather with learners' level of competence.

The analysis of the second statement shows that 85% students enjoy completing the tasks with each other. It shows the TBLT principle of working in pair and group to accelerate mutual learning and cooperation is successful here. However, 5% had no opinion and 10% disagreed. Teacher has to ensure that group members are cooperating with each other. In assessing group collaboration, in addition to measuring individual academic performance, the teacher needs to observe how group members respond to each other and whether joint attention to the task can be maintained (Barron, 2003).

The analysis of the third statement shows that 70% students admitted that the vocabulary provided by the teacher helped them form some new structures. As the vocabulary was used in a particular context, students acquired it more naturally. Moreover, teacher also assigned them the task based on vocabulary, which further helped them use it in real life situations for meaningful interaction. It fulfills the fundamental principle of TBLT approach.

8 students also admitted during the interview that they learnt many new words about the village-marina-yachts.

The analysis of the forth statement shows that only 50% students admitted that they understood the use of 'be' forms. 30% students had no idea. 15% disagreed while 5% strongly disagreed. As the TBLT focuses more on meaning than forms, students need some more practice to practise form-based activities to improve. 5% students admitted during the interview that it was difficult to form grammatically correct sentences. TBLT succeeded in achieving the goal of conveying the meaning but could not get much success to form correct structures of sentences. It is a matter of focus only as TBLT focuses more on function than form.

The analysis of the fifth statement shows that 90% students admitted that the activity provided them real-life situation to practice the language for communicative purposes. The lesson succeeded in implementing the basic principle of TBLT. In a TBLT class, the task must be a reflection of real world as Richards and Rodgers (2001) state about one of the characteristics of TBLT that teachers have to ensure, "Whether the task mirrors a real world activity or is a pedagogical activity not found in the real world" (p.235).

The analysis of the sixth statement shows that 60% students accepted that the activity helped them to enrich their general knowledge and collect information in target language. 35% had no idea while 5% disagreed to the statement. It may be because the focus of the activity was not to enrich the general knowledge rather providing the real life context to the task assigned so that students might feel confident. Students could not read much about the village-marina-yachts to increase their general knowledge, as the language used in google search engine was very difficult and above the level of learners. Students need more practice as Richards and Rodgers (2001) state, "Many tasks will require learners to create and interpret messages for which they lack full linguistic resources and prior experiences. In fact, it is considered the point of such tasks. Practice in restating, paraphrasing, using paralinguistic signals (where appropriate), and so on, will often be needed". (p.235)

The analysis of the seventh statement shows that 95% students admitted that the activity helped them acquire new vocabulary and structures and use them in meaningful interaction. Only 5% students disagreed. It proves a greater success of this approach as the fundamental principle of TBLT is achieved in the classroom. The overall analysis shows that the TBLT guaranteed big success in the classroom.

CHAPTER 12

Participatory Approach

Participatory Approach originated in the early sixties with the work of Paulo Freire (a Brazilian educator, who worked in adult education, teaching literacy). In his famous work, The Pedagogy of the Oppressed, Freire (2000) argued against what he saw as the traditional form of education 'a banking system' in which, "Knowledge is a gift bestowed by those who consider themselves knowledgeable upon those whom they consider to know nothing" (p.72). For Freire, there was a need to move away from this model to one, which would empower learners. Teachers needed to see themselves as part of the learning process, and as learners themselves. Freire advocated a critical pedagogy, where learners were transformed and empowered by the learning they are involved in. Participatory educational approaches are emancipator.

Participatory approach follows Paulo Freire's theory of knowledge. This approach does not distinguish between the person who has knowledge and the person who has no knowledge. He has attacked the concept of education as 'a banking system'. This approach treats everyone equally and requires everyone's equal participation in learning process as it must involve everyone. One may add to one's knowledge in the best way when one not only learns but also shares one's knowledge with each other. Here, there is no distinction between a learner and a teacher and teacher himself becomes one of the learners. He participates in learning process and facilitates teaching and learning process. Learners have primary importance in the classroom and play a vital role in the classroom activities.

Participatory teaching approach is a form of a reflective teaching, which is sometimes termed as interactive teaching method or learner-centered teaching method. This method stresses the subjectivity of learners and the self-construction of knowledge. It is a shift from a belief that learners are empty plate who are supposed to be imparted with knowledge (teach concept) to a belief that learners can construct knowledge and learn on their own if properly guided (learn concept) (Kafyulilo, n.d.). However, there are scholars who slightly differentiate between the objectives of learner-centered method and participatory approach as Auerbach (1993, as qtd. in Wiggins, 2004) states:

> Participatory approaches focus on social transformation and draw curriculum from the context of learners' lives. The role of the teacher is to identify issues and problems in the learners' lives and to use these in the content of the class to promote dialogue, reflection, and action. Learner-centered approaches focus on self-realization and on involving participants in the curriculum development

process. They are based on the idea that adults learn best when they are in charge of their own learning and when curriculum is based on their needs. The role of the teacher in this approach is to act as a facilitator. Although these approaches vary in their objectives they both place the learner at the center of pedagogy (p.8).

Though the objectives may be different, their main emphasis is on learners. Learners are always in focus with participatory approach. This approach precedes other approaches like content-based and task-based approaches as Freeman (2001) states, "Although it originated in the early sixties with the work of Paulo Freire, and therefore antedates modern version of content-based and task-based approaches, it was not until the 1980s that the participatory approach started being widely discussed in the language teaching literature"(p.150). It is one of the reasons that this approach shares much with other approaches, which succeeded it. For example, participatory approach is more like content-based approach in the sense that contents are again on focus in this approach and play an important part in language learning. However, it is a little bit different from content-based approach as it primarily focuses on real life experiences, personal experiences and situations one might face in everyday life. It ascertains that all the participants are actively taking part in learning. The participants get more excited to participate in the class because teacher takes into account different experiences of the learners and how they responded in that particular situation. Language is learnt more naturally when the focus is on its usage in daily life. This approach engages learners mentally as teacher deals with their issues. Kucharcikova and Tokarcikova (2016) share a research conducted in Slovakia:

> Much of the criticism has been directed to higher education in Slovakia over the decades. It is argued that the current education focuses more on acquiring encyclopedic knowledge rather than promoting the creativity to develop ability to identify problems. As a result, students are less able to analyze specific situation, to present and evaluate alternative solutions, stand up for their own opinions and use their knowledge in practical applications. These applied tools will help us enhance the quality of education and attract the attention to more effective learning at the universities as the imperative of successful preparation of students for both their professional and personal life. (p.82)

Though there have been several theoretical applications of this approach that may facilitate learning process, one cannot guarantee its success and predict the impediments until implemented in an EFL/ESL situation.

Experience

Let us share an experience of international students studying at AMU, Aligarh, India. There is a class of twenty adults from different countries like Iraq, Oman, Indonesia, Jordan etc.

They come for evening classes to improve English language so that they can cope with their curriculum at the university as well interact with people in their surroundings. Teacher greets all students in English and the students respond the greetings in English language. Teacher asks them how they feel in India and what problems they face. Students told that they were having many problems in the university as well as in their surroundings. Teacher asks them first to discuss their problems with the people around them. One of the students reports that there are many things at his apartment, which are not working properly, but he cannot tell this problem to his landlord. While he communicates these problems, he explains with the help of expressions/gestures and incorrect structures of sentences like I problem washing machine, refrigerator not working etc. After students finish, teacher takes out one picture from his beg out of many pictures, which particularly deal with the problems stated by the students. As five of the students had more or less the same problem, teacher makes it subject of teaching and learning.

Image 1. (https://pixabay.com/photos/rustic-kitchen-logs-log-home-2041017/)

When students look at the pictures, they point to the objects they have problems with like water tap, exhaust fan, microwave, oven, table, chair, cabinet etc. They identify the objects they have problem with. In this way, teacher connects the classroom learning to the outer world experiences. Teacher asks them to write the names of each object in English. He allowed them use dictionary. They orally named different objects in the picture. Now the teacher asked them to write problems associated with different objects. They wrote with some spelling and structural mistakes like refrigerator not cooling, oven holes block, micro-wave wire broken, cabinets broken etc. They report these problems to teacher and teacher pairs the students. In the pair, one student has the problem while the other one did not face it on personal level. Teacher provided them with a structure in the present continuous tense like, 'Refrigerator is not cooling,' 'Oven holes are blocking,' 'I am facing problems,' etc. Thus, teacher provided them with a structure of the present continuous tense and asked them to induce the rules from the structures. Then teacher asked them to form different sentences based on the same tense in pairs. He then asks one of the members of the pairs to come forward and present their sentences orally in the classroom. Students come up with different sentences. Some of them are here to assess their performance:

1. I am having problem with water tap.
2. I am going to change the broken glass of the kitchen door.
3. Cabinet is not working properly.
4. I am cleaning my kitchen etc.
5. Refrigerator is not cooling.
6. Oven holes blocking.
7. The roof of the kitchen is leaking.
8. One of the switches are not working.

Students come up with eight different sentences with a few mistakes (see sentences: 6 and 8). Teacher does not correct mistakes in the beginning while students present their sentences before the class.

Observation

Teacher noticed that students were very enthusiastic as if teacher was giving a voice to their problems. They were able to form sentences on the problems they were facing in daily lives. They were more confident to communicate their problems with the landlord as they knew exactly what they had to say to him. This way, they learnt structure and vocabulary related to the issues they had. They took great interest in their class as the class was discussing how to communicate their ideas into English so that their problems could be solved. In the next class, teacher dealt with another problem, provided the vocabulary on the same issues and selected the grammatical structures to convey their ideas. The class was serving the real purpose of language learning. As the primary purpose of language is to communicate, the class was exploiting the language for the same reasons.

The participatory approach was successfully applied in the class as students used language for the real purpose. They used language to convey their problems. They also learnt how to convey their various issues to their landlord. Students were very enthusiastic as it provided them with what they exactly needed.

However, it was teachers' perspective regarding the application of the participatory approach. Teacher picked up one common problem faced by learners and made it a topic of teaching. Students were encouraged to come up with new structures in target language. Teacher emphasized more on fluency. Teacher overlooked a few grammatical mistakes as it might have discouraged the students and broken their rhythm of speaking the target language. Though this approach seemed to do well, success of this approach cannot be truly measured, until, students, the target group, are given an opportunity to express their opinion and share their experiences. In order to record students' observation and experiences, a questionnaire set was given to them focusing on the key elements of the participatory approach especially on the contents, which were taught in the classroom. In addition to the questionnaire, students were also interviewed with a set of open-ended questions to assess whether they had any query, doubt or confusion, which were not the part of the questionnaire. The open-ended questions provided enough space to students to put forward their opinion frankly.

Analysis of Students' Feedback

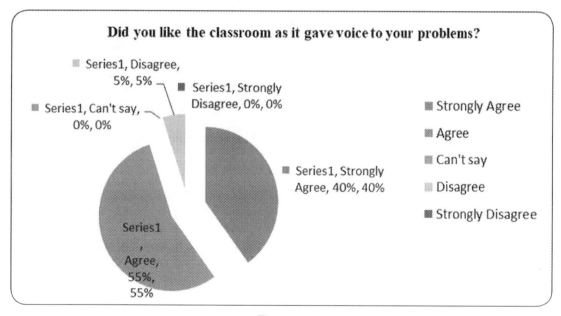

Figure 1

The first statement in the questionnaire if *they liked the classroom as it gave voice to their problems* reveals that there are 40% participants who strongly agreed that *they liked the classroom as it gave voice to their problems*. 55% of the participants agreed to it. 5% of the participants disagreed.

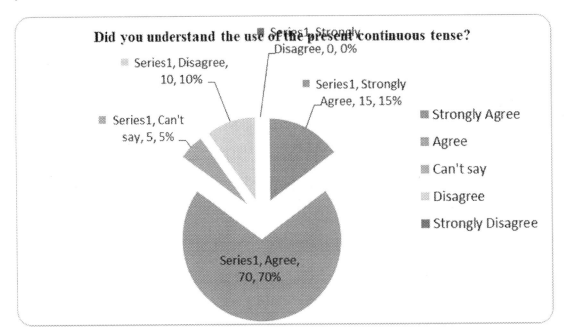

Figure 2

The second statement in the questionnaire if *they understood the use of the present continuous tense* displays that there are 15% of the participants who strongly agreed that *they understood the use of the present continuous tense*. 70% of the participants agreed though (5%) of the participants had no idea. 10% of the participants did not accept the statement

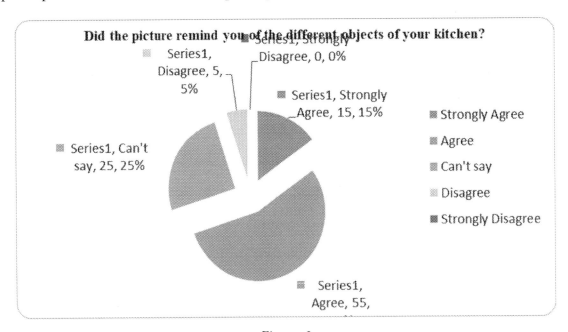

Figure 3

The third statement in the questionnaire if *the picture reminded them of the different objects of their kitchen* shows that 15% of the participants strongly agreed that *the picture reminded them of the different objects of their kitchen.* 55% of the participants agreed to the statement though 25% of the participants had no opinion. 5% of the participants dissented.

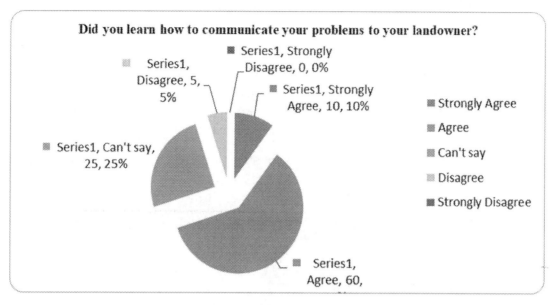

Figure 4

The fourth statement in the questionnaire if *they learnt how to communicate their problems to their landowner* exhibits that there are 10% of the participants who strongly agreed that *they learnt how to communicate their problems to their landowner.* 60% of the participants also admitted to it though 25% of the participants had no opinion. 5% of the participants disagreed to the statement.

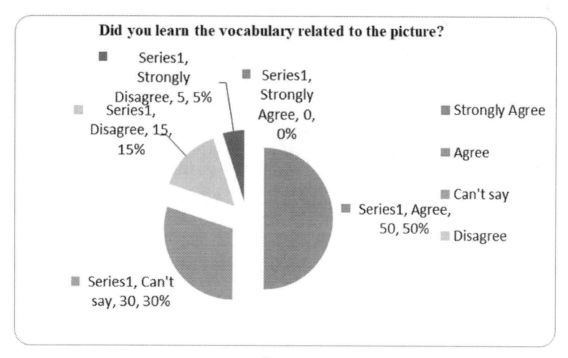

Figure 5

The fifth statement in the questionnaire if *they learnt the vocabulary related to the picture* divulges that there is none who strongly agreed to the statement that *they learnt the vocabulary related to the picture.* 50% of the participants agreed with the statement though 30% of the participants did not express their opinion. 15% of the participants disapproved and 5% of the participants strongly disagreed with the statement.

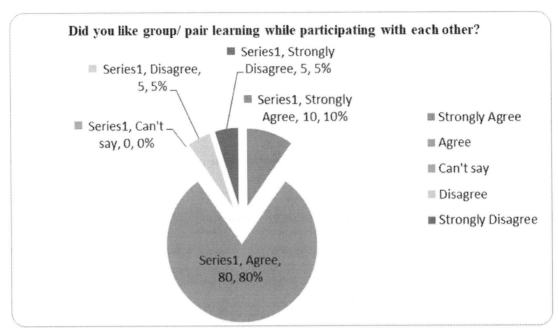

Figure 6

The sixth statement in the questionnaire if *they liked group/ pair learning while participating with each other* unveils that 10% of the participants were in absolute agreement to the statement that *they liked group/ pair learning while participating with each other.* A big no 80% of the participants agreed while there was none who did not state an opinion. 5% of the participants did not agree with the statement and the same number 5% of the participants had absolute disagreement.

Interview analysis

Another method used to collect the data was interview method. Twenty samples were selected out of 30, which were filled in with complete information. The participants responded to the following questions in the interview:

1. Learners rate (on a scale of 1-5) the effectiveness of this method where 1 represents the lowest and 5 represents the highest value:

2. Mention some common learning difficulties faced in class.

3. Mention some confusions, doubts or queries you had.

4.   Why do you like this method?

Table 1: Results of Interview Question no. 1

Q. No	Number of learners	Scale
1.	6	2
	4	3
	10	4

As shown in the table 1, in response to the first question, 6 learners rated the effectiveness of the method as 2 on a scale of 1-5 as mentioned above. 10 learners rated the effectiveness of the method as 4 and 4 other teachers rated as 3. The overall effectiveness of the method was rated 1-4s from learners' point of view.

Table-2: Results of Interview Question no. 2

Q.2.	Number of participants	Some common learning difficulties faced in class:
	5	It was difficult to name the different objects of pictures in English.
	8	Problems with singular and plural subjects and 'BE' forms
	7	Did not get a chance to be group leader. So, could not get chance to present the performance of my group.

As shown in Table 2, in response to question number 2, there were varied responses, only common responses were placed in the table here. Most of the learners (8) agreed that they had problems with singular and plural subjects and 'BE' forms. Some learners (7) did not get a chance to be group leader. So, could not get chance to present the performance of my group. Five learners said that it was difficult to name the different objects of pictures in English.

Table-3: Results of Interview Question no. 3

Q. 3.	Number of participants	Some confusions, doubts or queries you had.
	5	The picture of the kitchen did not have all the objects of our kitchen.
	8	Some of the pictures were not very clear.
	7	Could not understand the accent of teacher and other colleagues.

As shown in Table 3, in response to question number 3, there were varied responses, only common responses were placed in the table here. Most of the learners (8) agreed that some of the pictures were not very clear. Some learners (7) said that they could not understand the accent of teacher and other colleagues. 5 learners said that the picture of the kitchen didn't have all the objects of their kitchen.

Table-4: Results of Interview Question no.4

Q.4	Number of participants	Why do you like this approach?
	5	The objects in the picture provided a very good practice.
	8	This class helped a lot in understanding our own problems and expressing them in English.
	7	Language was learnt for real communication.

As shown in Table 4, in response to question number 4, there were varied responses, only common responses were placed in the table here. Most of the learners (8) accepted that this class helped a lot in understanding their own problems and expressing them in English. Some learners (7) said that language was learnt for real communication. 5 learners said that the objects in the picture provided a very good practice.

Discussion and Conclusion

The first statement in the questionnaire if they liked the classroom as it gave voice to their problems shows that 95% students (if the scales agree and strongly agree are merged) admitted that the classroom dealt with their everyday problems. 8 students also accepted during the interview that the class helped a lot in understanding their own problems and expressing them in English. Teacher followed the basic principle of the participatory approach as it deals with the real life issues. Opportunities which allow the learners' voices to be recognized, heard and used purposefully within the language-learning framework can be viewed as participatory.

The second statement in the questionnaire if they understood the use of the present continuous tense displays that 85% of students agreed that they understood the use of the present continuous tense as teacher used the tense as a tool to voice the problems of students. Seven students also appreciated during the interview that language was learnt for real communication. However, 5% did not have an opinion and 10% disagreed to the statement. Eight students accepted during the interview that they had problems with singular and plural subjects and 'BE' forms. Teacher needs to conduct some remedial classes especially for these students.

The third statement in the questionnaire if the picture reminded them of the different objects of their kitchen exhibits that 70% students agreed to the statement. However, 25% did not have an opinion while 5% disagreed to the statement. It makes sense, as one picture provided by the teacher cannot have all the objects of every student as every student has different settings and objects in the kitchen. Five students also admitted during the interview that the picture of the kitchen did not have all the objects of their kitchen. Nevertheless, there was a lot of interaction and communication among learners as they were enquiring how to pronounce the name of each object as presented in the picture of the kitchen. Richards and Rodgers (2001) rightly state, "People learn a second language more successfully when they use the language as a means of acquiring information, rather than as an end in itself" (p.207).

The fourth statement in the questionnaire if they learnt how to communicate their problems to their landowner states that 70% students agreed with the statement. 25% students had no opinion whereas 5% students disagreed to the statement. It shows teacher needs to pay special attention on these students or reform the pairs and group so that they can learn from teacher and with each other and improve their linguistic competence. Methods, tasks and activities that give learners the opportunity to own the language are used in the classroom and learners feel empowered as they do so. Teacher also has to pay attention on accent as seven students admitted that they could not understand the accent of teacher and other colleagues. If they cannot understand each other, speaking skills cannot be developed.

The fifth statement in the questionnaire if they learnt the vocabulary related to the picture reflects that 50% of students agreed to the statement. 30% had no opinion. 15% disagreed while 5% strongly agreed to the statement. The analysis suggests that teacher needs to provide students with some more practice as vocabulary learning takes time. Students need to repeatedly use them in order to acquire it. Teacher needs to provide a big and clear picture as five students admitted during the interview that the pictures in the worksheet were not very clear.

The sixth statement in the questionnaire if they liked group/ pair learning while participating with each other shows that 90% students agreed to the statement. Teacher successfully exploited the principle of cooperative learning in the classroom, which requires participation of each student. However, 5% students disagreed whereas 5% strongly disagreed to the statement. It proves teacher needs to pay special attention on those students who could not participate with the group. Seven students admitted during the interview that they did not get a chance to be group leader. Therefore, they could not get chance to present the performance of their group.

CHAPTER 13

Cooperative Learning Approach

Language is the product of society. It cannot be dissociated from the society it is used in. Language cannot be learnt in isolation. It can be best learnt with the people in a society. CLL (Cooperative Language Learning) is inspired by the same idea that language can be acquired more productively when people in groups or pairs learn it. We usually use language to exchange information with each other in society. Language is a tool for communication and communication is possible only in society with people. The same idea is adopted in cooperative language learning. Olsen and Kagan (1992) have rightly stated:

> Cooperative learning is group learning activity organized so that learning is dependent on the socially constructed exchange of information between learners in groups and in which each learner is held accountable for his or her own learning and is motivated to increase the learning of others. (p.8)

John Dewey, the US educator, is generally associated with the origin of cooperative learning into regular classroom on a systematic basis (Rodgers, 1988). The same approach was used in order to teach different disciplines not only language but also Mathematics etc. in schools. As mathematics has different puzzles/ problems related to specific laws, group and pair work prove to be beneficial in Mathematic class. The same is true about English language too. Students solve different sorts of 'jigsaw' activities related to English language. Here process is more important than product. As students work in pairs and groups, they aim to complete activities with cooperation. Jigsaw is a cooperative learning technique rich in opportunities for promoting interaction (Aronson, 2008). There is a lot of use of target language while attempting activities in the classroom. This approach focuses more on learners and discourages teacher-centered approach to teaching. It encourages cooperation rather than competition among students. Richards and Rodgers (2001) state about this approach, "It was more generally promoted and developed in the United States in the 1960s and 1970s as a response to the forced integration of public schools and has been substantially refined and developed since then(p.192)"

As we analyzed different methods and approaches in the previous chapters, we observed that a minority of students was always lagging behind no matter which method or approach teacher used in the classroom. This approach attempts to focus on the learners as a whole as Johnson, Johnson, and Holubec (1994) state that Cooperative Learning aims to:

- raise the achievement of all students including those who are gifted or academically handicapped
- help the teacher build the positive relationship among students
- give students the experiences they need for healthy, social, psychological, and cognitive development (p.2)

Cooperative language learning, as the name suggests, is based on the cooperation of learners. This approach is learner-centered by its basic nature. Richards and Rodgers (2001) state that the goals of CLL are the following:

- to provide opportunities for naturalistic second language acquisition through the use of interactive pair and group activities
- to provide teachers with a methodology to enable them to achieve this goal
- to enable focused attention to particular lexical items, language structures, and communicative functions through the use of interactive tasks
- to provide opportunities for learners to develop successful learning and communication strategies
- to enhance learner motivation and reduce learner stress and to create a positive affective classroom climate (p.193)

CLL provides a more natural environment by providing a real life situation to learners. Freeman (2000) states, "Cooperative or collaborative learning essentially involves students learning from each other in groups. But it is not the group configuration that makes cooperative learning distinctive; it is the way that students and teachers work together that is important" (p.164).

In CLL, the way groups work is more important than the way they are formed. This approach stresses on maximum cooperation of people belonging to different classes and sections of society varying in their social and academic nature. Teachers should form the three-, four-, or five-member groups so that students are mixed as heterogeneously as possible, first according to academic abilities, and then on the basis of ethnic backgrounds, race, and gender. Their groups should not be allowed to be formed based on friendship or cliques. When groups are heterogeneously formed and the other indispensable elements are met, students tend to interact and achieve in ways and at levels that are rarely found in other instructional strategies. They also tend to become tolerant of diverse viewpoints, to consider others' thoughts and feelings in depth, and seek more support and clarification of others' positions (Slavin, 1991).

Even with its increasing popularity, a large majority of the group tasks that teachers use, even teachers who claim to be using "cooperative learning," continue to be cooperative group tasks-not cooperative learning group tasks. For instance, nearly all "jigsaw" activities are not cooperative learning jigsaw activities. Merely because students work in small groups does not mean that, they are cooperating to ensure their own learning and the learning of all others in their group (Johnson, Johnson, and Holubec, 1993). This emphasis on academic learning success for each individual and all members of the group is one feature that separates cooperative learning groups from other group tasks (Slavin, 1991). Cuseo (1992) states:

> Cooperative learning is at the other end of the collaborative learning spectrum, since it is a carefully planned learning strategy that involves forming appropriate, sustained learning groups of interdependent members who have been assigned a specific learning goal. Emphasis is placed on student involvement in active learning and the development of social skills. Since the outcomes of cooperative learning are strongly dependent on detailed planning and implementation, cooperative learning has become the most operationally well-defined and procedurally structured form of collaborative learning. (as qtd. in Kaufman, Sutow & Dunn, 1997p. 38)

CLL focuses more on collaborative and mutual learning as it is the essence of this approach. In order to assess the practical application and outputs of this method, one study is shared here which was conducted at an intermediate level class at S.S.S. (Boys) at AMU, Aligarh, India.

Experience

There are 16 students in this class. Teacher forms the group of four students in each group. Teacher assigns them a jigsaw activity. The groups are formed heterogeneously as they consist of students belonging to different academic, social and cultural levels. As the AMU hosts students from the various states of India, teacher forms groups, which represent four states at the same time in each group. Teacher allows students to choose their leader unanimously from the group. Students have to work cooperatively with each other in the group. Now teacher assigns them an activity, which is of common interest to every student. He asks the four different groups to collect information about the founder of the University, Sir Syed Ahmed Khan, and a well-known figure. They were assigned the task in the following way:

- Group 1 has to collect information about Sir Syed Ahmed Khan and his family
- Group 2 has to collect information about his views on education
- Group 3 has to collect information about his views on politics
- Group 4 has to collect information about his views on social reformation

He asks every group to write a paragraph consisting of at least ten sentences. He allows students to use internet on their mobiles or look up for information in any book, journal or newspaper. He allows every group ten minutes' time to go to library adjacent to their classroom and select the books, newspaper paper or journals to collect the materials on the given topic. Teacher allows them half an hour to complete the task. He allows them to cooperate with each other. Teacher encourages them to read the materials and form their own sentences based on it. He strictly prohibited copying the materials from any book, journal, newspaper or website. After half an hour, students wrote the following passages as a group work:

Sir Syed Ahmed Khan and his family

Sir Syed Ahmed khan was born on 17 October 1817 in Delhi. He started his career as a civil servant. His family was highly respected by the Mughal dynasty. His maternal grandfather Khwajah Farid was a 'wazir' (minister) in the court of Akbar Shah II. Syed Ahmed's father, Mir Muttaqi was also close to Akbar Shah but rejected the position and titles offered to him. Perhaps he did not like the materialistic world. He died when Syed Ahmed was about 21 years of age. His mother's name was Azizunnissa Begum. She was a strong willed woman. She showed great interest in the education, character building and upbringing of her son. She was a strict and God-fearing lady.

His views on education

He always stressed on education. He considered ignorance as mother of poverty. He tried his best and prepared himself to popularize western education and science among the Muslims. He paid equal attention to both religious and scientific knowledge. He established the Mohammadan Anglo Oriental College for the same reason. It later on became the Aligarh Muslim University, Aligarh. He also established many schools in Moradabad and Gazipur. He was a pioneer of Muslim education in India. He also promoted professional education. He used education to remove poverty.

His views on politics

Sir Syed Ahmed Khan was an eminent political figure. He saved the lives of many Englishmen during mutiny of 1857. The Government gave him the title of 'Sir'. He cleared misunderstanding between the English and the Muslims. He won the confidence of the British Government. He wrote a book on the causes of Indian revolt of 1857. He helped the British to know the causes of the revolt. He bridged the gap between the British and the Muslims.

His views on social reformation

Sir Syed was against the superstition. He worked hard to spread education among masses. He stressed on job opportunities for the people. He united the Hindus and the Muslims. He issued a magazine *Tahzibul Akhlaq* to address social evils. He stood and advocated of simplicity, honesty and integrity. He discussed the etiquettes of eating and dining in Islam.

After students had searched and googled the information on Sir Syed Ahmed Khan, teacher asked all the groups to sit together and synthesize the materials under different heads. All the four groups had to sit together to complete the draft about Sir Syed which was divided in four sections as given to four groups. They helped each other to organize the contents and edit the draft.

Observations

Teacher observed that students took great interest in working together. They cooperated with each other while working on the task given by the teacher. All of them were working to achieve the same goal. As teacher formed heterogeneous groups, they were a bit hesitant but still cooperated with the group members. They extracted the information from different sources like internet; books etc. and then rephrased them. Teacher was just facilitating the classroom to ensure that every student was participating in the group. Though students could not complete ten sentences under each head because of shortage of time, they had a lot of cooperation while finalizing the draft. Students are placed in groups where team building is emphasized and students learn together while completing the task (Johnson & Johnson, 1989). There was a lot of social interaction among learners as Johnson and Johnson (1989) acknowledged about cooperative learning that "accountability to peers, ability to influence each other's reasoning and conclusions, social modeling, social support and interpersonal rewards all increase" (p. 71)

However, it was teachers' perspective regarding the application of CLL that it followed the learner-centered approach and involved them in learning process. Though this approach turned out to do well, success of this approach cannot be truly assessed until students, the target group, are given an opportunity to express their opinion and share their experiences. In order to record students' observation and experiences, a questionnaire set was given to them focusing on the key elements of CLL especially on the contents, which were taught in the classroom. In addition to the questionnaire, students were also interviewed with a set of open-ended questions to assess whether they had any query, doubt or confusion, which were not the part of the questionnaire. The open-ended questions provided enough space to students to put forward their opinions frankly.

Analysis of Students' Feedback

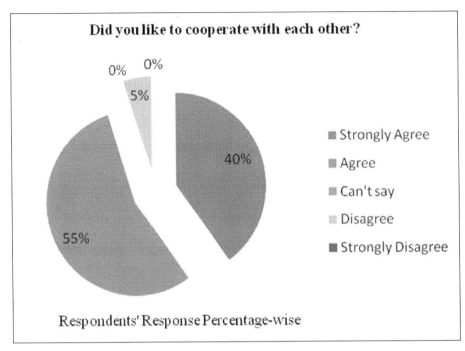

Figure 1

The first statement in the questionnaire if *they liked to cooperate with each other* reveals that there are 40% participants who strongly agreed that *they liked to cooperate with each other*. 55% of the participants agreed to it. 5% of the participants disagreed.

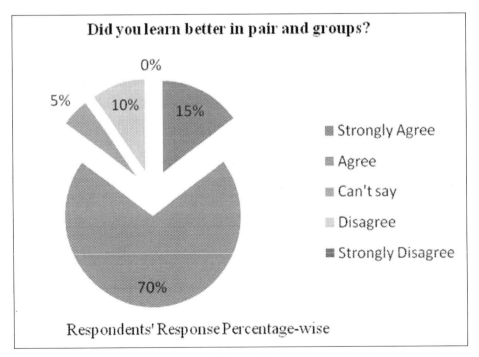

Figure 2

The second statement in the questionnaire if *they learnt better in pair and groups* displays that there are 15% of the participants who strongly agreed that *they learnt better in pair and groups*. 70% of the participants agreed though (5%) of the participants had no idea. 10% of the participants did not accept the statement

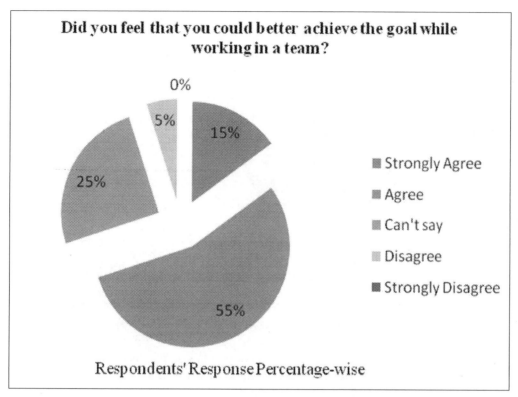

Figure 3

The third statement in the questionnaire if *they felt that they could better achieve the goal while working in a team* shows that 15% of the participants strongly agreed that *they felt that they could better achieve the goal while working in a team*. 55% of the participants agreed to the statement though 25% of the participants had no opinion. 5% of the participants dissented.

The fourth statement in the questionnaire if *this class made them learn something new and added to their knowledge* exhibits that there are 10% of the participants who strongly agreed that *this class made them learn something new and added to their knowledge*. 60% of the participants also admitted to it though 25% of the participants had no opinion. 5% of the participants disagreed to the statement

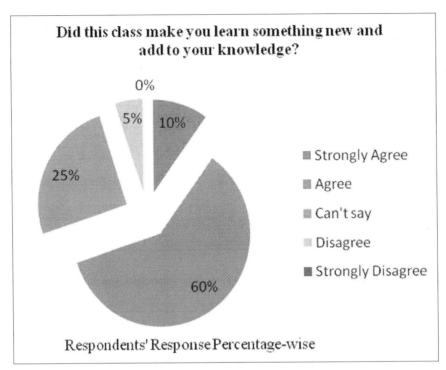

Figure 4

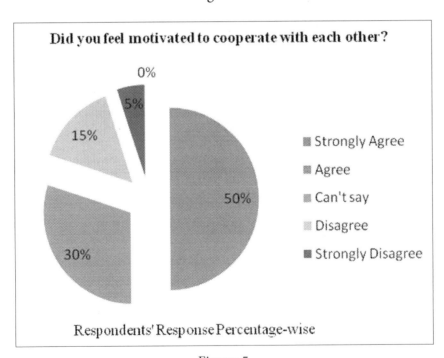

Figure 5

The fifth statement in the questionnaire if *they felt motivated to cooperate with each other* divulges that there is none who strongly agreed to the statement that *they felt motivated to cooperate with each other.* 50% of the participants agreed with the statement though (30%) of the participants did not express their opinion. 15% of the participants disapproved and 5% of the participants strongly disagreed with the statement.

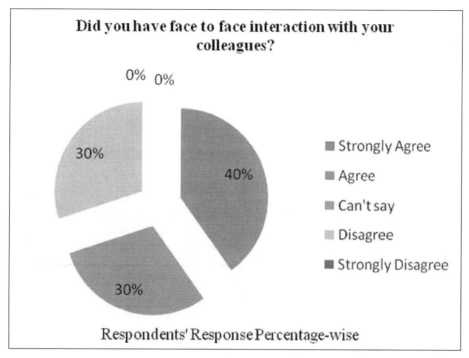

Figure 6

The sixth statement in the questionnaire if *they had face-to-face interaction with their colleagues* discloses that there is none who strongly agreed to the statement. 40% of the participants concurred that *they had face-to-face interaction with their colleagues*. 30% of the participants were not sure about it. 30% of the participant disagreed.

Interview analysis

Another method used to collect the data was interview method. Twenty samples were selected out of 30, which were filled in with complete information. The participants responded to the following questions in the interview:

1. Learners rate (on a scale of 1-5) the effectiveness of this approach where 1 represents the lowest and 5 represents the highest value:

2. Mention some common learning difficulties faced in class:

3. Mention some confusions, doubts or queries you had:

4. Why do you like this approach?

Table 1: Results of Interview Question no. 1

Q. No	Number of learners	Scale
1.	6	5
	4	4
	10	3

As shown in the table 1, in response to the first question, 6 learners rated the effectiveness of the approach as 5 on a scale of 1-5 as mentioned above. 10 learners rated the effectiveness of the approach as 3 and 4 other teachers rated as 4. The overall effectiveness of the approach was rated 1-5s from learners' point of view.

Table-2: Results of Interview Question no. 2

Q.2.	Number of participants	Some common learning difficulties faced in class:
	5	Group members were hesitant talking to each other.
	8	Time was too short for the activity
	7	Did not get a chance to be group leader. So, could not get chance to preset the performance of my group.

As shown in Table 2, in response to question number 2, there were varied responses, only common responses were placed in the table here. Most of the learners (8) agreed that time was too short for the activity. Some learners (7) did not get a chance to be group leader. So, could not get chance to preset the performance of their group. Five learners said that group members were hesitant talking to each other.

Table-3: Results of Interview Question no. 3

Q.3	Number of participants	Some confusions, doubts or queries you had:
	5	We were confused about different resources as which one should be selected.
	8	The internet was too slow.
	7	The language used in the book and internet was too difficult to understand.

As shown in Table 3, in response to question number 3, there were varied responses, only common responses were placed in the table here. Most of the learners (8) agreed that the internet was too slow. Some learners (7) said that the language used in the book and internet was too difficult to understand. 5 Learners said that they were confused about different resources as which one should be selected.

Table-4: Results of Interview Question no.4

Q.4	Number of participants	Why do you like this approach?
	5	It was very enthusiastic to work with each other, which helped a lot in completing the task.
	8	Going to the library and surfing the internet to collect information about Sir Syed was very exciting.
	7	The class provided a better chance to be familiar with each other.

As shown in Table 4, in response to question number 4, there were varied responses, only common responses were placed in the table here. Most of the learners (8) accepted that going to the library and surfing the internet to collect information about Sir Syed was very exciting. Some learners (7) said that the class provided a better chance to be familiar with each other. 5 Learners said that it was very enthusiastic to work with each other which helped a lot in completing the task.

Discussion and Conclusion

The first statement in the questionnaire if they liked to cooperate with each other reveals that 95% students agreed to the statement. It shows that teacher and students succeeded in implementing the basic principle of this approach, which is based on cooperation for language learning. Students also admitted that they were benefitted cooperating with each other and they learnt with each other. The group members, after completion of the task, reflected upon its success. Providing students the opportunity to reflect upon the quality of their group work will ultimately determine the success of cooperative learning teams (Johnson, Johnson and Smith, 1991).

The second statement in the questionnaire if they learnt better in pair and groups reveals that 85% of students agreed to the statement. 5 students also admitted during the interview that it was very enthusiastic to work with each other which helped a lot in completing the task. This way, learners could also evaluate their own strengths and weaknesses, utilizing the diversity of the group to accomplish their mutual goal. By considering how well the group worked together, the effectiveness of social skills used as well as the creation of goals for further growth, cooperative learning encourages students to become reflective practitioners and strive for continuous improvement (Williams, 2007). However, 5% students did not have an opinion while 10% disagreed to the statement, which shows that teacher needs to work harder on the group, as all the members of the group have to work together but learn individually. As a pillar for cooperative learning, individual accountability ensures that "students learn together, but perform alone" (Johnson, Johnson and Smith, 1991). Therefore, the learning of every student has to be ensured.

The third statement in the questionnaire if they felt that they could better achieve the goal while working in a team reveals that 60% students agreed to the statement. Jones (2008) states, "It enables students with the mindset that one must exercise their collaborative skills and work with others to achieve a common goal" (p.64). However, 25% of students did not state and opinion whereas 5% disagreed with the statement which shows that spirit of working together for collaborative learning was lacking among some students. Teacher has to make sure that he has to use such techniques in the classroom, which could make cooperative leaning 100% successful.

The fourth statement in the questionnaire if these classes made them learn something new and added to their knowledge reveals that 70% students agreed with the statement. It shows that this approach benefitted a large number of learners and they learned with each other in cooperative learning. They are secondary level students. It shows that cooperative learning is also helpful with secondary level students though for decades there have been hundreds of studies, which ultimately have come to the same basic conclusion, post-secondary students learn more, are better able to remember and then transfer their knowledge when taught with the cooperative learning model than other instructional methods (Cooper et al., 1990, Goodsell et al., 1992).

The fifth statement in the questionnaire if they felt motivated to cooperate with each other reveals 50% students agreed with the statement. 30% had no opinion. 15% disagreed with the statement whereas 5% strongly disagreed with the statement. It means that many of the learners were not motivated to cooperate with each other. 5 students also admitted that the group members were hesitant talking to each other. The reason may be there were some psychological barriers, which did not allow learners to work and learn together. They were also from different states, which might also be the reason of lack of interaction among learners. Moreover, 7 students admitted that they didn't get a chance to be group leader. Therefore, they could not present the performance of their group. Teacher must ensure that every member of the group gets a chance to be group leader. Teacher can provide the chances to other members to be group leaders in the successive classes. Group leaders must also ensure that they provide chances to every student to participate in classroom activities. Research indicates as compared to other forms of instruction, cooperative learning helps students become better communicators and listeners, cooperative members of a team and effective leaders (Strom and Strom, 2003; Lie 2008; Goodwin, 1999).

The sixth statement in the questionnaire if they had face-to-face interaction with their colleagues exhibits that only 40% of the participants agreed with the statement. It shows that there was a distance among the learners, which is a great obstacle in implementing the principles of cooperative learning. Probably, different linguistic and cultural backgrounds of learners did not allow them to come together and interact with them. Teacher has to bridge this gap in the class and ensure learners fully cooperate with each other in the class.

CHAPTER 14

Post-Method Era

As we have read in the previous chapters, there have been various methods and approaches evolving from time to time to teach language, specially, English. All these methods served to the needs of learners at a particular time and then they were replaced by one another. The new ones substituted old methods. For instance, in the 18th century, Grammar-Translation method came into existence. In the beginning of 19th century, Direct Method dominated the stage of language teaching. In the 1960s, the Audiolingual Method became well known in the language-teaching world because of its overemphasis on oral drills and production. Suggestopedia emerged in the 1970s, addressing the psychological fears students come with in a language classroom. In a way, it improved the business of learning by suggesting the fears of students and converting their negative energy into positive ones. Simultaneously, the Silent Way presented the belief that language students were responsible for their own learning and teachers maintained silence most of the time during their classes. Afterward, Total Physical Response (TPR) focused on listening followed by a physical response, similar to how children learn their first language. From the 1980s to 2000s, one of the most long-lasting methods was Communicative Language Teaching (CLT), which primarily focused on linguistic communicative competence aiming to improve communication skills of students. To this date, all methods were mainly concerned with teaching linguistic features, while other important aspects (socio-cultural, ethnic, psychological, political etc.) were neglected, resulting in issues in language learning.

The 2000s introduced the post-method era: a shift from using methods in the purist sense to recognizing that the nature of language learning is complex and non-linear. Choosing one method and expecting that a prescribed set of instructions will be effective with every learner is discouraged (Freeman, 2011). Therefore, in the post-method era, methods lost their impact on language teaching but their principles were not obsolete and continued to guide and equip novel teachers with several language-teaching tools and enable them to implement them in their classes as required. Nevertheless, post-method era presented many concepts and theories, which brought a complete shift in the realm of language teaching.

Kumaravadivelu (1994) talks about the Post-method condition which is a situation where it is mandatory to refigure the relationship between "theorizers" and "practitioners". This condition has three distinct features that are, search for an alternative to method, teachers' autonomy and "principled pragmatism" (a proposition different from eclecticism since it is more systemic, principled and critical). In 2008, he states that these three major attributes are useful to create a concrete foundation on which the parameters of Post-method pedagogy can be constructed and considered (Kumaravadivelu, 2008, p. 34).

While Post-method does not essentially point to the death of methods entirely, it, according to Richards and Rodgers (2001) "endorses the attempt of the teachers to make necessary adjustments and modifications to an already-established method with the realities of their local contexts in order to recreate them as their own" (p.251). It can thus be seen that Post method is a more democratic approach to teaching. It provides teachers more opportunities and liberty to decide how to teach in the classroom without blindly following any method. Methods were criticized for being inefficient to serve their desired purpose. Traditionally, teachers believed in a more top-down approach to language teaching. According to Nunan (2004), "The top-down approach is characterized by curriculum plans, syllabus outline and methodological procedures which are made by researches and syllabus designers. In such cases the teachers are restricted to using externally developed syllabus, materials and methods" (p.177). Nunan is right as teachers did not have any role to play. They had to follow the methodology designed by researchers and syllabus designers. Mostly, the researchers were not teachers and they were not very well familiar with students' issues.

On the other hand, Nunan (2004) also presents bottom-up approach inspired by the post-method, and has surfaced as the methods had started to fail. Unlike the top-down approach, there is no "prescriptive edicts" attached to this one; but is more a "documentation and systematization" of the classroom, practices designed according zthe needs analysis of the learners (p.177). The post-method era is not only a paradigm shift from researchers to teachers but also from a specific method and approach to a general approach to teaching. It considers many other aspects, which are directly concerned with language teaching and learning. For example, the post-method era emphasizes on the need of context in language teaching.

Context

The context of language learning, including the use of pragmatics, cultural and social awareness, is an important aspect to be considered. Kumaravadivelu (2001) presents the concept that language cannot be separated from society and is the inevitable need of society. The emphasis on context, including ethnic, social, and economic, corroborates with the underlying belief that one single method can no longer be applied to every classroom (Bell, 2003), if it ever could. Bearing in mind two different contexts, one in which learners share the same first language and their social and economic backgrounds are somewhat similar and another in which learner's first languages and their social and economic backgrounds are dissimilar, ELT is likely to be applied in different ways.

Identity

Lately, the concept of identity in language learning has been broadly explored with research suggesting that language learners' identities are multiple and subject to variations across time and place (Norton, 2000; Janks, 2010; Norton and Toohey, 2011). Learners' identities play an important role and cannot be neglected in the classroom. Kramsch (2009) argues that it is common for learners' identities to be ignored during the completion of communicative tasks in the context of English language teaching. It is imperative that one particular path to guide learners through their language learning without considering their identities is not an option in the post-method era.

Affective and Cognitive Variables

The post-method era stresses more on metacognitive, cognitive and socio-affective strategies than any particular method of teaching. Brown (2014) has stressed to go beyond methods to guide students to language learning. He rather stresses that teachers should implement metacognitive, cognitive, and socio-affective strategies. Students should reflect on their own learning process. They should be given complete freedom to choose their own learning style to facilitate language learning in a better way. For example, the way one learner learns the vocabulary may be different from the way another learner learns it. Instead of having all learners kowtow to one particular path, it is better to orient them to several strategies to learn vocabulary and encourage them to choose the ones they find most suitable for themselves. A useful strategy suggested by Brown (2014) is to implement activities that lower learners' inhibitions, encourage risk-taking, and build self-confidence. Teacher should build confidence of learners and motivate them for learning.

Critical Practice

Critical practice also plays an important role in language teaching and learning in the post-method era. Also known as critical pedagogy, critical practice provides learners an opportunity to promote dialogue with other learners and the teacher(s), encouraging a reflective and critical questioning of the pedagogical material in relation to their own life, biases, social and historical contexts (Benesch, 1999). For example, if students are aware why a specific methodology is chosen, it can help them understand the reason of a chosen path. An audio-lingual drill can help students with pronunciation of particular sounds of English. It is doubtful that oral drills will achieve the goal of learners reach "native-like" pronunciation level. However, oral drills improve comprehensibility in English that is, maintaining an accent from another language, but becoming easier to understand (Galante, 2014).

The Post-method Learner

One of the chief features of the post method learner is that he is an autonomous one. He takes charge of his own learning. He has complete freedom to choose the contents and style of his learning. According to Kumaravadivelu (2001) the Post-method learner is an autonomous one. He quotes Henri Holec (the writer of *Autonomy and Foreign Language Learning* published in 1979) who said learning becomes autonomous only when learners take charge of it. (p.545) In the year 2001 he suggests that there are three types of learner's autonomy: academic, social and liberatory. However, in 2006, he narrows it down to two: academic and liberatory. Kumaravadivelu considers the academic view as a narrow view, which develops the learners' capacity to learn, whereas the liberatory view goes beyond just capacity to learn and focuses on learning to liberate at the same time.

Learners' autonomy advocates that learners are free to learn the way they want as per their needs and can reflect on their progress from time to time. It makes learners to not only participate whole-heartedly in learning the language but also develop their own social autonomy by seeking the facilitators' intervention as per their requirement. They interact with peers and engage in conversation with native speakers of the target language through various cultural and social activities. Kumaravadivelu (2001) further adds that learners' autonomy are interpersonal, unlike academic autonomy, through which learners not only develop a sense of responsibility to shoulder their own learning but also a sense of sensitivity towards other learners. As learners take charge of their own learning, it creates a sense of responsibility among them. Learners become thinkers that are more critical and better problem solvers. Although it might seem that the teachers do not have much participation in this kind of learning environment, it is not possible to achieve desired results without guidance provided by the facilitator.

The Post-method Teacher

The post method teacher also enjoys more freedom in a language classroom than ever before. He is not bound to follow a particular method or approach in the classroom. Similar to the learners, the Post-method era also provides teachers their autonomy. Teacher gets prime importance in the classroom. His experiences, values and beliefs have a greater importance than before in the classroom. Teachers are also no less than a significant tool in this entire teaching-learning procedure since they not only directly deal with learners, but also understand them and also their context in the best way (Prabhu, 1990). Teachers' autonomy consists of his personal experiences and competence to teach and face challenge in a sociopolitical environment of the classroom. Teachers have to act as decision makers. Chen (2014) illustrates a study by Wallace who states that teacher's autonomy not only provides them to implement their personal experiences and beliefs but also encourages them to follow a reflective approach through which they will be able to analyze and evaluate their teaching acts within the classroom. Teaching is a process subject to amendment wherever necessary as per the requirement of the learners in the particular setting; Wallace further adds that it is necessary for teachers to monitor the effects of such changes.

The Post-method Teacher Educator

The Post-method Teacher Educator aims to equip perspective teachers with all necessary strategies that they might need in the classroom. The interesting point is that it goes beyond academic. Teacher has to take into consideration not only academic aspects of a learner but also socio-political, cultural, ethnic aspects, which cannot be separated from a learner's identity. Previous studies by (Philipson, 1992; Pennycook 1994; Tollefson, 1995; and Canagarajah, 1999) shed light on similar issue and said that it is important to introduce prospective teachers to the parameter of possibility so that they are better aware of the social, political and racial inequalities that persists and can prepare themselves to eliminate them through language teaching as students will strive to construct their identity within and beyond the classroom premises (Kumaravadivelu, 2001).

The Post-method Teacher Educator primarily deals with providing "preselected" and "presequenced" knowledge to the prospective teachers. In a Post-method setting, Kumaravadivelu (2001) states that it is important to emphasize on "as much on the teacher part of teacher education as on the education part of it" (p. 552). As mentioned before, it is imperative for autonomous teachers to reflect on their own knowledge and experience to shape their pedagogic experience based on the teaching and learning context. Teacher educator facilitates the teachers to reach their teaching goals by incorporating the prospective teachers' voice and visuals into an ongoing dialogue (Huq, 2015).

Kumaravadivelu (2001) also mentions that teacher educator would educate the future teachers to think critically, encourage them to make decisions on their own, articulate voices as well as encourage them to use their basic skills effectively in the classroom. However, educating the teachers is most effective when an idea of the students' beliefs, values and knowledge are incorporated in the dialogue. That way the prospective teachers would get an idea of what to expect once they step into the classroom.

Learners' Interactions in Teaching

In this category, three macro-strategies are put into consideration, namely maximizing learning opportunities, facilitating negotiated interaction and minimizing perpetual mistakes. The first strategy i.e. maximizing learning opportunities stands for providing as many opportunities as possible to learn. It considers teaching as a process of creating and making use of those opportunities for learning purposes. Allwright (1984) emphasized on this and says that teachers are not allowed to ignore any sort of contributory discourse and simply cannot categorize teachers and learners into separate segments, but has to deem both of them as "managers of learning" (p.156).

On the other hand, minimizing perpetual mismatches defines the perceptual mismatch between the interaction and interpretation between teachers and learners in a classroom. It is perceived that learners are not always able to interpret classroom activities the way the teacher has decoded it.

There is a mismatch between what teacher intends and what learner understands. Teacher must prepare himself for the possible sources of mismatch in advance. Some of the important points, which arise out of mismatch, include cognitive, communicative, linguistic, pedagogic, strategic, cultural, evaluative, procedural and attitudinal. Though it might not be possible to address all these predetermined set of mismatches in the actual setting, it is important for teachers to carry at least some background information about these before going into the classroom so that they may be ready to tackle them in the classroom (Kumaravadivelu, 2008, p.203).

Finally, facilitating negotiated interaction refers to meaningful learner-learner and learner-teacher interaction in the classroom. Learners should actively participate in the classroom activities. They should clarify, confirm, and check comprehension, request, repair, react and take turn. Learners should be active participants rather than passive receivers of knowledge. They should work to develop linguistic and communicative competence rather than memorizing the contents without context.

Technique of Teaching

As discussed in the previous heading, learners should not memorize the contents without proper context. The Post-method teacher stresses on contextualizing the linguistic contents so that students may learn the use of language in the real life. For instance, grammar teaching is considered a monotonous activity in an EFL/ESL classroom. Over the years, scholars such as (Krashen, 1985; Prabhu 1987 and Rutherford 1987) questioned, "whether L2 system can be analyzed and explicitly explained" to learners with a view to assist grammar construction. Scholars are of the opinion that it is not feasible to teach the entire range of grammatical structure through instruction and explanation, as Macintyre (1970) states, "teachers should include grammatical exercises in the classroom activities to create a rich linguistic environment for the intuitive heuristic that human beings automatically process" (p.108). The post method era curriculum appreciates the communicative language teaching and task based language teaching. Both of the approaches encourage contextual use of linguistic input. Grammar is not taught in the traditional way rather teachers are suggested to make quality textual data available to learners so that they can internalize and infer underlying rules governing grammatical usage and communicative uses rather than simply memorizing the structures.

Contents of Teaching

In the Post-Method Era, there is more emphasis on integration rather than on segregation. It stresses on the need of integrating syntactic, semantic and pragmatic component of language learning. It also emphasizes to merge the language skills i.e. reading, writing, speaking and listening, too. Swaffer, Arens & Morgan (1982) and Titone (1985) believe that skill separation is a concept that remained after audio-lingual era, which possess very little empirical or theoretical justification which ultimately is inadequate for developing functional skills. Words, sentences and meaning are all inter-related. They cannot be segregated. If they are segregated, they will lose their existence and they will not be able to provide context to language.

Resultantly, it is imperative to explain learners the necessity of integrated nature of language. It is evident the language skills are interrelated and it would not be practical for one to function without the other. Therefore, language knowledge and language ability are best developed when learnt and used holistically (Rigg, 1991).

Post-Method Pedagogy for Teacher Growth

In contrast to the concept of method, post-method pedagogy does not have the limitations mentioned above as it is not an alternative method but as Kumaravadivelu (2003) states "an alternative to method" (p.32). Post-method pedagogy puts the teacher at the center of language learning and teaching and values his or her beliefs, experiences and knowledge. For long, teachers had been neglected and they were being denied their place in a language classroom. They had to strictly follow a particular method and approach in the classroom. There is no one who can better understand students than their teachers, as they are their regular observers. They directly deal with learners, address and solve their issues. That is why, teachers are considered as great resources because of their experience in the past with students. Experience of teaching, knowledge of one or more methods gained throughout their training as teachers, knowledge of other teachers' actions and opinions and their experience as parents or caretakers are of extreme importance (Prabhu, 1990). Therefore, post-method teachers are encouraged to develop and create their own methods out of their experiences with students as their experiences are based on their classroom context and knowledge of other methods and approaches. As a result, the constructed method reflects teachers' beliefs, values and experiences (Richards & Rodgers, 2001). In this sense, post-method teachers are autonomous, analysts, strategic researchers and decision-makers. Such teachers are also reflective as they observe their teaching, evaluate the results, identify problems, find solutions, and try new techniques wherever possible. Based on this, there is a movement from "science-research conceptions" towards "art-craft conception of teaching" (Arikan, 2006, p. 4) as well as a shift from top-down process to bottom-up process as teachers "theorize what they practice or practice what they theorize" (Kumaravadivelu, 2003a, p. 37). One should notice that post-method does not deny the knowledge of existing methods and approaches because these methods make you aware of your beliefs and principles and provide inexperienced teachers with some valuable initial knowledge (Richards & Rodgers, 2001).

Post-method has three pedagogic parameters, which make it distinct from the concept of method: particularity, practicality, possibility. Kumaravadivelu (2006) states, "post method pedagogy must be sensitive to a particular group of teachers teaching a particular group of learners pursuing a particular set of goals within a particular institutional context embedded in a particular socio-cultural milieu" (p. 171). By practicality, what is meant is that method should be applicable since a theory is useless if it cannot be practiced (Khaki, n.d.). As for possibility, the method should be appropriate socially, culturally and politically (Khaki, n.d.) in contrast to method as a colonial construct. All these concepts are interconnected and cannot be dissociated from each other. They can be better comprehended in relation to each other as Huq (2015) states:

> The way pedagogy of practicality cannot exist without that of particularity, in the same way pedagogy of possibility cannot function without that of practicality. This notion of pedagogy of possibility is a blend of the context-sensitive theories teachers construct in a classroom and the socio-political experiences both set of participants bring into the pedagogical setting. This means that a learner's understanding of the language is not just a culmination of what s/he has learnt in the past years, but is also shaped by social, economical, political and cultural context that s/he has grown up in. (p.11)

Does Post-Method Pedagogy Mean Total Freedom?

Post-method pedagogy has, in no way, imparted complete freedom to teachers. In a way, teacher becomes more responsible and alert in post-method era. When he has to make decisions regarding the learning of students, he has to keep in mind some principles to conduct an effective lesson. Can (2009) states:

> Three-dimensional and the Macro-strategic frameworks provide teachers with such principles that are generalizable, open-ended, descriptive, theory-neutral, method-neutral and thus, not restrictive. Teachers taking into account their experiences, the frameworks and even their knowledge of the conventional methods can construct their own methods and thus, act as evaluators, observers, critical thinkers, theorizers and practitioners. (n.p.)

These frameworks prove to be very useful especially for inexperienced teachers as it can orient them to effective teaching level before they could get experiences in their field as Kumaravadivelu (2003) states, "practicing and prospective teachers need a framework that can enable them to develop the knowledge, skill, attitude, and autonomy necessary to devise for themselves a systematic, coherent, and relevant personal theory of practice" (p. 40)

Eclectic Method or Post-method?

Many teachers describe their teaching methodology as eclectic as Bell (2007) gives example of a teacher who says, "I have an eclectic method. I like to take a piece from here and a piece from there and I just combine them all" (p. 136). However, it was also seen that the concept of method was not conceived in a proper way and was generally considered as adaptation of techniques, which are open to any method. It is also very difficult to construct an eclectic method and merely putting together a package of techniques from various methods randomly cannot constitute a method. Stern (1992) states, "Weakness of the eclectic position is that it offers no criteria according to which we can determine which is the best theory..., therefore, it is too broad and too vague" (p. 11). It seems that what many teachers have been doing so far is actually going beyond methods as they have seen not only the usefulness of methods but also their limitations and felt the need to go beyond them to build their own (Can, 2009).

Bibliography

Abdul, N. B. (2016). The Use of Audio-Lingual Method in Teaching Listening Comprehension at the Second Year Students of SMK YAPIP Makassar Sungguminasa. *Exposure Journal, 5(1),* 43-52. Retrieved December 3, 2018, from: https://www.researchgate.net/publication/322066608 THE USE OF AUDIOLINGUAL METHOD IN TEACHING LISTENING COMPREHENSION AT THE SECOND YEAR STUDENTS OF SMK YAPIP MAKASSAR SUNGGUMINASA.

Ahmad, S., & Rao, C. (2013). Applying Communicative Approach in Teaching English as a Foreign Language: A Case Study of Pakistan. *Porta Linguarum, 20,* 187-203.

Allwright, R. L. (1984). The importance of interaction in classroom language learning. *Applied Linguistics, 5,* 156-17 1.

Anthony, E. M. (1963). Approach, Method and Technique. *English Language Teaching, 17,* 63-67.

Ariffin, S. R. & Mohamad, S. (1996). *Pemikiran Guru cemerlang: kesan teradapprestasipengajaran. Kertaskerja seminar isu-isupendidikan Negara. Fakultipendidikan,* Universiti Kebangsaan Malaysia, Bangi, 26-27 November.

Arikan, A. (2006). Postmethod condition and its implications for English language teacher education. *Journal of Language and Linguistics Studies, 2*(1), 1-11.

Aronson, E. (2008). *Jigsaw classroom.* Retrieved July 18, 2008 from http://www.jigsaw.org/

Asher, J. (1977). *Learning another language through actions: the complete teacher's guidebook.* Los Gatos, Calif: Sky Oaks Publications.

Asher, J. (1969). The total physical response approach to second language learning. *Modern Language Journal, 53,* 3-17

Barron, B. (2003). "When smart groups fail". *Journal of the Learning Sciences, 12,* 307–359.

Becker, A. (1986). Language in particular: A lecture. In D. Tannen (Ed.), Linguistics in context: Connecting observation and understanding (pp. 17–35). Norwood, NJ: Ablex.

Brown, H. D. (2002). Strategies for success; a practical guide to learning English. New York: Pearson Education.

Brown, H. (1994). Teaching by Principles – An Interactive Approach to Language Pedagogy. Englewood Cliffs, NJ: Prentince Hall Regents. (2nd ed.). White Plains. NY:Longman.

Brown. A, & Dowling. P. (1998). Doing Research/Reading Research: A mode of Interrogation for Education. London: The Falmer Press.

Brown, H. D. (2014). Principles of Language Learning and Teaching (6th ed.). NY: Pearson Education.

Bell, D. M. (2003). Method and Post-Method: Are they really so incompatible. *TESOL, Quarterly, 37* (2), 325-336.

Bell, D. M. (2007). Do teachers think that methods are dead? *ELT Journal, 61(2), 135-143.*

Breen, M. P. (1987). Learner Contributioiis to Task Design. In C.N. Candlin and D. Murphy (eds.). *Lunca.srer Prucfical Papers in English Languuge Educufion.* Vol. 7. *Lunguage Learning Tasks,*23-46. Englewood Cliffs, NJ: Prentice Hall.

Boumova, V. (2008). *Traditional vs. Modern Teaching Methods: Advantages and Disadvantages of Each* (Unpublished master's thesis). Masaryk University, Brno.

Benesch, S. (1999). Thinking Critically, Thinking Dialogically. *TESOL Quarterly, 33,* 573–580.

Brinton, D. (2003). Content-Based Instruction. In Nunan, D. (Ed.), Practical English Language Teaching. McGraw-Hill Contemporary.

Cael, J. (2010). *Teaching Pronunciation As A Core Skill Using The Silent Way Approach*(Unpublished master's thesis). SIT Graduate Institute. Retrieved November 15, 2018, from https://digitalcollections.sit.edu/cgi/viewcontent.cgi?referer=https://www.google.co.in/&httpsredir=1&article=1490&context=ipp_collection.

Can, N. (n.d.). Post-Method Pedagogy: Teacher Growth behind Walls. In *Ings of the 10th METU ELT Convention.* Retrieved March 25, 2018, from http://dbe.metu.edu.tr/convention/proceedingsweb/Pedagogy.pdf

Canagarajah, A.S. (1999). *Resisting linguistic imperialism in English teaching.* Oxford: Oxford University Press.

Carroll, J. (1963). "Research on Teaching Foreign Languages". In N. Gage (ed.), Handbook of Research on Language Teaching. (Chicago: RandMcNally). Pp. 1060-1100.

Carter, J. (1984). Relaxation handwriting improvement program with learning disabled and emotionally disturbed children. Journal of the Society of Accelerative Learning and Teaching. 9. 221-240

Chamot, A.V. & O"Malley, J.M.(1994). *The CALLA handbook: Implementing the cognitive academic language learning approach.* Reading, M.A. Addison Wesley.

Chang, S. C. (2011). A Contrastive Study of Grammar Translation Method and Communicative Approach in Teaching English Grammar. *English Language Teaching, 4*(2), 13-24. Retrieved from file:///C:/Users/tmkhan/Desktop/books/Chapter%202%20The%20 Grammar-%20Translation%20Method%20(Indicative%20and%20Deductive)/ critic%20one%20chang.pdf

Chen, H. K. (2011). Analysis of English Cognitive Direct Method from the Perspective of Knowledge Management. *The Journal of Human Resource and Adult Learning, 7*(2), 71-78. Retrieved from file:///C:/Users/tmkhan/Desktop/books/Chapter%203%20The%20 Direct%20Method/8%20Han-Kwang%20Chen.pdf

Chen, M. (2014). Postmethod Pedagogy and Its Influence on EFL Teaching Strategies. *English Language Teaching,7*(5), 17-25. doi:10.5539/elt.v7n5p17

Cooper, J., Prescott. S., Cook, L., Smith L., Mueck R. & Cuseo J. (1990). *Cooperative Learning and College Instruction.* Long Beach, CA: California State University Foundation.

Dipamo, B., & Job, R. S. (1991). A methodological review of studies of SALT (Suggestive-accelerative learning and teaching) techniques. *Australian Journal of Educational Technology,7*(2), 127-143. Retrieved November 15, 2018, from https://ajet.org.au/index. php/AJET/article/viewFile/2284/1115.

Elliott, J. (1993). Reconstructing teacher education: Teacher development. London: Falmer Press.

Ellis, N. (January, 2011). Language acquisition just Zipf's right along. Conference, Université du Québec à Montréal.

Feez, S. (1998). *Text-Based Syllabus Design.* Sydney: National Centre for English Teaching and Research

Freeman, D. L. (2001). *Techniques and Principles in Language Teaching* (2nd ed.). Delhi, India: Oxford University Press.

Freeman, D. L.(2011). A Complexity theory approach to second language development/ acquisition. In D. Atkinson (Ed.), *Alternative approaches to second language acquisition* (pp. 48–72). NY: Routledge.

Freeman, D. L. (2000). *Techniques and principles in language teaching* (2nd edition). Oxford: Oxford University Press.

Freeman, D. L. (1986). Techniques and Principles in Language Teaching. Oxford University Press.

Freeman, D. L. (2000). *Techniques and Principles in Language Teaching.* New York: Oxford University Press.

FREIRE, P. A. U. L. O. (2000). *Pedagogy of the Oppressed.* (M. B. Ramos, Trans.) (30th ed.). The Continuum International Publishing Group. Retrieved November 1, 2018, from https://envs.ucsc.edu/internships/internship-readings/freire-pedagogy-of-the-oppressed.pdf

Galante, A. (2014). English Language Teaching in the post method era. *TESL Ontario.* Retrieved June 25, 2018, from https://www.researchgate.net/publication/280734191

Goodsell, A., Maher, M. & Tinto, V. (1992). *Collaborative Learning: A Sourcebook for Higher Education.* University Park, PA: National Center on Postsecondary Teaching, Learning, and Assessment.

Ghani, M. Z., & Ghous, N. H. (2014). The Effectiveness of Total Physical Response (TPR) Approach in Helping Slow Young Learners With Low Achievement Acquire English as a Second Language. *International Journal of Research In Social Science, 4(6),* 127-13. Retrieved August 26, 2018, from http://ijsk.org/uploads/3/1/1/7/3117743/1_total_physical_response_tpr_approach.pdf

Goodwin M.W. (1999). Cooperative Learning and Social Skills: What Skills to Teach and How to Teach Them. *Intervention in School and Clinic, 35(1),* 29-33.

Hansler, D. (1985). Studies on the effectiveness of the cognition enhancement technique for teaching thinking skills. (Eric Document Reproduction Service No. ED 266 432)

Holleny, L. (2012). The effectiveness of Total Physical Response Storytelling for language learning with special education students (Unpublished master's thesis). Rowan University. Retrieved August 26, 2018, from https://rdw.rowan.edu/cgi/viewcontent.cgi?article=1196&context=etd

Holt, J. (1983). *How children learn.* Delacorte Press/Seymour Lawrence.

Howatt, A. P. R. (1984). *A History of English Language Teaching.* Oxford: Oxford University Press.

Huq, R. (2015). *Post-Method Pedagogy: A Survey of the English Medium Schools in Dhaka* (Unpublished master's thesis). BRAC University, Bangladesh. Retrieved July 25, 2018, from http://dspace.bracu.ac.bd:8080/xmlui/bitstream/handle/10361/4482/13363012. pdf;sequence

Janks, H. (2010). *Literacy and Power.* New York, NY: Routledge.

Jin, G. (2008). Application of Communicative Approach in College English Teaching. *Asian Social Science, 4(4)*, 81-85. Retrieved November 4, 2018, from **http://ccsenet.org/ journal/index.php/ass/article/download/1604/1518**

Johnson, D.W., R. T. Johnson, & E. J. Holubec (1993). Circles of Learning: Cooperation in The Classroom, 4th edition. Edina, MN: Interaction Book.

Johnson, D. W., Johnson, R.T. and Holubec, E.J. (1994). The new circles of learning: Cooperation in the classroom and school. Alexandria, VA: Association for Supervision and Curriculum Development.

Johnson, D. W., & Johnson, R. T. (1989). Making cooperative learning work. *Theory into Practice. 38 (2).* 67-73.

Johnson, D.W., Johnson, R.T., & Smith, K.A. (1991). *Active learning: Cooperation in the college classroom.* Edina, MN: Interaction.

Jones, K. A. (2008). Making Cooperative Learning Work in the College Classroom: An Application of the 'Five Pillars' of Cooperative Learning to Post-Secondary Instruction. *The Journal of Effective Teaching,* 8(2), 61-76. Retrieved November 18, 2018, from https://files.eric.ed.gov/fulltext/EJ1055588.pdf.

Ju, F. (2013). Communicative Language Teaching (CLT): A Critical and Comparative Perspective. *Theory and Practice in Language Studies,*3(9), 1579-1583. Retrieved November 2, 2018, from http://www.academypublication.com/issues/past/tpls/vol03/09/10.pdf

Jung, T., Osterwalder, H., & Wipf, D. (2000).*Teaching and Assessing Middle-Year Students' Speaking and Listening Skills. Teaching and Learning Research Exchange.* Retrieved from: http://www.mcdowellfoundation.ca/main_mcdowell/projects/research_rep/52_ teaching_assessing.pdf

205

Kafyulilo, A. C. (n.d): Training workshop for teachers on participatory teaching methods. http://www.slideshare.net/Vangidunda/training-workshop-for-teachers-on-participatory-teachingmethods?related=3

Kaufman, D., Sutow, E., & Dunn, K. (1997). Three Approaches to Cooperative Learning in Higher Education. *The Canadian Journal of Higher Education,27*(2), 3rd ser., 37-66. Retrieved November 18, 2018, from http://journals.sfu.ca/cjhe/index.php/cjhe/article/viewFile/183303/183261

Knight, P. (2001). English language teaching in its social context. Abingdon: Routledge.

Kucharcikova, A., & Tokarcikova, E. (2016). USE OF PARTICIPATORY METHODS IN TEACHING AT THE UNIVERSITY. *The Online Journal of Science and Technology,6*(1), 82-90. Retrieved November 1, 2018, from http://dergipark.gov.tr/download/article-file/210211

Kumaravadivelu, B. (2006). *Understanding language teaching: From method to postmethod.* Mahwah, NJ: Lawrence Erlbaum Associates.

Kumaravadivelu, B. (2008). *Understanding Language Teaching: From Method Postmethod.* Taylor & Francis e-Library.

Kumaravadivelu, B. (1994). The Post-method Condition: (E)merging Strategies for

Second/Foreign Language Teaching. *TESOL Quarterly, 26*(1), 27-50.

Kumaravadivelu, B. (1999). Critical Classroom Discourse Analysis. *TESOL Quarterly, 33,* 453–484.

Kumaravadivelu, B. (2001). Toward a Post-method Pedagogy. *TESOL Quarterly, 35*(4),537-560.

Kumaravadivelu, B. (2003). *Beyond Methods: Macrostrategies for language teaching.* New Haven, C.T.: Yale University Press.

Kumaravadivelu, B. (2006). TESOL Methods: Changing Tracks, Challenging Trends. *TESOL Quarterly, 40* (1), 59-80.

Kwambehar, S. T. (2015). Language Teaching Methods: *A Critique. Journal of Advances in Social Science-Humanities, 1 (1),* 26-33. Retrieved June 2, 2018, from jassh.in/index.php/jassh/article/download/5/3.

Kramsch, C. (2009). *The Multilingual Subject: What Foreign Language Learners Say about Their Experience and Why It Matters.* Oxford, UK: Oxford University Press.

Khaki, N. (n.d.). The Post-method Pedagogy [On-line]. Retrieved from: http://teachenglish. persianblog.ir/1385/5/

Krashen, S. D. (1985). *The input hypothesis: Issues and implications.* London: Longman.

Lie, A. (2008). *Cooperative Learning: Changing Paradigms of College Teaching.* Retrieved from:

http://faculty.petra.ac.id/anitalie/LTM/cooperative_learning.htm

Lozanov, G. (1978). Suggestology and Outlines on Suggestopedy. New York:Gordon and Breach.

Lozanov, G. (2009) Dear friend. Lozanov.org [online]. Available from: http://www.lozanov.org/

Macintyre, A. (1970). Noam Chomsky's view of language. In M. Lester (Ed.), *Readings in applied transformational grammar* (pp. 96- 113). New York: Holt, Reinhart & Winston.

Laili, M. (2015). Applying Communicative Language Teaching in Teaching English for Foreign language Learners. *Ahmad Dahlan Journal of English Studies, 2(3),* 1-8. Retrieved from: http://journal.uad.ac.id/index.php/ADJES/article/view/1723/1190

Manen, M. V. (1991). The tact of teaching: The meaning of pedagogical thoughtfulness. Albany: State University of New York Press.

Mart, C. T. (2013). The Audio-Lingual Method: An Easy way of Achieving Speech. *International Journal of Academic Research in Business and Social Sciences,3*(12), 63-65. Retrieved July 4, 2018, from https://www.researchgate.net/publication/269813000_The_Audio-Lingual_Method_An_Easy_way_of_Achieving_Speech

Mart, C. T. (2013). The Direct-Method: A Good Start to Teach Oral Language. *International Journal of Academic Research in Business and Social Sciences, 3*(11), 182-184.

Nagaraj, G. (1996). *English Language Teaching: Approaches, Methods and Techniques* (1ˢᵗ ed.). Kolkata, India: Orient Longman Limited.

Norton, B. (2000). *Identity and language learning.* London, UK: Longman.

Norton, B. & Toohey, K. (2011). Identity, language learning, and social change. *Language Teaching, 44,* 412–446.

Nunan, D (2004). Task- Based Language Teaching. Cambridge: Cambridge University Press.

Nurhasanah, S. (2015). The Use of Community Language Learning Method to Increase the Students' Participation in Classroom Conversation. *Register Journal, 8* (1), 81-98.

Retrieved from: https://media.neliti.com/media/publications/177289-EN-the-use-of-community-language-learning-c.pdf.

Olsen, R.E. W-B, & Kagan, S. (1992). About cooperative learning. In C. Kessler (Ed.), Cooperative language learning: A teacher's resource book (pp. 1-30). Englewood Cliffs, NJ: Prentice Hall.

Omoto, M. P., & Nyongesa, W. J. (2013). Content- Based Instruction: A Study of Methods of Teaching and Learning English in Primary Schools in Butula District. *International Journal of Business and Social Science*,4(5), 236-245. Retrieved November 15, 2018, from file:///C:/Users/tmkhan/Downloads/Dialnet-ContentBasedInstruction-5181354%20(1).pdf

Osman, T. (2017). *The Obstacles Against the Success of 'Suggestopedia' as a Method for ELT (English Language Teaching) in Global Classrooms*,6(5), 98-105. doi:10.11648/j.ajap.20170605.13

Paradis, M. (2009). Declarative and procedural determinants of second languages. Amsterdam, Netherlands/Philadelphia, PA: John Benjamins.

Paradis, M. (2004). A neurolinguistic theory of bilingualism. Amsterdam, Netherlands/Philadelphia, PA: John Benjamins.

Paradis, M. (1994). Neurolinguistic aspects of implicit and explicit memory: Implications for bilingualism. In N. Ellis (Ed.), Implicit and explicit learning of second languages (pp. 393-419). London, England: Academic Press.

Prabhu, N. S. (1987a). 'Language education, equipping or en abling', en Das, B. K. (ed). *Lunguuge Educution in Humun Resource Development*. Anthology Series 20. Singapore: RELC.

Prabhu, N. S., (1987b). *Second Lunguuge Pedugogy*. Oxford: OUP.

Prabhu, N. S., (1987). *Second Language Pedagogy*. Oxford: OUP.

Prabhu, N. S. (1990). There is no best method-why. *TESOL Quarterly, 24* (2), 161-176.

Pennycook, A. (1994). *The cultural politics of English as an international language*. London: Longman.

Phillipson, R. (1992). *Linguistic imperialism*. Oxford: Oxford University Press.

Qiu, Y. (2016). Research on the Application of Total Physical Response Approach to Vocabulary Teaching in Primary Schools. *International Journal of Arts and Commerce, 5(7)*, 18-24. Retrieved July 26, 2018, from https://www.ijac.org.uk/images/frontImages/gallery/Vol. 5 No. 7/3. 18-24.pdf.

Rao, D. B., & Ediger, M. (2014). *Methods of Teaching English.* New Delhi, India: APH Publishing Corporation.

Reed, V. (1989). Adolescent Language Disorders: General Strategies for Teaching Language Comprehension/Listening. Eau Claire, WI: Thinking Publications.

Richards, J. C., & Rodgers, T. S. (2001). *Approaches and Methods in Language Teaching* (2nd ed.). United Kingdom: Cambridge University Press.

Richards, J. C. & Theodore, T. S. (2010). *The Silent Way in Richards and Theodore's Framework.* Retrieved December 02, 2010 from Penn State University: http://www.personal.psu.edu/users/m/x/mxh392/insys441/methodology/silentway.html

Richards, J. C. and Rodgers, T. S. (1986). *Approaches and methods in language teaching: A description and analysis.* Cambridge: Cambridge University Press.

Richards, J.C. y T.S. Rodgers (1987). The Audio-lingual Method. En Approaches and Methods in language teaching. 44-63. Reino Unido: Cambridge University Press

Rodgers, T. S. (1988). Cooperative language learning: What's new? *PASSA: A Journal of Language Teaching and Learning, 18 (2):* 12-23.

Rogers, C. R. (1951). Client-Centered Therapy. Boston: Houghton Miffin.

Rutherford, W. E. (1987) Second Language Grammar: Learning and Teaching. Longman

Rigg, P. (1991). Whole language in TESOL. TESOL Quarterly, 25 (3), 521- 542

Rivers, W. M. (1964). The Psychologist and the Foreign Language Teacher. Chicago. University of Chicago Press.

Rivers, W. M. (1968). Teaching Foreign Language Skills. University of Chicago Press.

Robert, S. J. (n.d.). The Essential Elements of Cooperative Learning in the Classroom. Retrieved November 19, 2018, from https://www.learner.org/workshops/socialstudies/pdf/session6/6.CooperativeLearning.pdf.

Segalowitz, N. (2010). *Cognitive Bases of Second Language Fluency.* New York, NY/Oxon, United Kingdom: Routledge, Abingdon.

Slavin, R. E. (1991) Student Team Learning: A Practical Guide to Cooperative Learning. Washington, DC: National Education Association,. ED 339 518.

Sanchez, A. (2004). The Task-based Approach in Language Teaching. *International Journal of English Studies, 4*(1), 39-71. doi:DOI: 10.6018/ijes.4.1.48051 • Source: OAI

Satya, R. K. (2008). *Modern Methods of Teaching English*. New Delhi, India: APH Publishing Corporation.

Setterland, S. (1983). The teaching of relaxation in schools. University Goteborg. (Eric Document Reproduction Service No. ED 266 650).

Singh, J. P. (2011). Effectiveness of Total Physical Response. *Academic Voices A Multidisciplinary Journal, 1 (1)*, 20-22. Retrieved from: https://www.nepjol.info/index.php/AV/article/download/5303/4

Slavin, R. E. (1991). Student Team Learning: A Practical Guide to Cooperative Learning. Washington, DC: National Education Association, 1991. ED 339 518. Retrieved from: https://files.eric.ed.gov/fulltext/ED339518.pdf

Snow, M. (2001). Content Based and Immersion Models for Second and Foreign LanguageTeaching. In Celce-Murcia, M. (Ed.), Teaching English as a Second or Foreign Language. Third Edition. Boston, MA: Heinle & Heinle Thompson Learning.

Sophaktra, U. 2009. *Total Physical Response (TPR)*. Retrieved October 18, 2018, from: http://www.scribd.com/doc/23194878/Total-physical-Response-TPR

Stern, H. H. (1992). *Issues and options in language teaching*. Oxford: Oxford University Press.

Stern, H. H. (1983). *Fundamental Concepts of Language Teaching*. England: Oxford University Press.

Stevick, E. W. 1980. *Teaching Languages: A Way and Ways*. Rowley, Mass.: Newbury House

Stevick, E. (1996). *Memory, Meaning & Method* (2nd ed.). Boston, MA: Heinle & Heinle.

Strom P. & Strom R. (2003, April). *Student evaluation of cooperative learning: The Interpersonal Intelligence Inventory*. Presentation to the Annual Meeting of the American Educational Research Association, Chicago, IL.

Stryker, S. & Leaver, B. L. (1997). *Content-Based instruction in foreign language education: Models and methods*. Washington, DC: Georgetown University Press.

Suryani, N. (2012). *The Implementation Of Audio Lingual Method In Teaching English At The Fourth Year Of Sd N Bedoro 2 Sambungmacan-Sragen*. [Dissertation submitted as a Partial Fulfillment of the Requirements for Getting the Bachelor Degree of Education in English Department, Muhammadiyah University Of Surakarta]. Indonesia, Central Java. http://eprints.ums.ac.id/19633/14/PUBLICATION_ARTICLE.pdf

Swaffar, J., Arens, K., & Morgan, M. (1982) Teacher classroom practices: Redefining method as task hierarchy: *Modern Language Journal, 66,* 24-33

Thornbury, S. (2000). How to teach grammar. Harlow: Longman.

Titone, R. (1985). The four basic skills- Myth or reality. In K. R. Jankowsky (Ed.), *Scientific and humanistic dimension of language: Festchrift for Robert Lado* (pp-321-327). Amsterdam, Netherland: John Benjamins.

Tobin, K and Tippins, DJ. (1993). "Constructivism as a referent for teaching and learning". In Tobin, K (ed), The Practice of Constructivism in Science Education (3–21). Washington, USA. American Association for the Advancement of Science.

Tollefson, J. W. (Ed.). (1995). *Power and inequality in language education.* Cambridge: Cambridge University Press.

Villalobos, O. B. (2014). Content-Based Instruction: A Relevant Approach of Language Teaching. *INNOVACIONES EDUCATIVAS, 15 (20),* 71-83. Retrieved from: https://www.researchgate.net/publication/316258605_Content-Based_Instruction_A_Relevant_Approach_of_Language_Teaching

Widdowson, H. G. (1975). *Teaching Language as Communication.* Oxford: Oxford University Press.

Wiggins, H. L. (2004, August 11). *A Learner-Centered and Participatory Approach to Teaching Community Adult ESL* [Scholarly project]. Retrieved May 10, 2018, from https://scholarsarchive.byu.edu/cgi/viewcontent.cgi?article=1669&context=etd

Williams, R. B. (2007). *Cooperative Learning: A Standard for High Achievement.* Thousand Oaks, CA: Corwin Press.

Winitz, H. (Ed.). (1981). The Comprehension Approach to Foreign Language Instruction. New York: Newbury House.

Wordsworth, J. A. (1967). An Analysis of the Audi-Lingual Approach as Applied to Methods of Teaching Russian(Unpublished master's thesis). The University of British Columbia. Retrieved December 4, 2018, from http://summit.sfu.ca/system/files/iritems1/646/b11546384.pdf

Zaid, M. A. (2014). International Conference on Economics, Education and Humanities (pp. 110–116). Bali. Retrieved December 4, 2018, from http://icehm.org/upload/4700ED1214088.pdf

Printed in the United States
by Baker & Taylor Publisher Services